Business English Trainer

Sicher kommunizieren & verhandeln

Robert Tilley, Elke Schuch

compact

© Compact Verlag GmbH
Baierbrunner Str. 27, 81379 München
Ausgabe 2013

Chefredaktion: Dr. Matthias Feldbaum
Redaktion: Kerstin Nußhart, Tanja Böhm
Fachkorrektur: Oliver Astley
Produktion: Frank Speicher
Titelabbildung: www.iStockphoto.com, Abel Mitja Varela;
www.shotshop.com, Jozef Sedmák
Gestaltung: X-Design, München; satz-studio GmbH
Umschlaggestaltung: X-Design, München; Hartmut Baier

ISBN 978-3-8174-9328-9
381749328/1

www.compactverlag.de

Vorwort

Der Business English Trainer – effektives Sprachtraining für den Geschäftsalltag: Begleiten Sie Peter Brückner aus Deutschland, der von seiner Firma nach England versetzt wird, auf verschiedenen Stationen durch das Unternehmen und trainieren Sie so aktiv das sichere Kommunizieren und Verhandeln auf Englisch. Zu Peters Aufgabengebieten gehören: Geschäftskorrespondenz, Verhandlungen, Kundenbetreuung, Geschäftsreisen und vieles mehr. Um größtmöglichen Lernspaß zu garantieren, werden Peters Erlebnisse im englischen Berufsalltag auf humorvolle Weise dargestellt.

Alle Dialoge sind praxisnah und mit ihrer deutschen Übersetzung angegeben. Schlüsselbegriffe sind dabei farbig hervorgehoben. Zahlreiche Dialoge sind zudem vertont und können kostenlos über folgende Internetadresse heruntergeladen werden: http://www.compactverlag.de/download-93289. Geben Sie bitte folgenden Aktivierungscode ein: 9783817493289. Die einzelnen Tracks sind im Buch mit ◀)) gekennzeichnet. Durch aktives Mithören und Mitlesen trainieren Sie zusätzlich Hörverstehen und Aussprache.

Zwischen den Dialogen kann das Gelernte mithilfe kurzer Übungseinheiten vertieft werden. Die dazugehörigen Lösungen befinden sich am Ende des Buches. Nach jedem Kapitel werden alle wichtigen Vokabeln noch einmal aufgeführt und in einem ausführlichen Glossar am Ende des Buches zusammengefasst. Hinweise zu kulturellen Besonderheiten ergänzen die Kapitel und helfen so, Missverständnisse zu vermeiden.

Im Kapitel „Auf einen Blick" finden Sie die wichtigsten Redewendungen übersichtlich dargestellt, sodass sich das Gelernte schnell nachschlagen und wiederholen lässt.

Mit einem abschließenden Test im Anhang können Sie Ihren Lernerfolg überprüfen.

Viel Erfolg beim Englischlernen!

Inhalt

Here we go: kleine Einleitung am Anfang des Kapitels

Talk Talk Talk: praxisnahe Redewendungen mit deutschen Übersetzungen, die wichtigsten Stichwörter sind farbig markiert

🔊 **Audio-Download:** Kennzeichnung der Tracks

Background Information: Wissenswertes zu Business und Landeskunde

Dos and Don'ts: Tipps zum korrekten Verhalten in Geschäftssituationen

False Friends: Hinweise auf mögliche sprachliche Fehler

Correspondence |
Korrespondenz

Here we go

Die Korrespondenz stellt einen wichtigen Teil des Geschäftsalltags dar. Peter Brückners Vorgesetzter, James Morgan, betreut ihn mit der Aufgabe, sich um seinen persönlichen Posteingang und -ausgang zu kümmern.

Talk Talk Talk 1

(The office of James Morgan, Managing Director of ARGO Limited)

J. Good morning, Peter. Did you have a good weekend?

P. Good morning, Mr Morgan. Fine, thanks. I took advantage of the rainy weather and **caught up on some letter-writing**. A lot of my friends in Germany haven't heard from me for some time now.

J. I hope you haven't got **writer's cramp**. And I hope you haven't grown tired of writing letters because that's just what I want you to take over from me this week. During my absence last week, the **in tray** has become full of letters waiting to be answered. You know

(Das Büro von James Morgan, Managing Director von ARGO Limited)

J. Guten Morgen, Peter. Wie war Ihr Wochenende?

P. Guten Morgen, Mr Morgan. Danke, gut. Ich habe das Beste aus dem regnerischen Wetter gemacht und **ein paar überfällige Briefe geschrieben**. Viele meiner Freunde in Deutschland haben schon lange nichts mehr von mir gehört.

J. Ich hoffe, Sie haben keinen **Schreibkrampf** bekommen. Und ich hoffe, Sie sind des Schreibens dabei noch nicht leid geworden, denn genau das sollen Sie diese Woche für mich übernehmen. Während meiner Abwesenheit letzte Woche hat sich der **Eingangs-**

5

enough now about the business to reply to them for me. Just **dictate** them to Lucy and she'll **type** them **up** for you. When you've completed a **batch**, put them in my **out tray**. There are also some **emails to attend to**. You'll find them in the general ARGO **folder**.

korb mit Briefen gefüllt, die darauf warten, beantwortet zu werden. Sie kennen das Geschäft jetzt gut genug, um sie für mich zu beantworten. **Diktieren** Sie sie einfach Lucy und sie wird sie für Sie **abtippen**. Wenn Sie einen **Stoß** fertig haben, legen Sie ihn einfach in meinen **Ausgangskorb**. Es gibt auch noch ein paar **E-Mails, die zu bearbeiten sind**. Sie finden sie im allgemeinen ARGO-**Ordner**.

P. I'll do my best, Mr Morgan. But there are just a few questions of **style** I'd like to sort out first. I'm still a bit uncertain how **to end a letter** in English – there seem to be so many different forms of closing a letter...

P. Ich werde mein Bestes tun, Mr Morgan. Ich habe aber noch ein paar Fragen bezüglich des **Schreibstils**, die ich vorher noch klären möchte. Ich bin mir immer noch ein bisschen unsicher, wie man **einen Brief** im Englischen **beendet** – es scheint so viele verschiedene Arten zu geben, einen Brief abzuschließen ...

Dos and Don'ts – A matter of form...

When writing a **formal business letter**, the correct form of address is: **Dear Sir** or **Dear Madam**. The customary plural form is: **Dear Sirs**. If you are writing a business letter **to a person you know by name** then you may now begin your letter in the following way: **Dear Mr (Smith, Brown)**. Difficulty is encountered by the British (and Americans) when a woman is addressed. If you are replying to a letter written by a woman who gave her name as Mrs, then you can safely address her as: **Dear Mrs (Smith, Brown)**. A slight problem arises when you have to reply to a letter signed **simply with surname and first name** – Joan Brown, for instance.

Under no circumstances should you address her as Miss Brown. In the United States, the problem was solved by inventing a new form – **Ms** – and this has also won wide acceptance now in Britain. So, replying to a letter signed by Joan Brown, you can safely address her as **Ms Brown**. Another alternative in use is to address her as: **Dear Joan Brown**.
Titles must always be used: Dear Lord Salisbury, Dear Sir John (here the surname is dropped!), **Dear Dr Linklater, Dear Professor Maugham**.
Senior military ranks are also usually used in formal letter-writing: **Dear Major Rigby**.

And now – **how do you end a letter**?
Yours sincerely or **Yours faithfully**? The British use a simple rule in deciding whether to end a business letter with **sincerely** or **faithfully**. If the letter begins with a **Dear Sir**, they avoid employing a further S by ending the letter **Yours faithfully**. The same rule applies if the letter begins **Dear Madam** or **Dear Sirs**.
Yours sincerely is reserved for letters addressed to persons by name: Dear Mr Smith, Dear Mrs Brown etc. The form **Yours truly** is now found almost exclusively on correspondence sent by fax or electronic mail. The British have an almost limitless list of ways of ending letters addressed to people by their first name: **Dear John ... with best wishes, with kind regards, with regards, all the best ...**

Exercise 1

Wie würden Sie folgende Briefe beenden?

1. Dear Major Trowbridge, I hope you got home safely after the wedding... _____.

2. Dear Sirs, We are writing to request...

   _____.

3. Dear James, Thank you for your invitation to dinner...

   _____.

4. Dear Sir Charles, My society would like to invite you to address...

   _____.

5. Dear Mr Spencer, We would like to place an order with your company for... _____.

Talk Talk Talk

(Peter's office, Melissa Walker, the Marketing Manager, enters.)

M. Good morning, Peter. You look busy.

P. I have this **pile of letters to attend to**. They'll take a lot of **getting through**.

M. If you need any help or advice, give me a call – particularly if they concern marketing, of course.

P. That's very kind of you, Melissa. But I must try first of all to master these things myself.

(Peters Büro, Melissa Walker, die Marketingmanagerin, tritt ein.)

M. Guten Morgen Peter, Sie sehen beschäftigt aus.

P. Ich muss diesen **Haufen Briefe bearbeiten**. Es wird eine Weile dauern, bis ich sie **durch habe**.

M. Rufen Sie mich an, falls Sie Hilfe oder einen Rat brauchen – besonders, wenn es um Marketingfragen geht, versteht sich.

P. Das ist sehr nett von Ihnen, Melissa, aber ich sollte als Erstes versuchen, solche Aufgaben selbst zu bewältigen.

✉ Peter's first letter is a **formal request** from a large retail company for information about ARGO's range of products:

Dear Sirs,

We would be most grateful if you sent us **at your convenience** full information about the range of software products you are able to offer. We are particularly interested in any product you have which could lead to a streamlining of our sales and receipts accounting and recording systems.
I look forward to your reply,
Yours faithfully,

John Mitchell
Managing Director
The Rosings Group

Talk Talk Talk 2

(Peter's office)

(Peters Büro)

P. Steve? Hello, how are you today? I have a request here for information on **our full range of products**, but with special interest in anything in the **retail trade** area. We do have a **sales and receipts accounting program**, don't we?

P. Steve? Hallo, wie geht es Ihnen heute? Ich habe hier eine Anfrage nach Informationen über unsere gesamte **Produktpalette**, besonders über alles, was den Bereich **Einzelhandel** betrifft. Wir haben doch ein **Verkaufs- und Quittungs-Buchführungs-programm**, oder?

S. Yes, but we're not having a great deal of success with it. It's already a year old and, in computer terms, has long passed its **'sell-by' date.** But I'm expecting an updated system from America at any time.

S. Ja, aber wir haben keinen besonderen Erfolg damit. Es ist bereits ein Jahr alt und hat für technische Verhältnisse sein **Verfalls-datum** schon lange überschritten. Allerdings erwarte ich täglich ein

Can you put them off?

aktualisiertes System aus Amerika. **Können Sie die Leute noch ein bisschen hinhalten?**

P. Well, they seem to be in some hurry. Can I at least send off the other information?

P. Tja, sie scheinen es recht eilig zu haben. Kann ich ihnen wenigstens die anderen Informationen schicken?

S. Sure, but if they're retail trade they won't be interested in most of our other programs. But I'll let you have the lot. I'll tell you what – I'll do more. I have a new secretary. She'll help you **draft that letter** in such a way that they'll wait till next Christmas for the retail sales program. Her name's Beryl...

S. Klar, aber wenn sie im Einzelhandel tätig sind, werden sie sich für die meisten unserer anderen Programme nicht sonderlich interessieren. Ich werde Ihnen trotzdem den ganzen Schwung geben. Ich sage Ihnen was – ich tue noch mehr. Ich habe eine neue Sekretärin. Sie wird Ihnen helfen, **diesen Brief so zu entwerfen**, dass sie glatt bis Weihnachten auf das Einzelhandels-Programm warten. Ihr Name ist Beryl ...

 Peter und Beryl machen sich an die Arbeit:

Dear Mr Mitchell,

Thank you for **your enquiry** of 4 May. **We have great pleasure in enclosing** complete information on the full range of our products. You will, however, notice that one important product is missing: the ARGO retail sales and receipts logging and accounting program. This is because the program is being replaced by a revolutionary new software which will be reaching us from the United States shortly.

We would not want to interest you in a program which is so soon to be overtaken by the very latest technology, and we assure you that as soon as we

receive the new software we will get in touch with you again and arrange to demonstrate the new development to you personally.
I assure you of our best attention at all times.

Yours sincerely,

Peter Brückner
Assistant Managing Director
ARGO Limited

Background information
The British use the American spelling for "programme" in context of computers: "We want to install your **accounting program**."

Exercise 2

Bilden Sie die Substantive folgender Verben nach diesem Beispiel:
I **instructed** him to send me the documents as soon as possible.
Lösung: "instruction".

1. May I **request** a speedy reply? _____
2. I would like to **ask** you for something... _____
3. We are now forced to **demand** immediate payment of the outstanding account. _____
4. We have no alternative but to **refuse** payment until all the conditions have been met. _____

Talk Talk Talk

P. Well, that should do the trick. Thank you very much, Beryl.

B. That's quite all right, Mr Brückner. Any time. I'll put the letter in the **out tray for posting**, shall I?

P. I think I'd better show it to Mr Morgan first.

B. Just as you wish. The letter is **stored** anyway. I've created a **new folder** for the Rosings Group. You'll find it there.

P. Well, I hope there'll be more to go in that folder later on. Now for the next letter – oh dear, this one's a **complaint**.

P. Okay, so dürfte es klappen. Vielen Dank, Beryl.

B. Gern geschehen, Mr Brückner. Jederzeit. Ich werde den Brief jetzt in den **Postausgangskorb** legen, in Ordnung?

P. Ich glaube, ich zeige ihn besser zuerst Mr Morgan.

B. Wie Sie wollen. Der Brief ist auf alle Fälle **abgespeichert**. Ich habe eine **neue Datei** für die Rosings Group angelegt. Da finden Sie ihn.

P. Gut, ich hoffe, dieser Ordner wird später noch um einiges voller werden. Jetzt aber zum nächsten Brief – oje, eine **Beschwerde**.

 Dear Sirs,

I regret to have to inform you that my company is **not** at all **pleased with** the way in which the servicing contract for the ARGO office management system is being honoured. According to the contract, an ARGO representative should visit our offices in person once a month during the 12-month period after installation. Our system was installed seven months ago and your Newcastle representative, Mr Batty, has called on us personally just twice. He has phoned on occasion to check if the system is functioning satisfactorily. Fortunately, the system has given us no problems, but there are technical questions which we need to discuss on a one-to-one basis and not over the telephone.

I would be pleased if you rectified the situation and honoured the terms of the contract.
I hope to hear back from you very soon on this matter.

Yours faithfully,
George Robertson
Managing Director
The Newcastle Fine Produce Company

P. Lucy, I have a letter here to dictate, but first of all could you get me Mr Batty in Newcastle on the phone?

L. Certainly, Peter.

P. Hello, is that Desmond Batty? Peter Brückner of ARGO here. We've had a complaint from Newcastle Fine Foods that you haven't been following on their office management system installation as required in the contract.

D. I established that the system is working well and there was really no need to call by on a regular basis. George Robertson appeared to be in agreement.

P. Well, he's written us a pretty stiff letter of complaint. Can I tell him you'll be calling by as arranged monthly?

P. Lucy, ich habe hier einen Brief zum Diktieren, aber könnten Sie mich bitte zuerst mit Mr Batty in Newcastle verbinden?

L. Natürlich, Peter.

P. Hallo, spreche ich mit Desmond Batty? Hier spricht Peter Brückner von ARGO. Wir hatten hier eine Beschwerde der Newcastle Fine Foods darüber, dass Sie ihr Büromanagementsystem nicht betreut haben, wie es im Vertrag vereinbart ist.

D. Ich habe mich davon überzeugt, dass die Anlage einwandfrei funktioniert und dass es wirklich keinen Grund gibt, regelmäßig vorbeizukommen. George Robertson schien damit einverstanden zu sein.

P. Tja, er hat uns einen ziemlich deutlichen Beschwerdebrief geschickt. Kann ich ihm mitteilen, dass Sie in Zukunft wie vereinbart monatlich vorbeischauen?

D. Well, if that's really what he wants, then fine by me. But there's actually nothing to do.

D. Gut, wenn er das unbedingt will, dann ist mir das recht. Aber es gibt dort wirklich nichts zu tun.

P. I think he just wants the reassurance that somebody from ARGO is **on the spot** and taking a personal interest in his **office management**.

P. Ich glaube er braucht lediglich die Gewissheit, dass jemand von ARGO **vor Ort** ist und persönliches Interesse an seinem **Büromanagement** zeigt.

D. Fine, then tell him I'll come round next Monday – and then once a month.

D. Gut, dann sagen Sie ihm, dass ich Montag bei ihm vorbeikomme – und danach einmal im Monat.

 Dear Mr Robertson,

I am truly sorry you have had cause to complain about the way ARGO is honouring its contract with your company. There appears to have been a misunderstanding here. Mr Batty has not been calling personally as arranged because the system has been performing satisfactorily.
He most certainly would have visited your offices immediately if his help had been required.
I talked to Mr Batty by phone today and he has promised to visit personally next Monday and then once a month, as contractually arranged.
I assure you of our best attention at all times.

Yours sincerely,

Peter Brückner
Assistant Managing Director
ARGO Limited

Exercise 3

Welche Wörter passen in die Lücken?

scheduled | range | sent | reply | developed | areas | useful

operations | arrange | products (2x) | employ | grateful

Dear Sir,

We would be very _____ if you _____ us

information about your company's full _____ of

_____.

We are interested in various _____ which have been

_____ by your company, and we are sure we could

_____ them in various _____ of our

_____.

We have a board meeting _____ for next Wednesday,

so it would be particularly _____ if you could

_____ to send the information material to us by then.

I look forward to your _____.

Talk Talk Talk 3

(Steve enters Peter's office.)

(Steve betritt Peters Büro.)

S. Still **submerged in letters**? It's nearly lunchtime – I feel like a beer and a steak pie at the Duke of Rutland. Want to join me?

S. Immer noch **unter einem Berg von Briefen begraben**? Wir haben fast Mittag – ich hätte Lust auf ein Bier und eine Fleischpastete im Duke of Rutland. Möchten Sie mitkommen?

P. Oh, why not – I'll work late with the other letters if I have to.

P. Oh, warum nicht – ich werde wegen der restlichen Briefe eben länger arbeiten, wenn es nötig ist.

B. Wait for me then, I've **worked up a thirst** myself.

B. Warten Sie auf mich, ich bin **vom Arbeiten ganz durstig** geworden.

S. Make it snappy then, Beryl...

S. Dann **machen Sie schnell**, Beryl ...

(The Duke of Rutland pub)
S. What's it to be, Peter, the usual?

(Im Duke-of-Rutland-Pub)
S. Was darf's denn sein Peter, das Übliche?

P. Yes please, Steve.

P. Ja bitte, Steve.

S. And Beryl?

S. Und Beryl?

B. An alcohol-free beer, please. Writing letters in English must be quite different from how you compose letters in German, Peter?

B. Bitte ein Alkoholfreies. Briefe auf Englisch zu schreiben ist sicher etwas ganz anderes, als das auf Deutsch zu tun, oder, Peter?

P. There are small points of difference, but the general style is very similar. I had expected much less **formality** in English, but the rules are really just as rigid as in German.

P. Es gibt ein paar kleine Unterschiede, aber der generelle Stil ist ganz ähnlich. Ich hatte im Englischen viel weniger **Förmlichkeit** erwartet, aber die Regeln sind tatsächlich ebenso streng wie im Deutschen.

S. You're right there about formality and rules. But they're really only a cover, you know – I'll give you an example. Look at this letter I got this morning from my local council...

S. Sie haben Recht, was die Formalitäten und Regeln angeht. Aber sie sind lediglich eine oberflächliche Hülle – ich werde es Ihnen demonstrieren. Schauen Sie sich diesen Brief an, den ich heute Morgen von der Stadtverwaltung bekommen habe ...

 Dear Sir,

It has been brought to our attention that you are parking your car illegally on council land at the end of Lansdowne Drive, Wimbledon. Although the land has not yet been fenced off, there are two notices making it very clear that parking is prohibited. You have been observed on several occasions parking your car on this ground at night and driving your vehicle away the next morning before our parking wardens take up their duty. For security reasons, even night-time parking is prohibited. Hence, **we must ask you kindly to refrain from** parking your car on this terrain in future. Failure to comply with our request will result in legal action having to be taken against you.

Yours sincerely,

Edmond Tracey
Town Clerk

Exercise 4

Finden Sie einfachere Wörter oder Ausdrücke:

1. prohibited _____

2. observed _____

3. on several occasions _____

4. take up their duty _____

5. refrain from _____

6. terrain _____

Talk Talk Talk 4

B. So why are you getting so **het up**, Steve? It looks like an **open-and-shut** case to me.

B. Warum **regen** Sie sich so **auf**, Steve? Für mich sieht das wie ein **ganz klarer** Fall aus.

S. No. That's not it. Look at the style of that letter. They're basically telling me: "Hey, you **berk,** stop parking your **lousy** car on our ground". But this guy Tracey has decided to use sugar-coated words.

S. Nein, darum geht es nicht. Sehen Sie sich den Stil an, in dem dieser Brief geschrieben wurde. Was sie mir eigentlich sagen, ist: „Hey du **Dussel**, hör endlich auf, dein **lausiges** Auto auf unserem Grundstück zu parken." Aber dieser Tracey will alles durch die Blume sagen.

B. Oh, come on, Steve. He's just being polite.

B. Ach, kommen Sie, Steve. Er ist doch nur höflich.

S. Yes, in that typically English way where it means **zilch**.

S. Ja, aber eben auf diese typisch englische Art und Weise, die ungefähr **gar nichts** bedeutet.

P. Well, I don't want to take sides here, but official letters like that are also **couched** in polite terms in Germany.

P. Na ja, ich möchte hier zwar keine Partei ergreifen, aber offizielle Briefe wie dieser sind in Deutschland auch in höfliche Formulierungen **eingebettet**.

Background information

And don't forget to stamp your letters – but with which stamps?
Letters within the UK are sent by two alternative routes:
a. First Class – delivery usually takes one or two days
b. Second Class – delivery can take two or three days

Exercise 5

**Beryl kann Steve zu einem freundlichen Antwortbrief überreden.
Können Sie die Lücken darin füllen?**

| vicinity | opportunity | in question | cause | appeal | refrain | inform |

| used | unaware | prohibiting | assumed | defence |

Dear Mr Tracey,

Thank you for your letter of 4 June. I am sorry you have had
_____ to _____ me that I have been ille-
gally parking on council land. In my _____, I must say
that I was _____ that the land _____ be-
longed to the council. I certainly saw no notices _____
parking. I had _____ that at night at least the land could
be _____ to park cars on. If this is not the case, I shall
of course _____ from parking my car there in future. But
may I take this _____ to _____ for more
parking spaces in Lansdowne Drive and the _____.
Yours sincerely,

Steve Blackman

Exercise 6

In Großbritannien gibt es verschiedene Möglichkeiten zum Versenden eines Briefes. Wie kann man diese am besten umschreiben? Kreuzen Sie an!

Registered post

a) The recipient signs for the letter.

b) The sender receives a receipt confirming the letter has been sent.

c) A description of the letter's contents is officially registered.

Recorded delivery

a) The sender must sign a declaration assuming responsibility for the letter's delivery.

b) The post office takes responsibility for the safe delivery of the letter.

c) The recipient signs an official receipt confirming acceptance of the letter.

Talk Talk Talk

(James Morgan enters Peter's office.)

J. Peter, I have a letter here I'd like you to reply to today, if you can. It's a **job enquiry** which has been hidden among my **papers** for the past few days.

(James Morgan betritt Peters Büro.)

J. Peter, ich habe hier einen Brief, den Sie bitte noch heute beantworten sollten, wenn es Ihnen möglich ist. Es ist eine **Bewerbung**, die ein paar Tage lang unter meinen **Unterlagen** versteckt lag.

P. Certainly, Mr Morgan. But how should I reply to it?

P. Natürlich, Mr Morgan. Aber wie soll ich darauf antworten?

J. Just say we have no immediate vacancies but that we'll **put the application on file**. The young man certainly has qualifications which we might be able to use some time in the future. Just dictate the letter to Lucy.

J. Sagen Sie einfach, dass wir derzeit keine freien Stellen haben, **das Stellengesuch** jedoch **in die Datei aufnehmen**. Der junge Mann hat offensichtlich Qualifikationen, die uns in Zukunft vielleicht einmal nützlich sein könnten. Diktieren Sie den Brief einfach Lucy.

P. May I see the application?

P. Darf ich die Bewerbung mal sehen?

Dear Sir/Madam,

I am writing to inquire if your company has **an opening for a trainee in business management**. I have just completed my Master's degree in Business Administration at the University of Aston and am now looking for an opportunity to add practical experience to the theoretical knowledge I have gained in five years of study. Your company was recommended to me by the University's professional counselling service. I am attaching a brief **CV** which summarizes my educational background.

Yours faithfully,

Martin Russell

P. Lucy, could you **take a letter** please?

P. Lucy, können Sie bitte einen **Brief aufnehmen?**

L. Certainly, Peter…

L. Natürlich, Peter …

 Dear Mr Russell,

Thank you for your letter of 22 May. **We regret to inform you** that at the moment we have no vacancy which would suit your qualifications. However, we would be most interested in meeting you if such a vacancy occurrs in the future and we shall be glad to put your enquiry in our files. **In the meantime**, please accept an up-to-date information brochure on ARGO Limited.

Yours sincerely,

Peter Brückner
Assistant Managing Director

Der folgende Beschwerdebrief landet auf Peters Schreibtisch:

 Dear Sir,

Your sales representative in Birmingham promised one month ago to call by our offices and explain the advantages of the ARGO Accounting 2000 package. We suspended inquiries we had begun with other companies pending the outcome of the meeting with your representative. To this date, no ARGO representative has reported to us. I **regret** to have to inform you that our Board has decided that, unless we hear from your representative within one week of the date of this letter, we shall be compelled to **strike** ARGO **from** our shortlist of possible suppliers and look elsewhere for the product we urgently need.

Yours faithfully,

Eric Simpson
Director
Titan Products

Exercise 7

Helfen Sie Peter dabei, James Morgan vom Inhalt des Briefes zu unterrichten, indem Sie die richtige Form der Verben benutzen!

Mr Simpson of Titan Products `write` _____ to us `complain` _____ that although our sales representative in Birmingham `promise` _____ to call by his offices `explain` _____ our Accounting 2000 system, he `not turn up` _____. Mr Simpson `tell` _____ us that Titan `suspend` _____ enquiries with other possible suppliers until the company `look at` _____ our product. He `say` _____ the Titan Board `decide ... give` _____ us one more week for our representative `call` _____. If he `not do so` _____ within that time, Titan `strike` _____ us from its shortlist of possible suppliers and `look` _____ elsewhere for a supplier.

Talk Talk Talk

(Melissa enters Peter's office.)

M. Peter, how are you getting along in your search for a place to live?

(Melissa betritt Peters Büro.)

M. Wie kommen Sie bei Ihrer Suche nach einer Wohnung voran, Peter?

P. Two agents are now looking for me, but frankly I just get more confused with each email I receive from them.

P. Ich habe jetzt zwei Makler, die für mich auf der Suche sind, aber ehrlich gesagt verwirrt mich jede Mail mehr, die ich von ihnen bekomme.

M. What's wrong with them?

M. Was stimmt denn damit nicht?

P. Well, maybe I'm a bit too demanding, but whenever they send me descriptions of property I might be interested in and I arrange for a viewing, I never find what I expect. Here's the latest example…

P. Tja, vielleicht verlange ich einfach zu viel, aber jedes Mal, wenn sie mir Beschreibungen von Wohnungen schicken, die mich eventuell interessieren könnten und ich einen Besichtigungstermin vereinbare, finde ich nicht das vor, was ich erwarte. Hier das jüngste Beispiel …

 Dear Mr Brückner,

We are very pleased to offer you a **highly desirable** property in one of the areas which you indicated to us might be of most interest to you as a **permanent location** to live. The property is on the first floor of a magnificently converted Victorian-era mansion. It **boasts** a representative entrance hall, two **generously proportioned** bedrooms, a stately living room with separate dining area, Adam fireplace and corniced, built-in book-shelves, a spacious kitchen with every possible modern appliance, a luxurious bathroom with jacuzzi, substantial brass fittings and a pastel-toned suite. There are also panoramic views to Hyde Park.
We **urge** a very early viewing of this unique property and **would be pleased to arrange an appointment at your kind convenience**.

Yours sincerely,
…

Exercise 8

Schreiben Sie den Brief neu, indem Sie folgende Wörter und Ausdrücke durch passende aus der Auswahlliste ersetzen:

| wanted | ask | recommend | luxurious | large | site | has |

| possesses | extensive | needed | attractive |

1. highly desirable _____

2. permanent location _____

3. boasts _____

4. generously proportioned _____

5. urge _____

Talk Talk Talk 5

M. Well, sounds quite a place!

P. Doesn't it just? There were even a couple of photographs with the letter. Here...

M. Wow! Now that's something...

P. The photographer who took them must have been quite something, too. They're not at all like what I saw with my own eyes!

M. Das hört sich doch gut an!

P. Nicht wahr? Dem Brief waren sogar einige Fotos beigefügt. Hier ...

M. Donnerwetter! Das macht schon was her ...

P. Der Fotograf, der sie gemacht hat, muss auch ganz schön was draufhaben. Sie sehen nicht im geringsten so aus wie das, was ich mit meinen eigenen Augen gesehen habe!

M. Have you viewed the place?

P. Of course. Would you like my description of it?

M. I'm **dying to** hear it!

P. Right! Let's start with the entrance hall. "Representative" was the description. What it represented was a small space behind the front door, not large enough to put a coat-stand. Neither of the "generously proportioned" bedrooms was larger than 12 square metres. "Stately" living room? It was **in a bit of a state,** that I'll admit. The "separate dining area" just didn't exist. The "Adam" fireplace was a plaster **mock-up,** and the bookshelves were a DIY job. Modern kitchen appliances? They might have been complete if there had been a dishwasher and a microwave. The "luxurious" bathroom was a converted cupboard with no window. And so on. Want to hear more?

M. Sie haben sich die Wohnung angesehen?

P. Natürlich. Würden Sie gern meine Beschreibung davon hören?

M. Ich **sterbe vor** Neugier!

P. In Ordnung! Beginnen wir mit der Eingangshalle. „Repräsentativ" lautete die Beschreibung. Was sich mir präsentierte war ein kleiner Raum hinter der Eingangstür, nicht einmal groß genug, um eine Garderobe hineinzustellen. Keines der „großzügig geschnittenen" Schlafzimmer war größer als zwölf Quadratmeter. Wohnzimmer in „prächtigem Zustand"? Es war in einem **schlechten Zustand**, das muss ich zugeben. Der „separate Essbereich" existierte einfach gar nicht. Der steinerne Kamin war eine **Nachbildung** aus Gips und die Bücherregale waren selbst gemacht. Moderne Kücheneinrichtung? Sie wäre vielleicht komplett gewesen, wenn es eine Geschirrspülmaschine und eine Mikrowelle gegeben hätte. Das „luxuriöse" Badezimmer war ein umgewandelter Schrank ohne Fenster. Und so weiter, und so fort. Wollen Sie noch mehr hören?

M. (laughs) No, that's enough, Peter. You've learnt another important lesson in Britain – never trust an estate agent's **hype**. Or learn how to read between the lines.

P. Between the lines?

M. Estate agents have their own language. If the bedrooms had been really large they would have been described as "huge" not "generously proportioned", that kind of thing.

P. Oh dear! I don't think I'll ever find a place to live.

M. Patience, Peter, patience – a very English virtue!

M. (lacht) Nein, das reicht, Peter. Sie haben eine weitere wichtige, englische Lektion gelernt – traue nie den **Übertreibungen** eines Wohnungsmaklers. Oder lerne, zwischen den Zeilen zu lesen.

P. Zwischen den Zeilen?

M. Wohnungsmakler haben ihre eigene Sprache. Wären die Schlafzimmer tatsächlich groß gewesen, wären sie als „riesig" und nicht als „großzügig geschnitten" beschrieben worden oder so etwas in der Art.

P. Ach du meine Güte! Ich glaube, ich werde nie eine richtige Bleibe finden.

M. Geduld, Peter, Geduld – eine englische Tugend!

Background information

As Peter has now discovered, there are **various forms of English, employed in distinct situations and most visible in written letters**. A letter containing a very real threat of **dire** action will be written in as polite a form as the most harmless **missive**. But of all the various forms of English employed in official communications, the most curious and most difficult to construe is the language used by estate agents in describing the properties they hope to sell. If you are renting or buying property in Britain through the services of an estate agent, you would be well advised to engage the additional advice of somebody fluent in English.

Exercise 9

Setzen Sie die korrekte Form des Verbs „to write" ein!

1. I would _____ if I had only known your address.

2. I'll _____ just as soon as I arrive.

3. He _____ regularly won't he?

4. She has never _____ to me in that tone before.

5. I have better things to do than _____ to you all the time.

6. They _____ that they would be returning tomorrow.

7. I _____ to you right now, while waiting for the train.

Talk Talk Talk

P. Melissa, now here's a letter I really don't understand at all. It seems to belong in your department, but I'm not sure.

P. Melissa, ich habe hier einen Brief, den ich wirklich überhaupt nicht verstehe. Es scheint so, als würde er in Ihre Abteilung gehören, aber ich bin mir nicht sicher.

M. Let me take a look...

M. Zeigen Sie mal ...

✉ Dear Sirs,

Thank you for your letter of 15 inst., **to which we now have pleasure in replying positively**. Your interest in participating in the joint InterConnect initiative has been noted and we have pleasure in enclosing formal application forms. In view of the brief amount of time now remaining, may we urge you to forward us your application as soon as possible, together with the registration fee. The absolute deadline for applications is 31 July, and any applications received after that date can unfortunately not be accepted. I look forward to your reply.

Yours faithfully,
Robert Clarke

M. Oh dear, I don't know how that letter ended up on James's desk. I quite forgot that we had asked for information about participation in the InterConnect **marketing push**. I'll really have to get busy on this one – it's no wonder it had you puzzled, Peter.

M. Oje, ich weiß nicht, wie dieser Brief auf James' Tisch gelandet ist. Ich hatte fast vergessen, dass wir um Informationen über die Teilnahme an der InterConnect-**Marketinginitiative** gebeten hatten. Darum muss ich mich wirklich kümmern – kein Wunder, dass Sie verwirrt waren, Peter.

P. Well, there's one expression – or abbreviation there – that really **foxed** me, is that what you say? That "inst." What does that mean?

P. Tja, es gibt da einen Ausdruck – oder eine Abkürzung – die mich wirklich **verblüfft** hat, ist das das richtige Wort? Dieses „inst." – was bedeutet das?

M. Oh, that! It's just a formal way of referring to the month – in this case our letter was dated 15 July, or 15 "inst." The form is becoming obsolete, but you'll still meet it and it's good for you to know what it means.

M. Ach das! Das ist lediglich eine formelle Art und Weise, sich auf den jeweiligen Monat zu beziehen – in diesem Fall ist der Brief datiert auf den 15. Juli oder den 15. „inst." Dieser Ausdruck ist langsam veraltet, aber er kommt manchmal noch vor und es ist gut, dass Sie jetzt wissen, was er bedeutet.

P. So today is 21 "inst."?

P. Also ist heute der 21. „inst."?

M. Yes, but only in letter form – speaking of which, do you have any more **to reply to**?

M. Ja, aber nur in schriftlicher Briefform – und da wir gerade davon sprechen, haben Sie noch welche **zu beantworten**?

P. Stacks – I'd better get down to them.

P. Haufenweise – ich kümmere mich besser darum.

M. Peter, a tip: divide them up into categories. You'll save a lot of time that way. And then concentrate on those that have to be replied to urgently.

M. Peter, ein Tipp: Teilen Sie sie in Kategorien ein. So sparen Sie sich eine Menge Zeit. Und dann konzentrieren Sie sich auf diejenigen, die dringend beantwortet werden müssen.

P. Well, I suppose these **letters enquiring about** our products are the most pressing – I'll get down to those first...

P. Tja, ich vermute, die **Briefe, in denen man sich nach** unseren Produkten **erkundigt**, sind die dringendsten – die werde ich zuerst bearbeiten ...

Exercise 10

Wählen Sie die richtigen Wörter, um die Lücken zu füllen!

reply   early   best   grateful   receipt   assured   appreciate

prompt   sent

1. We have pleasure in acknowledging _____ of your letter.
2. Looking forward to a _____ reply.

3. We would _____ an _____ reply.

4. Please be _____ of our _____ attention
at all times.

5. Would you please _____ to the above address.

6. We would be _____ if you _____ us
information about your product line.

(Peter **tackles some letters of enquiry**...)

(Peter **geht ein paar Anfragen durch** …)

 Dear Sir,

My attention was caught by your company's advertisement in Techno-News. **I am particularly interested in** the Reddy program, which your company claims can contribute to large savings of time in sorting bulk orders. Our growth in wholesale trade has now reached the point where a highly developed technological system is needed to keep pace with increasing orders. I would, therefore, be most obliged if you arranged to send me further, detailed information on the Reddy program.

Yours faithfully,

Frank R. Gilpin
Managing Director
Top Trading

P. (reaches for his telephone)
Steve, do you have the **information brochures** and **catalogues** on the Reddy program?

S. Hang on a moment, I'll have a look. Yes, I've got a pile of stuff here.

P. I have an **enquiry** here for as much information as we can send, brochures and catalogues. I'll give you a copy of my reply – you'll want to alert your man in Birmingham, there could be a sale here.

S. Yes, **please keep me informed**. It's good of you to take over this **correspondence**, dear chap. I have so much to do at the moment.

P. No problem, Steve. It's a pleasure.

P. Lucy, can you **take a letter**?

L. Peter, you have a **dictaphone** in your desk, you know. Why don't you use that? It'll save us both time.

P. (greift nach dem Telefonhörer)
Steve, haben Sie die **Informationsbroschüren und die Kataloge** über die Reddy-Programme?

S. Bleiben Sie einen Augenblick dran, ich sehe nach. Ja, ich habe einen Stapel von dem Zeug hier.

P. Ich habe hier eine **Anfrage** nach so viel Informationen, wie wir schicken können, Broschüren und Kataloge. Ich werde Ihnen eine Kopie meiner Antwort geben – Sie werden Ihren Mann in Birmingham sicher darauf aufmerksam machen wollen, dass hier ein Geschäft zustande kommen könnte.

S. Ja, **halten Sie mich auf dem Laufenden**. Es ist nett von Ihnen, diesen **Briefwechsel** zu übernehmen, alter Freund. Ich habe im Augenblick so viel zu tun.

P. Kein Problem, Steve. Ist mir ein Vergnügen.

P. Lucy, können Sie **einen Brief aufnehmen**?

L. Peter, Sie haben ein **Diktiergerät** in Ihrer Schreibtischschublade. Warum benutzen Sie es nicht? Damit würden wir beide Zeit sparen.

P. Well, bless my soul, I should have known a high-tech company would have a device like that.

P. Meine Güte, ich hätte wissen sollen, dass ein Hightech-Unternehmen so einen Apparat haben würde.

P. Well, here we go...

P. Also, los geht's...

 Reply to letter from Mr Frank Gilpin, Managing Director, Top Trading, Aston Road 14–20, Birmingham, dated 14 July.

Dear Mr Gilpin,

Thank you for your letter of 14 July (Lucy, make that 14th of July or 14.07., if you like, whatever our style is). **I have great pleasure in sending you full information** on the Reddy program which you requested. This is the **very latest development** in electronic order-sorting, and **we are sure it will match your requirements.**

If you have any further questions please do not hesitate to contact me. My telephone and telefax numbers are as above.

Yours sincerely,

Peter Brückner
Assistant Managing Director
ARGO Limited

P. Steve, how would you like a **copy** of this letter? A **hard copy** or shall I put it **on file**?

P. Steve, in welcher Form hätten Sie die **Kopie** dieses Briefes gerne? **Auf Papier** oder soll ich sie **in einer Datei** speichern?

S. Can you create a folder for Top Trading and save it in that? You'll find a general file for business enquiries under "ARGO-Enquiries". I have access to that and it keeps me up to date on possible **sales follow-ups**. I'm sure we'll be hearing more from Top Trading – at least, I hope we do.

S. Könnten Sie einen Ordner für Top Trading erstellen und ihn darin abspeichern? Unter „ARGO-Anfragen" finden Sie einen allgemeinen Ordner für Geschäftsanfragen. Ich habe Zugriff darauf und er hält mich auf dem Laufenden über mögliche **Nachfolge-Verkäufe**. Ich bin mir sicher, wir werden noch mehr von Top Trading hören – wenigstens hoffe ich das.

Exercise 11

Peter findet es einfacher, seine Briefe mithilfe des Diktiergeräts an Lucy weiterzureichen. Geben Sie in den folgenden Sätzen die korrekten Komparativformen an.

1. This letter was much clear _____ than the first one.

2. His last letter was brief _____ than usual, but still long _____ than hers.

3. Although it was written by hand, the letter was legible _____ than I thought it would be.

4. The tone of that letter was insulting _____ than I expected.

5. Why was the letter lengthy _____ than the others?

6. The letter arrived soon _____ than I had expected.

(Peter takes the next letter from the pile.)

(Peter nimmt den nächsten Brief vom Stapel.)

 Dear Mr Morgan,

I am taking the liberty of writing to you following our meeting at the Chamber of Trade lunch. I was very interested in your description of the range of activities of your company, and I would like to learn more. I would be most honoured if you accepted an invitation to lunch with me at my club next week. May I suggest Friday?
I look forward to hearing back from you.

Yours sincerely,

Henry Rowbotham

Talk Talk Talk

(Peter knocks at James Morgan's office door and enters.)

(Peter klopft an James Morgans Büro und tritt ein.)

P. Mr Morgan, I believe this is a **personal letter** for you to answer. It was among the correspondence you gave me to attend to.

P. Mr Morgan, ich glaube dies ist ein **persönlicher Brief**, den Sie beantworten sollten. Er lag unter der Korrespondenz, die Sie mir zur Bearbeitung gegeben hatten.

J. Oh, Peter, I wanted to talk to you about that. I can't face a meeting with that man Rowbotham. He has absolutely no interest in ARGO – I think he's just looking for a drinking partner. Could you reply for me, telling him I am **indisposed** for the next couple of weeks?

J. Oh Peter, darüber wollte ich mit Ihnen sprechen. Ich möchte mich auf keinen Fall mit diesem Rowbotham treffen. Er hat absolut kein Interesse an ARGO – ich glaube, er sucht nur jemanden, der mit ihm einen trinken geht. Könnten Sie für mich antworten und ihm mitteilen, dass ich die nächsten paar Wochen **unabkömmlich** bin?

P. I'll try, but I'd like to show you the letter before I send it...

P. Ich werde es versuchen, aber ich würde Ihnen den Brief gerne zeigen, bevor ich ihn wegschicke.

 Dear Mr Rowbotham,

Mr Morgan has asked me to reply to your letter and to your kind invitation to lunch. He is unable to do so himself because he is **unfortunately indisposed**. He much appreciates the interest you showed in the work of ARGO Limited, and he has asked me to forward all the available information on the activities of our company. **If you have further questions** about the company, **I shall be happy to answer** them for you.
Mr Morgan joins me in sending greetings.

Yours sincerely,

Peter Brückner
Assistant Managing Director
ARGO Limited

Talk Talk Talk

J. **That'll do very well**, Peter. Thank you. But you might have opened yourself to an invitation to lunch with Rowbotham...

J. **Sehr gut gemacht**, Peter. Allerdings könnten Sie sich jetzt selbst der Gefahr einer Einladung zum Mittagessen von Mr Rowbotham ausgesetzt haben ...

P. I think **I can handle that**, Mr Morgan. Don't worry. That was a comparatively easy one – let's see what's next in the pile...

P. Ich denke, **damit komme ich klar**, Mr Morgan. Keine Sorge. Das war ein vergleichsweise einfacher Brief – mal sehen, was als Nächstes auf dem Stapel ist ...

Exercise 12

Sie sind zum Essen mit dem Managing Director einer großen Firma, Mr Gerald Green, eingeladen. Nachdem Sie zuerst angenommen haben, stellen Sie fest, dass Sie an dem Tag auf Geschäftsreise außerhalb der Stadt sind.

Wie würden Sie eine angemessene Absage formulieren?

_____

_____

_____

_____

_____

_____

Vocabulary

berk	Dussel/Idiot (ugs.)
to boast	prahlen (*hier:* etw. vorweisen können)
to catch up on letter-writing	überfällige Briefe schreiben
to couch a complaint	eine Beschwerde formulieren
dire	gräßlich; *hier:* weitreichend, unangenehm
to draft	entwerfen
to be dying to do sth.	„sterben" etw. zu tun (ugs.)
to end a letter	einen Brief beenden

✉ Korrespondenz

to enquire about	sich erkundigen nach
enquiry	Anfrage
fine by me	ist mir recht
foxed	verblüfft
generously proportioned	großzügig geschnitten
to get through	durchkriegen
het up	aufgeregt/erhitzt
highly desirable	höchst attraktiv
hype	zielgerichtete Übertreibung
in a state	*hier:* in einem schlechten Zustand
indisposed	unabkömmlich
in the meantime	in der Zwischenzeit
in tray	(Post-)Eingangskorb
lousy	lausig, verflixt
Make it snappy!	Machen Sie schnell/fix! (ugs.)
marketing push	Marketinginitiative
missive	Mitteilung
on occasion	bei Gelegenheit
on the spot	vor Ort
open-and-shut	klar und deutlich/eindeutig
out tray	(Post-)Ausgangskorb
permanent location	ständiger (Wohn-)Sitz
push	Initiative/Vorstoß (besonders im Marketing)
to refrain from	unterlassen
to reply to	beantworten
"sell-by" date	Haltbarkeitsdatum
stacks	Stapel
to streamline	rationalisieren
to strike from	ausstreichen/herausnehmen
to tackle some letters	ein paar Briefe durchgehen
to type up	abtippen
to urge	inständig bitten, drängen
to work up a thirst	sich durstig arbeiten
writer's cramp	Schreibkrampf
zilch	Nichts (ugs.)

Negotiations |
Verhandlungen

Here we go

Neben den alltäglichen Korrespondenzen, die in einem Unternehmen anfallen, bahnen sich natürlich auch wichtige geschäftliche Verbindungen an. Peter bekommt von James Morgan die Aufgabe übertragen, sich um einen bedeutenden Franchise-Vertrag von ARGO Limited mit einem amerikanischen Softwareanbieter zu kümmern.

Talk Talk Talk 🔊6

(James Morgan's office)

J. (on the telephone)
Peter, could you step into my office, please!

P. (enters) Good morning, Mr Morgan. What can I do for you?

J. I've been asked by **head office** in America to inquire into the possibility of obtaining a franchise for the United States for a new software product which Newcom in Manchester **has just brought out**. It was favourably written about in the American magazine "Computer World". We might be too late. Nevertheless, head office wants us to go ahead and approach Newcom.

(James Morgans Büro)

J. (ins Telefon) Peter, könnten Sie bitte in mein Büro kommen?

P. (tritt ein) Guten Morgen, Mr Morgan. Was kann ich für Sie tun?

J. Ich wurde vom **Hauptbüro** in Amerika darum gebeten, herauszufinden, ob es möglich ist, die amerikanischen Franchise-Lizenzen einer neuen Software zu erwerben, die Newcom in Manchester **gerade herausgebracht hat**. In dem amerikanischen Magazin „Computer World" wurde sehr positiv darüber berichtet. Wir kommen damit vielleicht schon zu spät, aber das

I'm really under pressure this week, therefore I'd like you to take this one over for me.

Hauptbüro möchte trotzdem, dass wir es versuchen und Newcom ansprechen. Ich bin diese Woche wirklich ziemlich im Stress, deswegen hätte ich gern, dass Sie die Sache für mich übernehmen.

P. Certainly, Mr Morgan.

P. Natürlich, Mr Morgan.

J. Head office has faxed us the "Computer World" article. You'll find everything you need there – even the address of Newcom and the name of their **Project Manager**. I'd be glad if you could get on to it right away...

J. Das Hauptbüro hat uns den Artikel aus der „Computer World" gefaxt. Sie finden darin alles, was Sie brauchen – selbst die Adresse von Newcom und den Namen ihres **Projektmanagers**. Es wäre schön, wenn Sie sich gleich darum kümmern könnten ...

Exercise 13

„Therefore" oder „nevertheless"?
Setzen Sie das richtige Wort in die folgenden Lücken ein!

1. We experienced delays in deliveries from our suppliers, _____ we were unable to complete your order in time.

2. Our production line let us down badly. _____ we shall do everything possible to get the goods to you by the end of next week.

3. We regret that we have not yet received payment for the last shipment. We are _____ not yet processing your second order.

Background information

Nevertheless is often replaced by **nonetheless** – particularly in written English. A less common alternative is **notwithstanding**. Notwithstanding means the same as despite but has the distinction of normally standing at the start of the sentence:

> Notwithstanding / Despite his objections, the company went ahead with its rationalization programme.

> The company went ahead with its rationalization programme despite his objections.

"Notwithstanding" is very rarely used in spoken English but is nevertheless often found in formal business correspondence.

Talk Talk Talk

(Peter dictates a letter to Newcom.)

(Peter diktiert einen Brief an Newcom.)

P. This letter is to Mr Trevor Payne, Project Manager of Newcom Technology – Lucy, you have the address on the fax.

P. Dieser Brief geht an Mr Trevor Payne, Projektmanager von Newcom Technology – Lucy, die Adresse finden Sie auf dem Fax.

 Dear Mr Payne,

Our attention was caught by the article on your company's software program "Instantweb", which was carried by the American magazine "Computer World". ARGO Limited markets a wide range of software products in the United States and Britain, including a successful newspaper copy-editing program which might well be complemented by "Instantweb". In combination, the two programs could contribute to an easier and more rapid access to the Internet by newspaper editorial offices.
Our head office in the United States was particularly interested in this pos-

sibility, and we **have been asked to approach you** with a view to obtaining the franchise for "Instantweb" in the United States. If the franchise is still available, we would be pleased to discuss with you all relevant details with a view to reaching a business contract of benefit to both enterprises.
I look forward to hearing from you.
Yours sincerely,

Peter Brückner
Assistant Managing Director
ARGO Limited

Background information
"Franchise" or **"licence"**?
A "franchise" is an official, contractual authorization to sell a company's products or services in a specified region or country.
A "licence" is the document of authorization.

Exercise 14

Im vorhergehenden Brief hat Peter einige Schlüsselsätze in der Passivform geschrieben. Das Aktiv ist jedoch dem Passiv immer vorzuziehen – also helfen Sie ihm und korrigieren Sie seinen Brief!

_____

_____

_____

_____

_____

Exercise 15

Verbinden Sie folgende Satzteile mit den passenden Konjunktionen „and", „but" oder „because".

1. We intend to place an order for items 1, 3 and 6, _____ first of all we would like to see your full price list.

2. We would like to order 100 units _____ look forward to a prompt delivery.

3. We regret having to return the delivered goods, _____ they arrived in a spoilt condition.

4. We regretfully have to cancel the contract, _____ you failed to honour an important clause.

5. We would normally have cancelled the contract _____ we recognize you acted in good faith.

6. Thank you for your prompt reply _____ we look forward to a fruitful cooperation.

Talk Talk Talk

(James Morgan's office. Peter enters.)

P. Good morning, Mr Morgan. I'm afraid the reply from Newcom doesn't sound very promising.

J. Let me see the letter...

(James Morgans Büro. Peter tritt ein.)

P. Guten Morgen, Mr Morgan. Ich fürchte, die Antwort von Newcom hört sich nicht sehr viel versprechend an.

J. Zeigen Sie mir mal den Brief ...

 Dear Mr Brückner,

Thank you for your letter of 21 May. **We were naturally pleased to hear that** our new software program "Instantweb" had caught the attention not only of "Computer World" but of your company, too.

Because of the "Computer World" publicity, we have received approaches from various companies and are at this time **involved in negotiations** with some of them. Nonetheless, we are not ruling out your company, and we would certainly welcome your more detailed proposals on a possible franchise for the United States.

Yours sincerely,

Trevor Payne

J. Hmm, how do we **take it from here**?	**J.** Hmm, wie sollen wir jetzt **weiter vorgehen**?
P. Well, as I see it, we have to convince them that we are the right company for the franchise. But how?	**P.** Nun ja, so wie ich das sehe, müssen wir sie überzeugen, dass wir die richtige Firma für ein Franchise sind. Aber wie?
J. Peter, let me think this one over, and I'll come back to you on it...	**J.** Peter, lassen Sie mich über diese Sache nachdenken, ich komme dann wieder auf Sie zu …

Background information

The software program impressed **both** Computer World **and** ARGO Limited. In his letter, Mr Payne writes he is pleased that it caught the attention **not only** of the magazine, **but also** of the company. Remember these useful constructions for shortlists!

Exercise 16

„Cost(s)" oder „price(s)"? Füllen Sie die Lücken mit den richtigen Wörtern!

1. Would you please send us your current _____ list.

2. We can't afford to pay such a high _____.

3. Production _____ were too high for the project to be a success.

4. We were able to keep _____ stable by cutting production _____.

5. The _____ is as stated. It would push our _____ to an intolerable level if we cut _____ any further.

Exercise 17

Peter muss drei dringliche Geschäftsbriefe beantworten. Beachten Sie dabei besonders den Gebrauch der Wörter „consequent" und „consequence".

1. Dear Sirs,

Our accountants inform me that a mistake in our costing department has resulted in a credit in your favour amounting to $2,560. **Consequently**, we have pleasure in sending you forthwith a cheque in this amount...

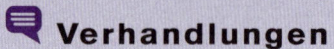

2. Dear John,

Our conversation over dinner last night has given me food (no pun intended!) for thought. As a **consequence**, I'd like to put forward the following business proposition...

3. Sirs,

I have the unpleasant task of informing you that your company's failure to live up to the terms of the contract and consequent non-payment force us to take legal action...

Finden Sie nun die richtige Form im folgenden Lückentext:

1. May we remind you of the legal _____ that may arise as a result of your actions?

2. We have waited two weeks for a reply to our letter, _____ we have no alternative but to look elsewhere.

3. Due to logistical problems and the _____ lack of stock, we are unable to dispatch your order as agreed.

4. We were most impressed by the results of the pilot project, _____ we have pleasure in placing an immediate order.

False friends

The English word **"consequent"** has nothing at all in common with German "konsequent". "Consequent" and **"consequence"** both describe anything that logically follows something else, the result of a previous happening or action.

Talk Talk Talk 7

(James Morgan's office)

J. Peter, I think the only way to tackle the Newcom issue is to make a **personal visit**. I don't think any amount of letter-writing is going to solve this one.

P. I **tend to** agree, but who should attempt it – Steve?

J. Steve's a good **sales director**. But this isn't a sale – it's a much more complicated matter.

P. So who have we got?

J. You, Peter. You!

P. Me? A **franchise contract**? I hardly know what a franchise is!

J. I know we haven't spent a lot of time together, but I have observed one thing – you are very quick to learn, Peter. I'll give you three days to **swot** up on this subject – and then Newcom is all yours!

(James Morgans Büro)

J. Peter, ich glaube, der einzige Weg, diese Newcom-Geschichte richtig anzugehen, ist ein **persönlicher Besuch**. Ich denke, ein noch so großer Haufen Briefe wird uns in dieser Angelegenheit nicht weiterbringen.

P. Ich **neige dazu**, Ihnen zuzustimmen, aber wer soll das versuchen – Steve?

J. Steve ist ein guter **Verkaufsleiter**. Aber hier geht es nicht um einen Verkauf – das ist eine viel kompliziertere Angelegenheit.

P. Wen haben wir denn sonst noch?

J. Sie, Peter. Sie!

P. Mich? Für einen **Franchise-Vertrag**? Ich weiß ja gerade einmal, was ein Franchise ist!

J. Ich weiß, dass wir uns noch nicht lange kennen, aber eins ist mir aufgefallen – Sie lernen schnell, Peter. Ich gebe Ihnen drei Tage, um sich in dieser Sache **schlau zu machen** – und dann gehört Newcom Ihnen!

P. Oh, no! And if I don't succeed?

J. Steve tells me he has an opening in sales!

P. Oh, nein! Und wenn ich keinen Erfolg habe?

J. Steve hat mir gesagt, er hätte noch eine offene Stelle im Verkauf!

Exercise 18

Ordnen Sie folgenden Slangausdrücken ihren passenden, formellen Begriff zu!

a) examine b) basic facts c) general information d) inform
e) essence f) true facts

1. ☐ There wasn't much to learn about the product. I got the **gist** of it in no time.
2. ☐ If you give me the **gen** I'll read up on the product at home tonight.
3. ☐ Give me the papers. I'd like to **take a look-see at** them.
4. ☐ I gave him the **low-down** on the terms of the contract.
5. ☐ Let's **gen** ourselves **up** on the background of the company before the meeting.
6. ☐ Just give me the **guts** of what the report has to say.

Background information

In the business world, people might ask for the **elevator version**. This expression comes from the American term for a lift and describes a short summary that lasts for as little as 30 seconds – or the duration of a ride in a lift!

Talk Talk Talk

(Peter's office)

P. I have an important letter for you, Lucy. Could you bring your note-book – and a cup of your excellent tea, if it's not too much trouble.

L. Certainly, Peter. I'll be right there…

P. The letter is to Mr Trevor Payne, Project Manager at Newcom Technology, Birmingham. You have the exact address **on file**, Lucy ...

(Peters Büro)

P. Ich muss Ihnen einen wichtigen Brief diktieren, Lucy. Könnten Sie bitte Ihr Notizbuch mitbringen – und vielleicht eine Tasse Tee, wenn es nicht zu viel Mühe macht.

L. Natürlich, Peter. Ich komme sofort …

P. Der Brief geht an Mr Trevor Payne, Projektmanager von Newcom Technology, Birmingham. Die exakte Adresse haben Sie **in Ihren Unterlagen**, Lucy …

 Dear Mr Payne,

Thank you for your letter of 26 May. **We fully understand** that other compa-nies have also expressed interest in the "Instantweb" program, **but we are confident that we are best placed to give it the fullest market exposure** in the United States. We have various ideas on how this could be achieved within the framework of a franchise agreement, and I would be very pleased to explain these to you in a personal meeting. **I would be only too happy** to travel to your offices in Manchester on any day of your choosing and shall keep my diary free for the next two or three weeks in anticipation of a favourable reply from you.
I look forward to hearing from you.

Yours sincerely,

Peter Brückner

P. Lucy, could you give a copy of that to Mr Morgan, and if he has no alterations to make then could you send it today by express post to Newcom?

L. Certainly, Peter.

(James Morgan enters Peter's office.)

J. Peter, the letter is fine. I've asked Lucy to send it right away. Now, I want to give you this – it's the **current annual report** of Newcom. It will **put** you **in the picture** – it's always best to know as much as you can about the company you're dealing with. If there's anything that's new to you or that you can't understand just let me know.

P. Lucy, könnten Sie Mr Morgan eine Kopie davon geben und den Brief, wenn er keine Änderungen mehr vornehmen will, noch heute per Express an Newcom schicken?

L. Aber sicher, Peter.

(James Morgan betritt Peters Büro.)

J. Peter, der Brief ist sehr gut. Ich habe Lucy gebeten, ihn sofort abzuschicken. Jetzt möchte ich Ihnen dies hier geben – das ist der **aktuelle Jahresbericht** von Newcom. Er wird sie **ins Bild setzen** – es ist immer gut, so viel wie möglich über die Firma zu wissen, mit der man es zu tun hat. Wenn es irgendetwas gibt, das neu für Sie ist oder das Sie nicht verstehen, lassen Sie es mich einfach wissen.

Background information

An **"annual report"** is a full account of a company's activities over the previous year. It contains a balance sheet showing income, expenditure and the value of company assets. The final balance shows either a profit or loss and any dividends payable to the company's shareholders. The annual report is presented at the annual meeting of shareholders, at which company officers also stand for re-election.

Exercise 19

Peter ist sich immer noch nicht so ganz sicher, wie er mit den Begriffen aus dem Jahresbericht von Newcom umgehen soll. Können Sie ihm helfen, die Bedeutung der folgenden Wörter richtig zuzuordnen?

1. balance sheet
2. board of directors
3. chief executive
4. current assets
5. multinational
6. profit and loss account
7. subsidiaries
8. supervisory board

a. A statement showing a company's expenditure and income over a period of usually one year

b. A company's total wealth, in terms of cash, cheques and payments due as well as property, equipment, stocks of goods, raw materials etc.

c. A body of elected officers who run the company and who stand for re-election at the annual meeting

d. A company's additional, semi-autonomous offices, usually distributed in various different countries

e. When a company has a network of such offices abroad it is described in this way

f. A financial statement showing a company's income, expenditures, assets and debts

g. A small group of officers whose job is to oversee the work of the Board of Directors

h. The head of a company's Board of Directors

Background information
"Net" or "gross"?

In financial transactions and statements, "net" describes an amount entirely free of taxes, expenses and other deductions. A company's net profit, for instance, is the amount of income remaining after subtracting all costs and expenses incurred in the production process.

"Gross" has the opposite meaning, describing the total of any amount before deductions. A company's **gross profit**, for instance, is the total earned before taxes and other deductions.

And **gross domestic product**? That's the annual total value of goods produced and services provided by an individual country. The gross domestic product of South Africa in the year following the fall of apartheid there was equivalent to 75 billion American dollars.

This figure (usually abbreviated to GDP) is often expressed in **"per capita"** ("per head") terms. South Africa has a population of 31 million – therefore the GDP per capita in the relevant period was equivalent to 2,400 American dollars.

Talk Talk Talk

(The offices of ARGO Limited)

L. Good morning, Peter. What a lovely day! Perhaps summer really is on the way. I have **a stack of** post for you!

P. Thanks, Lucy. A pot of tea would also be welcome. And do you have any more of those biscuits your sister makes?

(In den Büros von ARGO Limited)

L. Guten Morgen, Peter. Was für ein wunderbarer Tag! Vielleicht wird es wirklich langsam Sommer. Ich habe **einen ganzen Haufen** Post für Sie!

P. Danke, Lucy. Eine Kanne Tee wäre mir auch sehr recht. Und haben Sie vielleicht noch ein paar von diesen Keksen, die Ihre Schwester macht?

L. I kept some specially for you. Now you just take this **bundle** off to your office and I'll bring you tea **in a jiffy.**

L. Ich habe extra für Sie ein paar aufgehoben. Nehmen Sie diesen **Packen** hier einfach mit in Ihr Büro und ich bringe Ihnen **in Windeseile** Ihren Tee.

P. Lucy, you're a "Schatz"

P. Lucy, Sie sind ein Schatz.

(Melissa enters.)
M. "Schatz" is the word! Don't you listen to his sweet words, Lucy. He's a German charmer!

(Melissa tritt ein.)
M. Ein „Schatz", ja? Hören Sie nicht auf ihn, Lucy. Er ist ein deutscher Charmeur!

P. I **met my match** when I tried to charm you, though, Melissa!

P. Ich habe **mir die Zähne ausgebissen**, als ich versucht habe, meinen Charme bei Ihnen wirken zu lassen, Melissa!

M. Well, perhaps I can't make tea like Lucy. I certainly can't make biscuits like her sister!

M. Tja, vielleicht kann ich nicht so gut Tee kochen wie Lucy. Und ganz sicher backe ich nicht so gute Kekse wie ihre Schwester!

P. But you can serve up a marvellous English roast. Steve and I really enjoyed our meal with you.

P. Aber dafür servieren Sie einen wunderbaren englischen Braten. Steve und ich haben das Essen mit Ihnen wirklich genossen.

M. Well, if you're a good boy we might just repeat the experience. Now, off to work with you!

M. Nun ja, wenn Sie immer schön brav sind, können wir dieses Erlebnis ja noch einmal wiederholen. Und jetzt an die Arbeit!

P. I'm just sorting my post now – here's a reply from Newcom...

P. Ich sortiere gerade meine Post – hier ist eine Antwort von Newcom ...

 Dear Mr Brückner,

Thank you for your letter of 2 June. I would be very happy to meet you at our offices here in Manchester on any day convenient to you next month to discuss franchise possibilities. **I would suggest a morning meeting** to allow us to continue the discussions over lunch and possibly into the afternoon. You would naturally be our guest for the entire day.
May I suggest that you call my secretary on the above extension to fix a day. If you require hotel accommodation in Manchester, she will also be glad to attend to your requirements.
I look forward to meeting you and to a fruitful discussions.

Yours sincerely,

Trevor Payne

Exercise 20

Finden Sie die Lösung, die am besten passt:

1. My secretary will be glad to find / arrange / date an appointment for you.

2. If you require / seek / demand hotel accommodation please don't hesitate to let us know.

3. We would be very glad to organize / find / book your flight from London to Birmingham.

Talk Talk Talk 8

(Peter's office)

P. Lucy, could you put me through to Newcom, please? You have the number.

L. Certainly, Peter. Just one moment.

P. Hello, Newcom? **Could you put me through** to extension 210, please?

(Connection is made...)

P. Hello, is that Mr Payne's office? It's Peter Brückner of ARGO Limited here. Mr Payne wrote to me to suggest that I make an appointment for a meeting next month. 18th? Fine. At 11 a.m.? Yes, that suits me very well. No, I don't need hotel accommodation. I shall return to London the same day. Should I email **confirmation of my travel arrangements**? No? I'll do it all the same – I like to have these things on file. But thank you very much for all your help. I look forward to my visit to Newcom…

(Peters Büro)

P. Lucy, könnten Sie mich bitte zu Newcom durchstellen? Die Nummer haben Sie.

L. Natürlich, Peter. Einen Moment bitte.

P. Hallo, Newcom? **Könnten Sie mich bitte** mit der Durchwahl 210 **verbinden**?

(Verbindung wird aufgebaut ...)

P. Hallo, bin ich verbunden mit Mr Paynes Büro? Hier spricht Peter Brückner von ARGO Limited. Mr Payne hat mir geschrieben, um einen Termin für die nächste Woche vorzuschlagen. Am 18.? Sehr schön. Um 11 Uhr? Ja, das passt mir sehr gut. Nein, ich brauche keine Hotelreservierung. Ich reise noch am selben Tag nach London zurück. Soll ich Ihnen eine **Bestätigung für die Details meiner Reise zumailen**? Nein? Ich tue es trotzdem – ich habe so etwas immer gern schriftlich. Aber vielen Dank für Ihre Hilfe. Ich freue mich schon auf meinen Besuch bei Newcom …

 Fax to:

Mr Trevor Payne
Projects Manager
Newcom

Manchester

From:
Peter Brückner
Assistant Managing Director
ARGO Limited
London
Fax Nr. 003
Date: 04.06.2013

Dear Mr Payne,

This fax serves as confirmation that I will be travelling to Manchester
on 18 July in the morning for a meeting with you at Newcom headquarters
at 11 a.m. Thank you very much for finding the time for a meeting, to which
I look forward very much.

Yours truly,

Peter Brückner

Background information

You will see the 24-hour clock at airports and train stations, but most
British companies prefer the 12-hour clock. In business writing, the correct way to abbreviate 3 o'clock in the afternoon is **3 p.m.**, while 10
o'clock in the morning is **10 a.m.** These abbreviations come from the
Latin *(ante meridiem* and *post meridiem)*.

Exercise 21

Einladungen – Was gehört in die Lücken?

honour	inviting	invitation	pleased	engaged	convenient	glad

company	kind	mark	reception	attend	afraid	invite

1. If it is _____ for you, may I _____ you to tea at the Dorchester next Tuesday afternoon at 4?

2. To _____ the 25th anniversary of the company, we are _____ all employees to a champagne _____ in the conference room next Wednesday at 12 noon.

3. I would be very _____ if you and Mrs Smith accepted our _____ to dinner on the 25th. Cocktails at 7 p.m.

4. Thank you for your _____ invitation to _____ the concert and evening reception. My wife and I are very _____ to accept.

5. May we have the _____ of your _____ at dinner at the Ritz next Saturday?

6. Thank you so much for the invitation, but I'm _____ I am otherwise _____ on that evening.

Talk Talk Talk

(Peter's office, James Morgan enters.)

(Peters Büro, James Morgan tritt ein.)

J. Well, Peter, all **geared up** for the Manchester meeting?

J. Nun, Peter, **alles bereit** für das Meeting in Manchester?

P. I'm as ready as I ever will be, Mr Morgan.

J. Any questions before you set off? I have to leave the office in ten minutes.

P. No, I think I should be all right, Mr Morgan.

J. Then good luck, Peter. See you tomorrow...

(Melissa enters after a while.)

M. You're off to Manchester soon, then, Peter?

P. That's right. Wish me luck!

M. I'll do better than that. Come on, I'll buy you one at the "Nag's Head" – one for the road.

P. Actually, I might just have two – but that's very kind of you, Melissa. I accept **unconditionally**. But what about Steve?

M. No, I want you all to myself for half an hour Peter – I want to make sure you're prepared for what awaits you in Manchester. I've had

P. Ich bin so bereit, wie ich nur sein kann, Mr Morgan.

J. Noch irgendwelche Fragen, bevor Sie losfahren? Ich muss in zehn Minuten das Büro verlassen.

P. Nein, ich glaube, ich komme schon klar, Mr Morgan.

J. Dann viel Glück, Peter. Wir sehen uns dann morgen ...

(Etwas später tritt Melissa ein.)

M. Sie brechen also bald nach Manchester auf, Peter?

P. Stimmt. Wünschen Sie mir Glück!

M. Ich werde noch etwas viel Besseres tun. Kommen Sie, ich lade Sie auf einen Drink im "Nag's Head" ein – einen für unterwegs.

P. Vielleicht nehme ich sogar zwei – aber das ist wirklich sehr nett von Ihnen, Melissa. Ich nehme **ohne zu zögern** an. Aber was ist mit Steve?

M. Nein, ich möchte Sie für ein halbes Stündchen ganz für mich allein haben, Peter – ich möchte sicher sein, dass Sie auf das, was

some dealings in the past with
Newcom. They're tough customers.

Sie in Manchester erwartet, auch
gut vorbereitet sind. Ich hatte in
der Vergangenheit schon öfter mit
Newcom zu tun. Das sind schwierige Kunden.

Exercise 22

Setzen Sie jeweils „some" oder „any" ein:

1. Did you make _____ progress at the meeting?

2. Could you give me _____ advice on how to tackle the
   problem?

3. There are _____ entries in an old calendar.

4. I'd like to finish the meeting with a general discussion of the
   issue and ask if there are _____ questions.

5. Did the theatre production give you _____ pleasure at
   all?

6. I was able to get _____ meaning out of that letter.

7. Is there _____ sense at all in that book?
   – Well, I did find _____ things of interest.

8. _____ of the points in his lecture I found quite provo-
   cative.

Exercise 23

Wählen Sie zwischen „something" oder „anything".

1. Is there _____ on your mind?

2. Do you have _____ at all in that forgetful head of yours?

3. Would you like to see _____ in the castle or grounds?

4. I can't see _____ at all from where I'm standing.

5. May I ask you _____ very important?

6. Ask me _____ at all, I really don't mind.

7. Was there _____ left over from the buffet after the guests had gone?

Talk Talk Talk

(Peter's office)

P. Lucy, I have another very important letter I must send before leaving for Manchester.

L. I'll be with you after I've made this call, Peter.

P. I'll record it on the dictaphone, Lucy. Take your time.

(Peters Büro)

P. Lucy, ich habe hier noch einen sehr wichtigen Brief, den ich abschicken muss, bevor ich nach Manchester fahre.

L. Ich komme sofort zu Ihnen, nachdem ich diesen Anruf erledigt habe, Peter.

P. Ich spreche ihn einfach auf das Diktiergerät, Lucy. Lassen Sie sich Zeit.

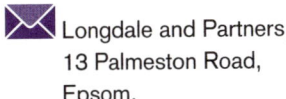 Longdale and Partners,
13 Palmeston Road,
Epsom.

(Lucy, fill in the exact postal code for me from the letterhead, please)

Dear Sirs,
Thank you for your enquiry about our Accounting 2000 Program. **I am arranging for you to receive all our available information on the system and for our regional sales representative,** Mr Simon Tucker, to call you and arrange a meeting. He will be happy to explain its qualities and functions and answer your questions.
Before contacting Mr Tucker, however, it would be useful for me to know the size of your accounting department and the nature of the accounting system you are now using. If I am not available, please feel free to contact our Sales Director, Mr Steve Blackman, who will be happy to answer any queries you may have.

Yours faithfully,

Peter Brückner
Assistant Managing Director

Background information

The conjunctions **before**, **while** and **after** follow a similar pattern. If the subject is the same in both halves of a sentence, it is often possible to use them with the -ing form of the verb to avoid repetition:
Before I contact/**Before contacting** my colleague, I would like to know some more information.
He often draws pictures while he talks/**while talking** on the phone.
We went for drinks after we left/**after leaving** the office.

Exercise 24

Füllen Sie die Lücken mit der richtigen Präposition und setzen Sie das Verb in die korrekte Zeitform!

before   after   during   while   meanwhile

1. _____ reply in full to your letter, I would like to remind you of one or two relevant facts.

2. It was only _____ read your letter that I became aware of the true state of the company's affairs.

3. _____ the time it took you _____, reply I was able to find answers to all my questions.

4. I must confess that I read your letter only _____ receive the subsequent reminder.

5. _____ agree in principle to your proposals, I must raise one or two objections.

6. I shall respond in full _____ examine your proposals; _____ please allow me a little time to study the situation.

Talk Talk Talk

(Peter prepares to leave the office. Lucy calls him back.)

(Peter will gerade das Büro verlassen, als Lucy ihn zurückruft.)

L. Oh, Peter! In this morning's post there was another letter from

L. Oh, Peter! In der Post von heute Morgen war ein Brief von Longdale

Longdale and Partners, which might **affect** your reply. I opened it because it was simply addressed to ARGO – but I think you should read it.

P. Lucy, I'm off to lunch now, but give me the letter and I'll read it in my break.

L. Here it is. Are you having lunch with Miss Walker? She's already left, but she said she thought you were joining her.

P. Yes, Lucy, that's why I'm in such a hurry. See you later...

(At the Nag's Head)

P. Hello, Melissa. Sorry I'm late but Lucy had an important letter to give to me.

M. Important? Who from?

P. Longdale and Partners. They are interested in our Accounting 2000 program. It would be **a very important sale** for us.

M. So what does the letter say?

and Partners, der **Auswirkungen** auf Ihre Antwort **haben** könnte. Ich habe ihn geöffnet, weil er nur an ARGO adressiert war – aber ich glaube, Sie sollten ihn besser lesen.

P. Lucy, ich bin gerade auf dem Weg zum Mittagessen, aber geben Sie mir einfach den Brief und ich lese ihn in meiner Pause.

L. Hier ist er. Gehen Sie mit Miss Walker zum Lunch? Sie ist schon gegangen, sagte aber, dass sie dachte, Sie würden mitkommen.

P. Ja, Lucy, deshalb habe ich es ja auch so eilig. Bis später ...

(Im Nag's Head)

P. Hallo, Melissa. Tut mir leid, dass ich so spät komme, aber Lucy hat mir noch einen wichtigen Brief gegeben.

M. Wichtig? Von wem?

P. Longdale and Partners. Sie sind an unserem Accounting 2000-Programm interessiert. Das wäre **ein sehr wichtiger Verkaufserfolg** für uns.

M. Also, was steht in dem Brief?

Dear Sirs,

Subsequent to our letter of 6 June, requesting full information on your Accounting 2000 system, we have been approached by Redstar Technologies with a very attractive offer which will undoubtedly have an **effect** on our final decision. **In all fairness to your company, we do not want to take this decision before comparing the various systems on offer**. Our problem is that the Redstar Technologies offer combines a highly **competitive price with a firm deadline** for our decision. We normally resist pressure of this kind, but the attractive nature of the offer compels us to take rapid action. Would your company be in the position of demonstrating to us your Accounting 2000 system within one week of receipt of this letter? In the meantime, you could perhaps send us relevant information on the system. **Additionally,** we would appreciate a call establishing direct communication between our accounting department and whoever is responsible in your company for the Accounting 2000 system. Our Chief Accountant, Mr Francis Staff, can be reached on extension 4435.

Thank you in advance for your prompt attention to this matter.

Yours faithfully,

Matthew Gilpin
Chief Executive

False friends

Be careful not to confuse **"affect"** and **"effect"**. The words are so similar that even the British have problems with them. "Affect" is most commonly used as a verb and "effect" is frequently the corresponding noun (although, to add to the confusion, the latter can also be used as a verb, meaning to bring about or accomplish something). To "affect" means to produce a result, a change or an "effect":

Mr Gilpin of Longdale and Partners says the offer from Redstar Technologies will inevitably **affect** his company's decision – it will inevitably **have an effect** on it.

Exercise 25

„Affect" oder „effect"? Füllen Sie die Lücken!

1. Alcohol has a very strange _____ on some people.

2. How will the downturn in profits _____ the company's future?

3. What _____ is Jim's promotion likely to have on his family?

4. Will the move to company headquarters in New York _____ his future plans?

5. How can we _____ this staff reshuffle without causing problems?

6. If you can _____ this plan successfully, you're assured of promotion.

Talk Talk Talk

(In the pub – continued...)

P. Well, Melissa, what do you make of that?

M. Well, I wouldn't worry your head about it. You've got **bigger fish to fry**. This is Steve's problem.

P. But he's not around.

(Im Pub – Fortsetzung …)

P. Tja, Melissa, was halten Sie davon?

M. Na ja, ich würde mir deshalb nicht den Kopf zerbrechen. Sie haben **einen größeren Fisch am Haken**. Das ist Steves Problem.

P. Aber er ist nicht da.

M. He's back tomorrow.
I'll pass on the letter to him in the morning.

M. Er kommt morgen zurück.
Dann werde ich ihm den Brief morgen früh weitergeben.

P. You're a treasure. Another drink?

P. Sie sind ein Schatz. Noch einen Drink?

Blättern Sie weiter bis S. 157, um zu erfahren, wie Peters Reise nach Manchester verlaufen ist.

Exercise 26

Sie müssen einen Brief beantworten, in dem nach Informationen über ein neues Produkt gefragt wird, für das Ihre Firma wirbt. Wie beginnen Sie Ihren Brief? Machen Sie mindestens drei Entwürfe und benutzen Sie jeweils die folgenden Wörter: „pleased", „pleasure" und „glad".

_____

_____

_____

_____

_____

_____

Dos and Don'ts – A matter of form...

Matthew Gilpin of Longdale and Partners begins his letter: **"Subsequent to..."**. He could have just as well written: **"After sending you our letter of..."**. English stylists actually prefer the latter version, arguing that it is simpler and easier to understand. In spoken English, "subsequent to" virtually never occurs, but it is a very entrenched form in official letter-writing – whatever the "stylists" say!

Equally, **"Thank you for your letter of..."** is often replaced by a very formal **"We acknowledge receipt of your letter of..."** or **"We are in receipt of your letter of..."**. The two forms are in common use, but you will be never wrong in writing a simple: **"Thank you for your letter of..."**

 **Vocabulary**

to affect	beeinflussen
bundle	Bündel/Packen
confirmation	Bestätigung
effect	Auswirkung
(to be) geared up	bereit sein (etwa: seine Sieben Sachen zusammen haben)
gross profit	Bruttogewinn
gross domestic product (GDP)	Bruttoinlandsprodukt
to have bigger fish to fry	einen größeren Fisch am Haken haben (etw. Wichtigeres vorhaben)
in a jiffy	im Handumdrehen/in Windeseile
in the picture	im Bild sein/Bescheid wissen
market exposure	Marktpräsenz
to meet one's match	„seinen Meister treffen"
on file	in den Unterlagen
per capita	pro Kopf
sales director	Verkaufsleiter
(a) stack of	ein ganzer Haufen (von)

stock	Vorrat
to swot	„büffeln; pauken" (ugs.)
to take it from here	jetzt weiter vorgehen
to tend to	dazu tendieren/neigen
unconditionally	bedingungslos/ohne Vorbehalte

On the phone | Telefonieren

Here we go

Die nächste Zeit wird Peter im Büro von Steve Blackman assistieren, um einen Einblick in die Welt des Verkaufs zu bekommen. Eine ganze Reihe von Telefongesprächen fordern dabei seine Englischkenntnisse heraus.

Talk Talk Talk 9

(Steve's office)

P. Good morning, Steve. Mr Morgan tells me I'm working for you this week.

S. That's right, Peter. I hope you don't pick up any bad habits. I tried to call you at home over the weekend, but there was no reply. Don't you have an **answering machine**?

P. I have ordered one, but it will take another week or so to be sent. I travelled down to Brighton at the weekend. German friends called me up on Saturday morning to invite me down there.

(Steves Büro)

P. Guten Morgen, Steve. Mr Morgan hat mir gesagt, dass ich diese Woche für Sie arbeite.

S. Stimmt, Peter. Hoffentlich gewöhnen Sie sich bei mir keine schlechten Eigenschaften an. Ich habe schon versucht, Sie am Wochenende anzurufen, aber da ging niemand ans Telefon. Haben Sie denn keinen **Anrufbeantworter**?

P. Ich habe einen bestellt, aber es wird noch etwa eine Woche dauern, bis er ankommt. Ich bin über das Wochenende in Brighton gewesen. Freunde aus Deutschland hatten mich über das Wochenende dorthin eingeladen.

S. Well, I hope you had a relaxing time because we've got a busy week ahead of us. Our **top salesman** called in sick this morning, and I can't get hold of his **replacement**.

P. How can I help out?

S. Look, can you keep on trying his numbers. I le's not even answering his **mobile**. Something must have happened to him over the weekend. He's usually very reliable and has his **report** on my desk first thing Monday mornings.

P. Report?

S. Each of our half dozen sales staff must submit a weekly **progress report**. Four are in. One man is sick – and one's gone missing! While I work through these reports, you can try to **track** him **down**. Keep trying to get him on the phone. You can also **phone around** the other salesmen to see if they have any idea where he is.

S. Tja, ich hoffe, Sie haben sich gut erholt, denn wir haben eine anstrengende Woche vor uns. Unser **Top-Verkäufer** hat sich heute Morgen krank gemeldet und ich erreiche seine **Vertretung** nicht.

P. Wie kann ich weiterhelfen?

S. Nun ja, Sie können versuchen, ihn weiter anzurufen. Er geht nicht einmal an sein **Handy**. Irgendetwas muss ihm am Wochenende passiert sein. Er ist normalerweise sehr zuverlässig und ich habe seinen **Bericht** immer Montagfrüh auf dem Schreibtisch.

P. Bericht?

S. Jeder unserer Vertreter und Vertreterinnen im Außendienst muss einen wöchentlichen **Erfolgsbericht** abliefern. Vier haben wir bereits. Einer unserer Leute ist krank – und einer wird vermisst! Während ich mich durch diese Berichte arbeite, können Sie versuchen, ihn **aufzuspüren**. Versuchen Sie weiter, ihn ans Telefon zu bekommen. Sie können auch bei den anderen Vertretern **herumtelefonieren** – vielleicht haben sie ja eine Ahnung, wo er stecken könnte.

P. No problem, Steve. Just give me the numbers.

P. Kein Problem, Steve. Geben Sie mir einfach die Nummern.

S. Here's his mobile number. He has instructions to have it **switched on** at all times. And here is his home number. He has voicemail and I've left **umpteen** messages on it already.

S. Hier ist seine Handynummer. Er hat eigentlich Anweisungen, es Tag und Nacht **eingeschaltet** zu lassen. Und hier ist seine Nummer von zu Hause. Er hat einen Anrufbeantworter und ich habe bereits **zig** Nachrichten hinterlassen.

P. I'll get down to it right away. Is there anything I should know about him?

P. Ich kümmere mich sofort darum. Gibt es etwas, das ich über ihn wissen sollte?

S. His name is Joe Sampson. Single, lives alone in Newcastle and **covers** the entire north-east for us from there.

S. Sein Name ist Joe Sampson. Er ist Single und lebt allein in Newcastle. Das ganze Nord-Ost-Gebiet **fällt in** seine **Zuständigkeit**.

Dos and Don'ts – A matter of form...

Even if it is not a condition of your contract, always call your employer if you are going to be late for work. If you need to take the day off, call as early as possible to say that you will be absent. Particularly on Monday mornings, it is common for people to pull a sickie or throw a sickie – to phone in and pretend they are ill so that they can have an extra day at home.

In America, and more recently in the UK, some companies have introduced **duvet days** to tackle this problem: staff are allowed to call in up to four times a year if they do not feel like going to work without having to invent a reason.

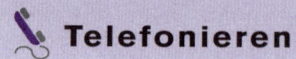

Exercise 27

Peter schafft es endlich, Joe Sampson auf seinem Handy zu erreichen. Wie verläuft die weitere Konversation?

P. Hello, Mr Sampson? _____ Peter Brückner from
ARGO in London. We have been trying to _____ you for
ages. Mr Blackman has _____ several messages on your
_____. He hasn't received your weekly report, either. Is
anything wrong?

S. I've just come out of hospital. I slipped and injured my shoulder
while putting up some cupboards on Saturday morning and the neigh-
bours carted me off to hospital. I'm sorry I didn't have my
_____ phone with me. Have you been trying very long to
_____ me?

P. I've been trying for more than an hour to _____ you,
but I just couldn't _____ through. I'll tell Mr Blackman
you're okay, and I'm sure he'll be _____ you shortly. He
wants your weekly report!

Background information

Salesman or salesperson?

Job titles sometimes end in "-person" instead of "-man" to avoid illegal
or unnecessary discrimination on grounds of sex. Use a dictionary to
check, because some forms (e.g. "postperson") do not exist!

Talk Talk Talk  10

(Steve's office)

(Steves Büro)

S. I'm glad to hear he's okay but he could have found some way of calling me. He should have his mobile on him and either have it switched on or check the voice-mail twice a day. That's part of his contract. You see the problems we have with the sales staff, Peter!

S. Ich freue mich zu hören, dass es ihm gut geht – aber er hätte eine Möglichkeit finden müssen, mich anzurufen. Er hätte sein Handy eingeschaltet haben müssen oder er hätte seinen Anrufbeantworter zweimal am Tag abhören sollen. Das gehört zu seinem Vertrag. Da sehen Sie mal, was wir für Probleme mit unseren Verkäufern haben, Peter!

P. I asked him to call you right away, and he said he would. That'll be him now.

P. Ich habe ihn darum gebeten, Sie umgehend anzurufen – und er sagte, er würde es sofort tun. Das müsste er sein.

S. Hello, Joe? I was just telling Peter here we're glad to hear you are okay, but you had us worried. Now what about that report? No, I can't wait for you to **punch it** back **into** the system and **email** it. That'll take hours. Fax it – as soon as possible, okay? Otherwise, did you have a good week? Give me a buzz later today and tell me all about it. And find an expert to put up those cupboards – you're paid to sell our systems!

S. Hallo Joe? Ich habe Peter gerade gesagt, dass wir froh sind, dass es Ihnen gut geht, aber wir haben uns Sorgen um Sie gemacht. Was ist jetzt mit dem Bericht? Nein, ich kann nicht warten, bis Sie ihn in den Computer **gehackt** haben und **per E-Mail herüberschicken**. Das wird ja Stunden dauern. Faxen Sie ihn – so schnell wie möglich, okay? Und hatten Sie ansonsten eine gute Woche? Rufen Sie mich doch später an und erzählen Sie mir davon. Und suchen Sie sich einen Fachmann, der Ihnen diese Regale aufstellt – Sie werden dafür bezahlt, unsere Systeme zu verkaufen!

Exercise 28

Sie fühlen sich nicht wohl und beschließen, einen Arzt zu konsultieren. Rufen Sie Lucy an und sagen Sie ihr, dass Sie zu spät zur Arbeit kommen werden.

Hello, Lucy. It's Peter Brückner. I'm just _____ to say I will be slightly late because I want to go to the doctor. Can you take any _____ for me? If any of the salesmen _____, please _____ them to _____ Dave, and he'll handle things. I have my _____ with me, so please try to _____ me on it if I'm needed urgently.

Exercise 29

Formen Sie aus untenstehenden Sätzen einen einzigen Satz, indem Sie Konjunktionen verwenden.

- I have a doctor's appointment.
- I won't be at the office until later.
- I just called to say...
- If there are any calls for me please take a message.

_____

_____

Talk Talk Talk 11

(Steve's office)

S. Peter, let me now **induct** you into the very secret world of sales!

P. Secret?

S. Our business is so **innovative** and **competitive** that our sales people **play their cards very close to the chest**. I have difficulty myself **winkling out** the details of their reports. Sometimes I'm on the phone for hours **clarifying** and **elaborating points**. Reaching them is also a problem, although they are supposed to be on duty practically around the clock. I'll give you a **test run** first of all. Geoff Burnes says he's **on the brink** of **sealing a** big **contract** with Metropolitan Newspapers. We're trying to **break into** the provincial newspapers with a new copy-editing software system, called Quick-Ed. Give Geoff a call – at least, try to reach him – and ask if he has anything new to report **on that front**. There's absolutely nothing about it in his weekly report.

(Steves Büro)

S. So Peter, jetzt werde ich Sie in die Geheimnisse des erfolgreichen Verkaufens **einführen**.

P. Geheimnisse?

S. Unsere Branche ist so **innovativ** und es **herrscht** so **ein starker Wettbewerb**, dass unsere Verkäufer **ihre Geheimnisse für sich behalten**. Ich habe sogar selbst Probleme, die Details ihrer Berichte zu **enträtseln**. Manchmal verbringe ich am Telefon Stunden damit, bestimmte **Punkte** zu **klären** und **ausführlich auszuarbeiten**. Sie zu erreichen ist außerdem auch immer ein Problem, obwohl sie eigentlich rund um die Uhr im Dienst sein sollten. Ich werde sie erst einmal durch einen **Testlauf** schicken. Geoff Burnes sagt, dass er **kurz davor** steht, **einen Vertrag** mit Metropolitan Newspapers **abzuschließen**. Wir versuchen, mit unserem neuen redaktionellen Softwaresystem Quick-Ed **in den Markt** der provinziellen Zeitungen **vorzudringen**. Rufen Sie Geoff an – oder versuchen Sie wenigstens, ihn zu erreichen – und fragen Sie ihn, ob es **in dieser Sache** etwas Neues gibt. In seinem wöchentlichen Bericht steht absolut nichts darüber.

(Peter reports back after ten minutes.)
P. I've tried his home number but he's not there. I left a message on his **answerphone** and another one on his mobile. I asked him to call back urgently.

S. Okay, give me a few minutes while I just clarify one or two points in this other report...

(Peter's office phone rings.)
P. Hello, Peter Brückner here.

L. Oh, Peter! I have a very **agitated** Mr Burnes on the phone. He says he's been trying **for ages** to get through to Steve, but the line is constantly engaged.

P. Steve has a lot of phoning to do this morning. Could you put Mr Burnes through to me please, Lucy? Hello, Mr Burnes?

G. Yes, may I speak to Steve Blackman?

(Peter meldet sich nach zehn Minuten zurück.)
P. Ich habe versucht, ihn zu Hause zu erreichen, aber er ist scheinbar nicht da. Ich habe sowohl auf seinem **Anrufbeantworter** als auch auf seinem Handy eine Nachricht hinterlassen. Ich habe ihn gebeten, dringend zurückzurufen.

S. Okay, geben Sie mir ein paar Minuten, in denen ich ein oder zwei Punkte in diesem anderen Bericht klären muss ...

(Peters Telefon klingelt.)
P. Hallo, Peter Brückner am Apparat.

L. Oh, Peter! Ich habe hier einen sehr **aufgeregten** Mr Burnes in der Leitung. Er meint, er würde jetzt schon **seit einer Ewigkeit** versuchen, zu Steve durchzukommen, aber die Leitung wäre ständig besetzt.

P. Steve hat heute Morgen eine Menge zu tun. Könnten Sie Mr Burnes bitte zu mir durchstellen, Lucy? Hallo, Mr Burnes?

G. Ja, könnte ich bitte mit Steve Blackman sprechen?

P. Not right now, **his line is busy.** He's asked me to contact you and ask if you have anything new to report on the possible Metropolitan Newspapers contract.

P. Er telefoniert gerade. Er hat mich gebeten, Kontakt zu Ihnen aufzunehmen und Sie zu fragen, ob Sie etwas Neues über den möglichen Vertrag mit Metropolitan Newspapers zu berichten haben.

G. Good Lord! I've only just knocked on the door there. **Give me a break!** Tell Steve to call me back. But he'd **better make it snappy** – I'm back **on the road** as soon as I can get myself some lunch.

G. Meine Güte! Ich habe da doch erst vorsichtig an die Tür geklopft! **Machen Sie mal halblang!** Sagen Sie Steve bitte, er soll mich zurückrufen. Aber er **sollte sich besser beeilen** – ich bin gleich wieder **unterwegs,** sobald ich mir etwas zum Mittagessen besorgen konnte.

Exercise 30

Sie sollen einen Verkäufer Ihrer Firma anrufen und ihm mitteilen, dass der Verkaufsleiter mit seiner Leistung nicht zufrieden ist. Wie drücken Sie sich hierbei taktvoll, aber bestimmt aus? Unterstreichen Sie den passenden Begriff.

Hello, Mr Burnes, Mr Blackman asked me to call and tell you he's not

totally happy / at all satisfied with your report.

He wonders if you could please / right away take another look at it

and improve / elaborate on some of the points. Mr Blackman feels

the report is not complete / is sketchy . He'd like you to call him when

it's ready – immediately / when you get the chance .

Exercise 31

Sie kritisieren schriftlich einen Verkaufsbericht. Wie drücken Sie sich dabei taktvoll aber bestimmt aus?

After reading John Simmonds's report, I must say I am not at all happy / satisfied with it. He has not shown the necessary care / dedication in writing / constructing / penning it. I would like to suggest that he be asked / instructed to rewrite it.

Talk Talk Talk  12

(Steve's office)

(Steves Büro)

S. Peter, could you **man** my phone for a while, please? I have to step out on an errand. I'm expecting to hear from ABC Electronics about that new accounting system of ours they're installing. I'll ask Lucy to put all my calls through to you...

S. Peter, könnten Sie bitte für eine Weile mein Telefon **übernehmen**? Ich muss etwas auswärts erledigen. Ich erwarte einen Anruf von ABC Electronics – es geht um unser neues Buchhaltungssystem, das bei Ihnen installiert wird. Ich bitte Lucy, alle meine Anrufe zu Ihnen durchzustellen ...

(Two hours later...)
P. Steve, **panic stations** at ABC! They can't install that software for **love nor money**! They sound very **irritated**. They can't read a thing on the discs and they're scared to **mess around** with it in case the whole system crashes.

(Zwei Stunden später ...)
P. Steve, es gibt eine **Krise** bei ABC! Sie können das Softwaresystem **auf Teufel komm raus** nicht installieren! Sie klingen ziemlich **verärgert**. Sie können nichts auf den DVDs lesen und haben eine **Heidenangst**, dass ihr ganzes System zusammenbrechen wird.

S. I'll handle it. Lucy, get me ABC right away, please!
Hello, ABC? Could you put me through to the Accounting Department, please? The extension is engaged? I'll hold, but please connect me as soon as you can. This call is urgent.

ABC. You're going through to Mr Baxter now, sir.

S. Hello, Mr Baxter? Steve Blackman here. **What seems to be the problem**? **Shut down** your system, **reboot** and try again. Still no good? Look, what exactly have you got there? Accounting 2000 ER? Good lord, that's **our** system. You've got our entire **accounting** records there! How on earth did that happen? It came in a bag with a packet of sandwiches? Wait a minute! I'll be damned! Your software is still sitting on my desk. Our courier grabbed the wrong package in his hurry to get to lunch. I'll send the right one round right away! I'll call you back to confirm it's on its way. Chip!!!

L. He's gone to lunch, Steve!

S. Ich kümmere mich schon darum. Lucy, verbinden Sie mich bitte sofort mit ABC!
Hallo, ABC? Könnten Sie mich bitte mit der Buchhaltung verbinden? Die Leitung ist besetzt? Ich warte, aber bitte verbinden Sie mich so schnell wie möglich. Es ist wirklich wichtig.

ABC. Ich verbinde Sie jetzt mit Mr Baxter, Sir.

S. Hallo, Mr Baxter? Hier spricht Steve Blackman. **Wo liegt denn das Problem**? **Fahren Sie Ihr System herunter** und **starten Sie es neu**. Es funktioniert immer noch nicht? Was für ein System haben Sie denn genau? Accounting 2000 ER? Du lieber Himmel, das ist unser System. Unsere gesamte **Buchhaltung** ist darauf gespeichert!
Wie konnte das nur passieren? Es kam in einer Tüte mit ein paar Sandwiches? Moment mal! Das gibt's doch nicht! Ihre Software liegt immer noch auf meinem Tisch. Unser Kurier muss es so eilig gehabt haben, zum Mittagessen zu kommen, dass er das falsche Paket erwischt hat. Ich schicke Ihnen das richtige sofort vorbei! Ich rufe Sie zurück, sobald es unterwegs ist. Chip!!!

L. Er ist zum Mittag gegangen, Steve!

☎ Telefonieren

Exercise 32

Stellen Sie aus den untenstehenden Sätzen ein Telefongespräch mit einer Kundenfirma zusammen!

a) He's not there? Could you ask him to call me back as soon as possible, please.

b) I just called to ask how the new software is performing.

c) No? Then I'll wait for Mr Baxter's call. Or perhaps I'll ring again later.

d) Hello! ABC? Steve Blackman here. Could I speak to Mr Baxter, please?

e) Oh, just a minute, please! Perhaps you have somebody else there who could help me with my enquiry?

1. _____ 2. _____ 3. _____ 4. _____ 5. _____

False friends

How irritating! No, "irritating" is not translated as "irritierend" in German. Irritating means "ärgerlich".
"They sound very irritated" is translated as "Sie scheinen sehr verärgert zu sein".
The German word "irritiert" is translated in English as "confused".

Talk Talk Talk  13

(Steve's office)

S. Well, Peter **let's get down to it!**
This is my Monday routine. What
a great way to start the week! We
call up the individual salesmen's
reports and **place** them in their
individual files, which are subdiv-
ided into various folders. Let's start
with Smales's. He's **responsible**
for the Midlands, and he's based
in Birmingham. Last week he got
as far as Stratford, **following up a
lead** at a new electronics company
there. He called in to report he was
optimistic about the chances of **a
deal**, so let's read what he has to
say! But first we have to complete
a **log** of his movements, day by
day, then **match** these with his
expenses sheet. That then goes
to Accounting. At the end of the
report, the salesman has to give an
assessment of the week's work
and a forward projection, but we
usually put that on **file** in our own
words.

(Steves Büro)

S. Na schön, Peter. **Stürzen wir uns
in die Arbeit!** Das ist mein üblicher
Montagstrott. Was für eine Art, die
Woche zu beginnen! Wir **rufen** die
einzelnen Berichte der Verkäufer
auf und **legen** sie in ihren individu-
ellen Ordnern **ab**, die wiederum in
einzelne Abschnitte gegliedert sind.
Fangen wir mit Smales an. Er sitzt in
Birmingham und ist für die Midlands
zuständig. Letzte Woche hat er sich
bis nach Stratford vorgearbeitet, um
dort einem **möglichen Kontakt** zu
einer neuen Elektrofirma zu **folgen**.
In seinem Bericht klang er sehr optimistisch, was die Möglichkeiten über
einen **Geschäftsabschluss** anbe-
langt, also lesen wir mal, was er zu
sagen hat! Aber zuerst mal müssen
wir einen **Ablaufplan** seiner Aktivitäten anfertigen, und zwar für jeden
einzelnen Tag. Und dann müssen wir
ihn mit dieser **Spesenabrechnung
abgleichen**. Das Ganze wandert
dann zur Buchhaltung. Am Ende seines Berichtes muss jeder Verkäufer
einen **Leistungsbericht** der vergan-
genen Woche abliefern und einen
Kommentar über die zu erwartenden
Entwicklungen abgeben. Aber das
tragen wir gewöhnlich mit unseren
eigenen Worten in die **Akten** ein.

Exercise 33

Der Bericht von John Smales richtet sich nach seinem Wochen-
plan. Können Sie aus den Einzelterminen einen vollständigen
Bericht machen?

Monday: Birmingham. Call Texo. No reply. Try again tomorrow. p.m.:
Cranford Foods, 2 p.m. Contract changes good. Call again Friday.
Tuesday: a.m. Stratford. Taylor Electronics. Meeting set for Friday.
Lunch: Stratford News Editor. Describe new copy-editing software.
Interested! p.m. Back to Birmingham, call at phone company on way.
Wednesday: a.m. Dentist appointment! p.m. Met Birmingham Cham-
ber of Commerce and Trade. Describe company objectives.
Thursday: a.m. Drive to Stratford for early start Fri.
Friday: Call Cranford Foods first thing – call again next Mon. 10 a.m.
meeting with Taylor Electronics – full board! Prospects must be good!

_____

_____

_____

_____

_____

_____

_____

Talk Talk Talk

(Melissa enters office.)

M. Morning Steve, good morning Peter!

S. My, you certainly seem to have had a fine weekend!

M. Not at all, nothing but work.

S. You're taking work home with you?

M. It's already there waiting for me. Look, I can't stand around here making polite conversation. I need to know if your people have made any progress with that new copy-editing software.

S. Peter can tell you more **on that score**. He's just spoken to the man responsible for the contract, Burnes. Burnes called me last week to say he was confident of getting the contract, but he didn't sound so optimistic when Peter contacted him this morning.

(Melissa betritt das Büro.)

M. Guten Morgen Steve, guten Morgen, Peter!

S. Meine Güte, Sie sehen aus, als hätten Sie ein großartiges Wochenende gehabt!

M. Ganz und gar nicht. Arbeit, nichts als Arbeit.

S. Sie nehmen Arbeit mit nach Hause?

M. Nein, sie wartet da schon auf mich. Okay, ich kann hier leider nicht nur herumstehen und ein Schwätzchen halten. Ich muss wissen, ob Ihre Leute Fortschritte mit der neuen Redaktions-Software gemacht haben.

S. Peter kann Ihnen mehr **über dieses Thema** erzählen. Er hat gerade mit dem Mann gesprochen, der für diesen Vertrag verantwortlich ist, mit Burnes. Burnes hat letzte Woche mit mir telefoniert, um mir zu sagen, dass er zuversichtlich sei, den Vertrag unter Dach und Fach zu bringen – aber er klang nicht mehr so optimistisch, als Peter heute Morgen mit ihm gesprochen hat.

P. He was actually **very short** on the phone. He sounded really under pressure.

P. Er war streng genommen sogar **ziemlich kurz angebunden**. Er klang, als würde er unter Druck stehen.

M. I'm not surprised! We're not the only company pushing new forms of this product. But if we can **get a lead** on the others we have a **head start** in the market. **Keep me posted** on this one. If we **score a hit** I'd like to include the product in our new **promotion**.

M. Das wundert mich nicht! Wir sind nicht die einzige Firma, die versucht, neue Versionen dieses Produkts auf den Markt zu bringen. Aber wenn wir es schaffen, den anderen ein wenig **voraus zu sein**, können wir uns auf dem Markt einen **Vorsprung** verschaffen. **Halten Sie mich** über diese Sache **auf dem Laufenden**. Wenn wir **einen Erfolg verbuchen** können, würde ich dieses Produkt gern in unsere neue **Kampagne** aufnehmen.

S. Of course, I'll call you right away. But don't keep your hopes up.

S. Natürlich, ich sage Ihnen sofort Bescheid. Aber machen Sie sich nicht zu viel Hoffnungen.

Exercise 34

Vervollständigen Sie folgendes Telefongespräch:

M. Hello, Mr Burnes. I'm _____ after a meeting today with the Sales Department Chief. I'd like to clarify the state of the Metropolitan Newspapers negotiations. Mr Blackman said you _____ him last week and that you were optimistic.

However, when Mr Brückner _____ you today he said you didn't sound so confident.

B. When I _____ to Blackman last week I _____ just _____ to the Chairman of Metropolitan Newspapers. The talks went very well, and I believe I shall be able to _____ you next week with good news. I was under pressure when Mr Brückner _____ this morning. Can you give him my apologies and tell him I shall _____ back later today.

Dos and Don'ts – A matter of form...

Do insist on clarity in all telephone business dealings, and don't allow pressure to lead you into giving the wrong impression. Before making your call, make a list on a notepad of all the important points you have to discuss. Tackle them one by one, carefully noting the replies for reference. Following the conversation, write an immediate report on the exchange with the other party and if necessary, for complete clarity, formulate it as a business letter. If you decide to record the conversation you should inform the other party beforehand.

Talk Talk Talk  14

(Steve's office)

S. Now, Peter, if Melissa will allow us to get on with our work, I'll show you how we put the department's own weekly report together.

(Steves Büro)

S. So, Peter, wenn Melissa uns jetzt wieder an unsere Arbeit lässt, werde ich Ihnen zeigen, wie wir den Wochenreport unserer eigenen Abteilung zusammenstellen.

P. That would really interest me. I don't know how you can **keep track of** what half a dozen salespeople out there in the field are up to.

P. Das würde mich wirklich interessieren. Ich habe keine Ahnung, wie man den **Überblick darüber behält**, was ein halbes Dutzend Vertreter im Außendienst so macht.

S. There are plans to **update** the computer program we use to make it more **user-friendly**. Now, since we've actually spoken to Burnes this morning on the phone, his report will be the most up to date. We go through it day by day, checking that every contact, every **lead** has been correctly **followed up**.

S. Es gibt Überlegungen, die Computerprogramme so **upzudaten**, dass sie etwas **benutzerfreundlicher** werden. Da wir ja heute Morgen mit Burnes telefoniert haben, wird sein Bericht sicher am aktuellsten sein. Wir werden ihn Tag für Tag durchsehen und aufpassen, dass jeder Vertrag korrekt ist und **jeder Ansatz** angemessen **weiterverfolgt wurde**.

Exercise 35

Sie sollen Burnes anrufen, um einige Punkte seines Berichts zu überprüfen. Wie führen Sie dieses Gespräch?

_____, Mr Burnes. _____ Peter Brückner here. I _____ you to elaborate on some of the points in your report. Do take notes if you like and then _____ me back later. I find it quicker to do this kind of thing _____ the phone. _____ you please tell me _____ company you visited on Tuesday. Did you _____ beforehand? Did they ask you to _____ personally or were they happy to do business initially _____ phone? Did you _____ them back?

Talk Talk Talk  **15**

(Steve Blackman's phone rings.)

S. Hello, Blackman here!

A. Mr Blackman. This is Arthur Smith from accounting. There's an irregularity here in last week's **expenses return** by Jim Ives. Have you got a minute – or are you busy?

S. Can you send Ives's file up? I'll look through it and then call you back. Perhaps I overlooked something.

A. Fine, but can we clear this up today before you send down last week's returns? We're pretty **inundated** down here – Miss Sykes is down with the flu. I don't have a soul to answer the phone, and it's been ringing all day.

(There's a knock at the door and Chip enters cautiously.)

(Steve Blackmans Telefon klingelt.)

S. Ja, Blackman?

A. Mr Blackman. Hier ist Arthur Smith von der Buchhaltung! Es gibt eine Abweichung in der **Spesen- abrechnung** von Jim Ives aus der letzten Woche. Haben Sie eine Minute Zeit – oder sind Sie gerade zu beschäftigt?

S. Können Sie Ives Unterlagen ein- fach heraufschicken? Ich sehe sie mir an und rufe Sie dann zurück. Vielleicht habe ich einfach etwas übersehen.

A. Gern, aber könnten wir das heute noch klären, bevor Sie die Abrechnungen der letzten Woche herunterschicken? Wir **ertrinken** hier unten **in Arbeit** – Miss Sykes liegt mit der Grippe im Bett. Ich habe hier keine Menschenseele, die ans Telefon gehen kann, und es klingelt den ganzen Tag.

(Es klopft an der Tür und Chip tritt vorsichtig ein.)

S. Well, hello, Chip! Smith, you can borrow Chip if you like. He's got nothing to do apart from his sandwich round.

S. Na so was, hallo Chip! Smith, wenn Sie möchten, können Sie sich unseren Chip ausleihen. Er hat eh nichts zu tun – außer Sandwiches durch die Gegend zu fahren.

A. Oh, God, no! But wait a minute, has he really got nothing to do?

A. Oh Gott, bitte nicht! Aber warten Sie – hat er wirklich nichts zu tun?

S. Well, he's just standing around. Wait a sec – I'll put this on **loudspeaker**...

S. Na ja, er steht nur herum. Sekunde bitte – ich schalte den **Lautsprecher** ein ...

A. Do you think he could run an **errand** for us?

A. Meinen Sie, er könnte einen **Botengang** für uns erledigen?

S. Chip?

S. Chip?

C. Sure.

C. Klar.

A. Could he run down to the pizzeria on the corner and bring us back an order? I've been trying for the last half an hour to call them to place an order but they're just not answering...

A. Könnte er vielleicht schnell zur Pizzeria um die Ecke laufen und uns etwas zu essen bringen? Ich versuche jetzt schon eine halbe Stunde, dort etwas zu bestellen, aber es geht einfach niemand ans Telefon ...

S. Pizzas? Sandwiches are Chip's speciality – and that's just what I want to talk to you about now, Chip...

S. Pizzas? Na, eigentlich sind ja Sandwiches Chips Spezialität – und genau darüber möchte ich mit dir jetzt noch ein Wörtchen reden, Chip...

Exercise 36

Was können Sie mit diesem Chaos anfangen?

Hello, _____ the Ergon Media Company?

No? _____ to? Who? Pronto Pizza? But I _____

the Ergon Media Company. What _____ do you have?

Well, that's the number I _____. At least, that's the

_____ I always _____ the Ergon Media

Company on.

I'll _____ up and _____ again. (After trying

repeatedly) Damn, now I can't _____ at all. The

_____ is always _____, Lucy. Lucy? Where

is the woman? (Chip calls out from the office.) She's _____

the phone, ordering pizza. Want one?

Background information

Despite the casual nature of business dealings in Britain, you'll still hear just the surname being used, even in social situations – and particularly between employees of rival firms. Don't take it as a sign of unfriendliness – it's said to be a throwback to English school tradition, where pupils were almost invariably addressed just by their surname. In fact, the surname can indicate a degree of intimacy which isn't necessarily expressed by the first name alone – and certainly not by the use of a "Mr" title. This is a further example of the subtle structure of English social behaviour. Avoid copying it until you're really part of the English scene!

Exercise 37

Wählen Sie das richtige Wort!

a) Could you call the shop and give this order on / with / over the phone.

b) He's just come off / from / away from the phone, so he's ready to see you now.

c) If you can't contact me today per / via / with the / by / through the phone you'll have to leave a message with my secretary.

d) He's been with / over / on the phone for hours, I can't think what he's addressing / speaking / thinking / talking about.

Talk Talk Talk

(Steve's office)

(Steves Büro)

S. Well, there you have had an **object lesson**, Peter, in the frustrations of an average day in the Sales Department.

S. Tja, Peter – das war ein erster **praktischer Anschauungsunterricht** darüber, wie frustrierend ein typischer Tag in der Verkaufsabteilung sein kann.

(Phone rings)

(Das Telefon klingelt.)

And here's another coming up... Hello, Steve Blackman here. Can I help you? Mr Tomkins? Mr Tomkins of Arco? **What can I do for you?**

Und da kommt schon das nächste Problem ... Hallo, hier Steve Blackman. Kann ich Ihnen helfen? Mr Tomkins? Mr Tomkins von Arco? **Was kann ich für Sie tun?**

Mr T. Your man in Sheffield promised to give me a call by the end of last week to **confirm the price and conditions** of the Accounting 2000 package. I haven't heard a thing from him.

Mr T. Ihr Mann in Sheffield hat mir versprochen, bis zum Ende letzter Woche zurückzurufen, um mir **den Preis und die Lieferbedingungen** für das Accounting 2000-Softwarepaket **zu bestätigen**. Ich habe noch kein Wort von ihm gehört.

S. Ferguson? He's normally very **reliable**. I'll try to reach him myself and get him to call you right away. Are you there all day?

S. Ferguson? Er ist normalerweise ziemlich **verlässlich**. Ich versuche, ihn selbst zu erreichen und sage ihm, dass er Sie sofort zurückrufen soll. Sind Sie den ganzen Tag im Büro erreichbar?

Mr T. I'll be **around**. If I'm not in the office, tell him to **leave a message** with my secretary and I'll call him back. But I've so much going on at the moment that I expect to be spending most of the morning on the phone, anyway. I just hope he catches me in a moment when I'm off the phone.

Mr T. Ja, ich werde **da sein**. Sagen Sie ihm, falls ich nicht da sein sollte, soll er doch meiner Sekretärin **eine Nachricht hinterlassen** und ich rufe zurück. Aber hier ist gerade so viel zu tun, dass ich vermutlich ohnehin den größten Teil des Vormittags am Telefon verbringen werde. Ich hoffe nur, er erreicht mich, wenn ich gerade nicht am Telefon bin.

S. If I manage to get him on the phone right now, I'll get him to call you immediately. I hope you'll be hearing from him in a minute or two.

S. Wenn ich ihn sofort am Telefon erwische, sage ich ihm, dass er sie gleich zurückrufen soll. Ich hoffe also, dass Sie in den nächsten ein oder zwei Minuten von ihm hören.

S. Lucy, can you get me Ferguson, please? Or at least try to reach him – either at home or on his mobile.

S. Lucy, können Sie mich bitte mit Ferguson verbinden? Oder versuchen Sie wenigstens, ihn zu erreichen – entweder zu Hause oder auf seinem Handy.

L. His home number is busy. **He's on the phone.** Shall I wait until **he's off**, or shall I try the mobile?

L. Seine Privatnummer ist besetzt. Also **telefoniert er gerade**. Soll ich warten, bis **er aufgelegt hat** oder es auf dem Handy versuchen?

S. Get him on the mobile. I have to speak to him right away!... Stan? I've had Arco on the phone **complaining** that you had promised them an Accounting 2000 package price last week. They're still waiting for your call.

S. Holen Sie ihn ans Handy. Ich muss sofort mit ihm sprechen! ... Stan? Ich hatte gerade Arco am Telefon – sie haben sich **beschwert**, dass Sie ihnen schon letzte Woche ein Paketpreis für unser Accounting 2000 machen wollten. Sie warten immer noch auf Ihren Anruf.

Mr F. What are they talking about? I called them last Thursday and told them the cost and explained the conditions of sale and so on. They'll get it all in writing, but at least they got it over the phone.

Mr F. Von was reden die eigentlich? Ich habe sie letzten Donnerstag angerufen, ihnen den Preis gegeben, die Lieferbedingungen erklärt und so weiter. Sie kriegen das natürlich alles noch einmal schriftlich, aber telefonisch habe ich ihnen bereits alles mitgeteilt.

S. I'll get back to you on this one. Let me first call Arco. There seems to have been a **misunderstanding** here. But can you let them have what they want in writing as soon as possible?

S. Ich rufe Sie deshalb noch einmal zurück. Aber lassen Sie mich zuerst noch mal bei Arco anrufen. Da scheint es wohl ein **Missverständnis** gegeben zu haben. Aber könnten Sie ihnen trotzdem alle Daten so schnell wie möglich schriftlich geben?

Mr F. Sure. No problem. They'll have it today by fax.

S. Lucy, be a dear and get me Mr Tomkins at Arco again. I've got something very important to clear up here. What, no reply? Then just keep trying please. God, what an **outfit**!

Mr F. Natürlich, kein Problem. Sie bekommen es heute per Fax.

S. Lucy, seien Sie doch bitte so gut und holen Sie mir noch einmal Mr Tomkins von Arco an den Apparat. Ich muss hier etwas sehr Wichtiges klären. Was, es geht niemand ans Telefon? Dann versuchen Sie es bitte weiter. Gott, was für ein **Saftladen**!

Exercise 38

Es gibt ein Missverständnis mit einem Kunden. Wie verläuft das Gespräch?

Hello, Arco? Could I _____ to Mr Tomkins, please. Mr Tomkins, it's Jeffreys _____ . I _____ if I _____ trouble you with a small problem. Someone at your office has just _____ to _____ that you are still waiting for word on the price of the system Arco is interested in. I _____ several days ago, and although your phone was constantly _____ , I spoke to one of the clerks and _____ him to _____ you a message. Didn't you _____ it? No? Then I'll dig the information out again and _____ you back. Oh, please don't _____ up. Keep me on the _____ . I have to _____ your accounting department.

 **Vocabulary**

accounting	Buchhaltung
assessment	Leistungsbericht
to be off the phone	aufgelegt haben, nicht sprechen
to be on the phone	gerade telefonieren
to break into the market	in den Markt vordringen
to call up sth.	etw. abrufen
competitive	wettbewerbsorientiert, konkurrenzfähig
to complain	sich beschweren
to confirm price and conditions	Preis und Lieferbedingungen bestätigen
to cover (a territory)	für (ein Gebiet) zuständig sein
deal	Geschäftsabschluss
to elaborate points	Punkte ausarbeiten
to email sth.	etw. per E-Mail schicken
errand	Botengang
expenses sheet/return	Spesenabrechnung
file (on sb.)	Akte (über jmd.)
to follow up a lead	an einer Sache dranbleiben; eine Möglichkeit verfolgen
to get down to sth. right away	sich sofort um etw. kümmern
to have a head start	einen Vorsprung haben
to induct sb. into sth.	jmd. in etw. einführen
innovative	innovativ
to keep sb. posted	jmd. auf dem Laufenden halten
to keep track of sth.	den Überblick behalten
to leave a message	eine Nachricht hinterlassen
log	Ablaufplan
loudspeaker	Lautsprecher/Mithörtaste
to make it snappy	sich beeilen
to man sb.'s phone	jds. Telefon übernehmen
panic stations	Krise
product line	Produktreihe
progress report	Erfolgsbericht

to punch sth. into	etw. einhacken
to put sth. on file	etw. in die Akten eintragen
to reboot	neu starten (PC)
to score a hit/goal	einen Erfolg verbuchen
to seal a contract	einen Vertrag abschließen
to shut down	herunterfahren (PC)
telephone company	Telefongesellschaft
test run	Testlauf
top sales representative	Spitzenverkäufer
to track sb. down	jmd. aufspüren
umpteen	zig
user-friendly	benutzerfreundlich

Customer service | Kundenbetreuung

Here we go

Nach seinen Erfahrungen in der Verkaufsabteilung kehrt Peter an seine eigentliche Position als Assistent bei James Morgan, dem Managing Director bei ARGO Limited, zurück. Er wird dort mit verschiedenen Kundenproblemen und deren Lösung konfrontiert und erhält weitere Aufträge ...

Talk Talk Talk  16

(James Morgan's office)

J. Hello! Morgan here!

L. Oh, good morning, Mr Morgan. It's Lucy here. Mr Brückner called to say he would be a little late this morning because he has to call at the Social Security Office on the way in. I tried to put him through to you, but the line was busy, and he was in a hurry, **so I took the message**.

J. Fine, Lucy. Don't worry. I don't really have anything for him to do yet...

(James Morgans Büro)

J. Hallo! Morgan am Apparat!

L. Oh, guten Morgen, Mr Morgan. Hier ist Lucy. Mr Brückner hat mich angerufen, um zu sagen, dass er heute wohl etwas später kommen wird, weil er auf dem Weg noch beim Sozialversicherungsamt vorbeischauen muss. Ich habe versucht, ihn zu Ihnen durchzustellen, aber die Leitung war besetzt und er hatte es sehr eilig – also **habe ich die Nachricht entgegengenommen**.

J. Schon gut, Lucy. Keine Sorge. Ich habe sowieso noch nichts Richtiges für ihn zu tun ...

(Peter enters after some time.)
P. I really am sorry I'm so late, Mr Morgan. I hope Lucy told you the reason.

J. No problem, Peter. Come in and make yourself at home. I'll call Lucy for some tea and then we'll **get down to business**.

P. I'm looking forward to working more closely with you again, Mr Morgan. And I hope I can be of some help, too.

J. That you can be, Peter! I was just sifting through the **paperwork** that has to be attended to during the week. You can certainly take some of that workload off me. You'll be very **au fait** by now with much of it after your time in Sales.

(Nach einer Weile tritt Peter ein.)
P. Tut mir wirklich leid, dass ich so spät komme, Mr Morgan. Ich hoffe, Lucy hat Ihnen den Grund dafür gesagt.

J. Kein Problem, Peter. Kommen Sie rein und machen Sie es sich bequem. Ich bitte Lucy, uns einen Tee zu bringen und dann **machen wir uns an die Arbeit**.

P. Ich freue mich schon darauf, wieder enger mit Ihnen zusammenzuarbeiten, Mr Morgan. Und ich hoffe, dass ich Ihnen eine Hilfe sein kann.

J. Oh, das werden Sie, Peter! Ich war gerade dabei, den **Papierkram** zu überfliegen, der im Laufe der Woche erledigt werden muss. Sie können mir bestimmt etwas von dieser Arbeit abnehmen. Nach Ihrer Zeit im Verkauf werden Sie mit dem meisten davon schon **vertraut** sein.

False friends

You **surely** know the difference between **safe** and **secure**? These three words can be translated as "sicher". Generally speaking, **safety** refers to protection from accidents, while **security** refers to protection from crime or future events (e.g. financial and social security).

Exercise 39

Sie müssen im Büro anrufen, um mitzuteilen, dass Sie sich leider verspäten werden. Wie gehen Sie dies am elegantesten an?

Hello, Lucy? I've tried to _____ Mr Morgan on his

_____, but the line is always _____. I have to

call at the Social Security Office on the way to work, so I'll be rather

late.

_____ please leave a message for Mr Morgan?

_____ please tell him I tried to _____ him but

I couldn't _____ through, and _____ please

tell him I'll be in late? If I'm delayed by more than half an hour or so,

I'll _____ again.

_____ you _____ able to do that for me?

Thank you so much, Lucy!

False friends

Remember that there is a difference between the adverbs **on time** and **in time**. Both are used to talk about punctuality, but they are not used synonymously.

If a train arrives **on time**, it is neither late nor early. It arrives at the scheduled time. However, passengers must arrive at the station in time to make their connection. In other words, they must arrive with time to spare.

Peter calls ahead to say he will be late: he lets his employer know **in time** that he will not be **on time** for work.

Exercise 40

Finden Sie das richtige Wort!

1. Please wait / hold / don't go away I'm trying to connect you.

2. Can you put through / speak to / try another line?

3. May I speak to / talk / contact Mr Brown, please?

4. The line is dead. I think I've been switched off / thrown out / cut off

5. Is he still on / at / in the phone?

6. Would you please leave / get off / relinquish the line. I'm busy.

7. Please try to get them by / with the / on the phone.

Talk Talk Talk 17

(James Morgan's office)

J. Now, Peter. Let's look at some of this paperwork. At the start of every week Steve sends in a **round-up** of what his people have been up to the previous week, a progress report and a **projection**. He also copies for me what he sends to **accounts** – a rough balance of outgoings, supported by receipts, and an account of receipts, actual and expected. I try

(James Morgans Büro)

J. Also, Peter, nehmen wir uns mal etwas von dem Papierkram vor. Steve schickt mir zu jedem Wochenbeginn eine **Übersicht** darüber, was seine Leute in der Vorwoche alles getan haben, einen Fortschrittsbericht und eine **Prognose**. Außerdem schickt er mir alles in Kopie, was er an die **Rechnungsstelle** weitergibt, eine grobe Aufstellung der Ausgaben, belegt

to get through it all on Monday morning, but it's usually Tuesday before I'm through. Anyway, Tuesday is our usual conference day.

durch Rechnungen, zusätzlich noch eine Zusammenstellung aller Rechnungen – der aktuellen und der noch erwarteten. Ich versuche, mich während des Montagmorgens da durchzuarbeiten, aber meistens brauche ich bis Dienstag, bevor ich damit fertig bin. Dienstag ist auf jeden Fall unser üblicher Konferenztag.

P. How can I help you here?

P. Wie kann ich dabei helfen?

J. Perhaps you'd like to take Steve's summary and match it with his accounts report. Accounting will pick up any irregularities, but it doesn't harm to be ahead of the **bean-counters**!

J. Sie könnten vielleicht Steves Aufrechnungen übernehmen und sie mit der Summe seiner Rechnungsbeträge abgleichen. Die Rechnungsstelle wird zwar alle Unregelmäßigkeiten aufspüren, aber es kann nichts schaden, diesen **Erbsenzählern** einen Schritt voraus zu sein!

P. Bean-counters?

P. Erbsenzähler?

J. Oh dear, there's my time in the Far East showing me up again. That's what the accounting staff were called in Hong Kong, and the expression has travelled as far as the United States and Britain now!

J. Oh je, da kommt meine Zeit im Fernen Osten wieder durch. So haben wir die Mitarbeiter der Rechnungsstelle in Hongkong genannt und dieser Ausdruck hat sich inzwischen bis in die Vereinigten Staaten und nach England verbreitet!

(The phone rings) And there's the first distraction of the day. Hello, Morgan here! But Mr Thomson, we tried to get you all last week. You

(Das Telefon klingelt.) Und da haben wir ja schon die erste Ablenkung des Tages. Hallo, hier Morgan! Aber Mr Thomson, wir

were never there. Look, can I call you right back? What's your extension? (Puts the phone down) That, Peter, was a bean-counter!

haben die ganze letzte Woche versucht, Sie zu erreichen. Sie waren nie da. Hören Sie, kann ich Sie zurückrufen? Wie lautet denn Ihre Durchwahl? (Legt den Hörer auf) Das, Peter, war ein Erbsenzähler!

Exercise 41

Sie wurden gebeten einen Verkäufer anzurufen, um ihn darauf hinzuweisen, dass sein Bericht nicht mit seiner Abrechnung übereinstimmt. Wie verläuft das Gespräch?

Hello, _____ Mr Harper? I'm _____ on the instructions of Mr Morgan to _____ you for clarification of your report. Mr Morgan says it doesn't tally with your accounting. I think the best thing is for you to _____ company headquarters and ask to _____ the head of accounting. When I _____ to him this morning I must confess I didn't understand the problem. Would you mind _____ him and _____ him to sort the problem out, and then _____ me to report on the situation. Mr Morgan also expects a _____ from you later in the day. If he's not there, ask to be _____ to me. Oh, before you _____ off, please give me a _____ where I can reach you this afternoon.

Background information

Tally-ho! A "tally" in the business sense is an account or a reckoning. The verb "to tally" means "to make an account", "to add up" – or, in the above context, "to make two separate things agree or correspond".

And tally-ho? That's a hunting term – a hunter's cry on sighting a fox!

Talk Talk Talk  18

(Morgan's office)

(Morgans Büro)

J. Peter, may I hand Thomson on to you? He's an absolute nuisance! He's the accountant at Sparrow Technologies, and he's not happy with the software we sent him, nor with the **payment agreement**. I've told him we'll send one of our people round to **talk him through** the system and that our accounting will handle the payment problem. But he simply insists on speaking to me. Give him a call, tell him you're my assistant and try and sort out his problems. If you manage to get him off my back, I'll buy you lunch tomorrow!

J. Peter, kann ich diesen Thomson an Sie übergeben? Der Mann ist ein absoluter Nervtöter! Er ist Buchhalter bei Sparrow Technologies und er ist nicht zufrieden mit unserer Software – und auch nicht mit den **Zahlungsbedingungen**. Ich habe ihm gesagt, dass wir einen unserer Leute zu ihnen schicken werden, der ihnen das System **erklärt** und dass unsere Buchhaltung sich um die Zahlungsmodalitäten kümmern wird. Aber er besteht einfach darauf, mit mir zu reden. Rufen Sie ihn bitte an, sagen sie ihm, dass Sie mein Assistent sind und versuchen werden, seine Probleme zu lösen. Wenn Sie es schaffen, ihn mir vom Hals zu halten, lade ich Sie morgen zum Mittagessen ein!

P. I'll do my best, Mr Morgan. But do you think I can do it all on the phone?

P. Ich werde mein Bestes versuchen, Mr Morgan. Aber glauben Sie, ich kann das alles über das Telefon erreichen?

J. The alternative is a long journey – he's in Scotland!

J. Die Alternative wäre eine lange Reise – er sitzt in Schottland!

Exercise 42

Sie wollen sich nach den Kosten für eine Geschäftsreise nach Schottland erkundigen und rufen ein Reisebüro an, um nach der billigsten und schnellsten Reisemöglichkeit zu fragen. Wie verläuft das Gespräch?

Hello, _____ the Oxford Street Travel Centre?

I _____ to travel to Scotland tomorrow, returning on Thursday. Do you have any special offers by air? The domestic desk? Can you _____ me through? Yes, I'll _____.

Hello, is that the domestic desk? Do you have any special offers to Glasgow or Edinburgh? No, not by train! By air! I'm on the wrong _____? Could you _____ me through to the right extension then, please? Yes, I'll _____.

Hello, hello! Damn, I've been _____. The phone is _____. I'll never get to Scotland at this rate. I'll do it all _____ phone.

Talk Talk Talk  19

(Peter's office)

(Peters Büro)

P. Hello, Mr Thomson? Mr Morgan asked me to call you and try and sort out your problems.

P. Hallo, Mr Thomson? Mr Morgan hat mich gebeten, Sie anzurufen und zu versuchen, Ihre Probleme zu lösen.

Mr T. Who am I speaking to?

Mr T. Mit wem spreche ich?

P. Oh, I am sorry – my name is Peter Brückner. I'm Mr Morgan's new assistant.

P. Oh, tut mir leid – mein Name ist Peter Brückner. Ich bin Mr Morgans neuer Assistent.

Mr T. Well, I hope you can assist me with my problems, young man!

Mr T. Tja, ich hoffe, Sie können mir bei meinen Problemen helfen, junger Mann!

P. I'll certainly try. What seems to be the matter?

P. Ich werde es zumindest versuchen. Wo scheint es denn ein Problem zu geben?

Mr T. Seems to be? Problem? I've got at least two for you to solve. Let's start with number one – the accounting software you delivered. I can't install it.

Mr T. Scheint? EIN Problem? Ich habe mindestens zwei, die Sie für mich lösen müssen. Fangen wir mit der Nummer 1 an – die Buchhaltungssoftware, die Sie mir geliefert haben. Ich kann sie nicht installieren.

P. We had a **call from a client with a similar problem**. He hadn't read our instructions carefully enough. A couple of phone calls should put the matter right.

P. Wir hatten bereits einen **Anruf von einem anderen Kunden mit einem ähnlichen Problem**. Er hatte unsere Installationsanweisung nicht sorgfältig genug gelesen. Mit ein paar Telefongesprächen sollte das Problem zu lösen sein.

Mr T. Phone calls? Phone calls? I want somebody round here **on the double**, my man!

Mr T. Telefongespräche? Ein paar Telefongespräche? Ich will jemanden hier an Ort und Stelle sehen, aber **in Nullkommanichts**, junger Mann!

P. Let's see. We have a man in Glasgow who can call on you tomorrow.

P. Mal sehen. Wir haben einen Mitarbeiter in Glasgow, der morgen vorbeikommen könnte.

Mr T. Tomorrow? Yesterday would have been better. But I'll **settle for** tomorrow.

Mr T. Morgen? Gestern wäre besser. Aber ich werde mich mit morgen **zufrieden geben**.

P. I'll tell him to call you right away and let you know when he will be around.

P. Ich werde ihm sagen, dass er Sie sofort anrufen soll, um Ihnen mitzuteilen, wann er da sein kann.

Mr T. I'll be waiting, young man, I'll be waiting...

Mr T. Ich warte, junger Mann, ich warte darauf ...

Exercise 43

Ordnen Sie die Positionen nach ihrem Rang in einem Unternehmen:

a) Secretary

b) Managing Director

c) Accountant

d) Department Head

e) Salesman

f) Trainee salesman

g) Assistant Managing Director

h) Chief Accountant

i) Chief Secretary

1. ____ 2. ____ 3. ____ 4. ____ 5. ____

6. ____ 7. ____ 8. ____ 9. ____

Talk Talk Talk 20

(Peter's office)

P. Lucy, do you have the number of our man in Glasgow? McLeod is his name. Roy McLeod.

L. I'll have it for you **in a jiffy**. Shall I call him for you and connect you?

P. That would be very kind of you, Lucy.

L. Mr McLeod? ARGO Limited, London, here. Mr Brückner would like to speak to you. **Please hold the line. I'm putting you through right now**...

P. Hello, Roy McLeod? Peter Brückner here. I'm helping Mr Morgan out this week. Sparrow Technologies are causing us problems – at least, they say they have problems.

R. Are you dealing with Thomson?

P. That's him, the company accountant. He has called several times, and frankly he's getting on Mr Morgan's nerves. Can you call round and try and sort things out?

(Peters Büro)

P. Lucy, haben Sie die Nummer von unserem Mann in Glasgow? Sein Name ist McLeod. Roy McLeod.

L. Ich suche sie Ihnen im **Handumdrehen** heraus. Soll ich ihn für Sie anrufen und Sie gleich durchstellen?

P. Das wäre sehr nett von Ihnen, Lucy.

L. Mr McLeod? Hier ARGO Limited, London. Mr Brückner würde gern mit Ihnen sprechen. **Bitte bleiben Sie in der Leitung, ich stelle Sie durch** ...

P. Hallo, Roy McLeod? Hier Peter Brückner. Ich assistiere Mr Morgan diese Woche. Wir haben Probleme mit Sparrow Technologies – zumindest sagen sie, dass sie Probleme hätten.

R. Haben Sie es etwa mit Mr Thomson zu tun?

P. Ganz genau, mit dem Buchhalter der Firma. Er hat schon mehrmals bei uns angerufen und, ehrlich gesagt, geht er Mr Morgan schon ziemlich auf die Nerven. Können

R. I've been round there several times, didn't he tell you? The man is impossible. He can't operate a computer and he doesn't seem able to read. I helped him install Accounting 2000 and within a week the whole system was down! But I'll give him a call – I hope I can do all this on the phone. He's got a fierce temper...

Sie mal vorbeischauen und versuchen, das zu regeln?

R. Ich war doch schon mehrfach dort, hat er Ihnen das nicht gesagt? Der Mann ist einfach unmöglich; er kann nicht mit Computern umgehen und offensichtlich nicht einmal lesen. Ich habe ihm dabei geholfen, Accounting 2000 zu installieren und innerhalb einer Woche ist das gesamte System zusammengebrochen! Aber ich werde ihn anrufen – ich hoffe, ich kann das über das Telefon regeln. Der Mann hat ein ziemlich unbeherrschtes Temperament ...

Exercise 44

Sie sprechen am Telefon mit einem sehr verärgerten Mr Thomson von Sparrow Technologies. Wie würden Sie ihn beruhigen? Sie müssen Ihre Worte sehr sorgsam wählen!

Hello, Mr Thomson! Yes, I understand / know you have problems, and that is why I am calling. I do confirm / assure you that we are doing everything we can / find possible to arrive / find a solution. I'm afraid / concerned it won't be easy, but I can assure / guarantee you we won't give up / stop work until you are entirely pleased / satisfied .

Dos and Don'ts – A matter of form...

"Sound" advice!

A telephone conversation puts a safe distance between the callers, but never allow that to affect your tone – particularly if you are talking in English. In business dealings, remain correct and polite at all times, even when provoked by difficult clients. Never, ever put the phone down in anger! However difficult or confrontational the conversation, direct it to a correct close. Remember the German saying: "Der Klügere gibt nach." Interestingly, the nearest English equivalent has a martial ring: "Discretion is the better part of valour." So discretion please, even in the most difficult telephone situation!

Talk Talk Talk 21

(At the bar in the Duke of Gloucester)

(An der Bar vom Duke of Gloucester Pub)

S. Okay, what's yours, Peter?

S. Okay, was möchten Sie trinken, Peter?

P. No, it's my round, Steve.

P. Nein, diese Runde geht auf mich.

S. Well, mine's a pint of best bitter. Now, tell me how you're getting along with Jimmy?

S. Na schön, dann nehme ich ein Glas „Best Bitter". Na, erzählen Sie mal, wie kommen Sie mit Jimmy zurecht?

P. Jimmy?

P. Jimmy?

S. Morgan. The old man!

S. Morgan. Der Alte!

P. Actually, he's very kind and helpful.

P. Eigentlich ist er sehr nett und hilfsbereit.

S. Well, I'm sure that's because you're being very kind yourself and helping him a lot!

P. I'm certainly helping him with the **workload**. Phoning, sorting out problems over the phone – that kind of thing.

S. Such as?

P. Well, I had to call this very difficult chap in Glasgow...

S. Don't tell me. Name of Thomson, perhaps?!

P. Yes. Fortunately, I was able to hand the problem on to McLeod.

S. McLeod can handle him. Thomson's our most difficult customer, and he doesn't like to sign a cheque!

P. That's the message I got from Mr Morgan.

S. Well, you're learning, my boy! Another?

P. Good lord, no! I'm due back in the office in five minutes.

S. Tja, das liegt sicher nur daran, dass Sie selber sehr freundlich sind und ihm viel Arbeit abnehmen!

P. Ich nehme ihm wirklich etwas von seinem **Arbeitspensum** ab. Telefonieren und versuchen, Probleme über das Telefon zu lösen – so was in der Art.

S. Zum Beispiel?

P. Na ja, ich musste diesen sehr schwierigen Typen in Glasgow anrufen ...

S. Nichts sagen! Heißt der zufällig Thomson?!

P. Ja. Zum Glück konnte ich das Problem an McLeod weitergeben.

S. McLeod kommt schon mit ihm klar. Thomson ist unser schwierigster Kunde und er schreibt nur sehr ungern Schecks aus!

P. Genau das hat Mr Morgan auch durchblicken lassen.

S. Tja, da lernen Sie ja einiges, mein Junge! Noch eine Runde?

P. Gott bewahre, nein! Ich muss in fünf Minuten zurück im Büro sein.

S. Well, you're really a management type now. Has Jimmy given you a **pager** yet?

S. Meine Güte, Sie sind ja schon ein richtiger Managertyp. Hat James Ihnen schon einen **Pager** gegeben?

P. A pager?

P. Einen Pager?

S. Joking, Peter, joking! If Jimmy wants you, you'll hear your mobile ringing frantically. He hasn't invested in pagers yet, thank goodness!

S. Das sollte nur ein Scherz sein, Peter! Wenn James etwas von Ihnen will, werden Sie schon hören, wie Ihr Handy hektisch klingelt. Er hat bis jetzt noch kein Geld für Pager ausgegeben, Gott sei Dank!

P. Well, he did mention something about "pagers".

P. Na ja, er erwähnte mal irgendetwas über „Piepser".

S. Oh, no! Spare me that! I sometimes long for the old days when you just left a number where you could be reached...

S. Oh, nein! Ersparen Sie mir das! Ich sehne mich manchmal nach den alten Tagen zurück, als man nur eine Nummer hinterließ, unter der man erreichbar war ...

Background information

Pager? A pager – or a "beeper" – is a device which is carried by a person who must be reachable at all times – a doctor in a hospital, for instance, or the manager of a hotel. It emits a beep or other sound to alert the person carrying it that he or she is required. It is a "one-way" transmission device with a panel showing details of a problem or the name and number of the person calling. It normally has a limited range – within a building or, at most, a city block.

Exercise 45

Wie nennt man die folgenden Geräte?

- a device for taking messages which you can play back at your leisure   _____
- a GPS device for finding your way in an unknown city or on long journeys   _____
- a device for recording conversations or presentations   _____
- a computer that is smaller than a PC but larger than a tablet   _____
- a portable device for making and receiving calls   _____

Talk Talk Talk  22

(James Morgan's office)

P. I'm sorry I'm late back from lunch, Mr Morgan.

J. That's all right, Peter. Ask Lucy to get some tea ready and then let's get down to work... I'd like you to take over the Accounting 2000 program for the next few days. We're

(James Morgans Büro)

P. Tut mir leid, wenn ich meine Mittagspause etwas überzogen habe, Mr Morgan.

J. Schon in Ordnung, Peter. Bitten Sie Lucy doch, uns etwas Tee zu kochen und dann machen wir uns an die Arbeit ... Ich hätte gern, dass Sie sich in den nächsten paar Tagen

having quite a lot of problems with it, chiefly because it does seem to be quite difficult to install.

P. Well, that was certainly Thomson's problem in Glasgow, but McLeod's working on it.

J. There are two Scots together. At least they're speaking the same language – or with the same accent, that is!

P. I've looked at the installation instructions, and I must confess I had problems following them. Perhaps it's because they were written by the American **manufacturers**. They seem to assume a high degree of computer literacy.

J. My, Peter! And you have assumed a high degree of English literacy since you've been with us! Congratulations!

P. I must thank you and my colleagues here if that is the case. I certainly feel very much at home in the English language now.

um das Programm Accounting 2000 kümmern. Wir haben einige Probleme damit, besonders, weil es schwer zu installieren zu sein scheint.

P. Tja, das war definitiv Thomsons Problem in Glasgow, aber McLeod arbeitet daran.

J. Na, zwei Schotten auf einem Haufen. Wenigstens sprechen sie dieselbe Sprache – oder wenigstens denselben Dialekt!

P. Ich habe selber einmal einen Blick in die Installationsanleitung geworfen und ich muss zugeben, dass ich Probleme hatte, ihr zu folgen. Vielleicht liegt es daran, dass sie von den amerikanischen **Herstellern** geschrieben wurde. Sie scheinen es dort gewohnt zu sein, ganz selbstverständlich Fachbegriffe aus dem Computerbereich zu verwenden.

J. Meine Güte, Peter! Und Sie benutzen seit Sie hier sind ganz selbstverständlich Fachbegriffe aus der englischen Sprache. Kompliment!

P. Wenn das wirklich so ist, verdanke ich das Ihnen und meinen Kollegen hier. Ich fühle mich mittlerweile in der englischen Sprache wirklich zu Hause.

J. Tell me – **how do we go about tackling the** Acc. 2000 **problems?**

J. Sagen Sie mir – **wie nehmen wir die Probleme** mit Acc. 2000 **am besten in Angriff**?

P. I think the best way would be to **assign** one of our computer staff to install each system personally. It will stretch the department and add to costs. But in the end I think it will benefit ARGO, in terms of **time, expense and customer-relations**.

P. Ich glaube, der beste Weg wäre es wohl, wenn wir einen Angestellten aus unserer Computerabteilung dazu **abstellen** würden, jedes System persönlich zu installieren. Das wäre natürlich eine zusätzliche Belastung für die Abteilung und würde das Budget strapazieren. Aber ich glaube, letztendlich würde ARGO davon profitieren – im Sinne von **Zeitersparnis, Kosten und Kundenbeziehungen**.

J. I think you're right. Can I leave that in your hands? I'm going to be away for a few days. It will mean calling all our sales team to alert them to what we intend to do.

J. Ich glaube, Sie haben Recht. Kann ich das Ihnen übertragen? Ich bin für ein paar Tage weg. Es würde bedeuten, dass wir alle unsere Verkäufer sofort darüber informieren müssten, was wir vorhaben.

P. McLeod should be installing Thomson's system right now and he'll call me back. I'll phone the others right away, and I'll follow up the calls with a **memo**.

P. McLeod sollte in diesem Moment schon dabei sein, das System von Mr Thomson zu installieren und danach wird er mich zurückrufen. Ich werde die anderen sofort anrufen und anschließend noch ein **Memo** verschicken.

Exercise 46

Setzen Sie die richtige Form des Verbs „to call" ein:

1. I _____ him yesterday but he wasn't there.

2. They told me he _____ although I had instructed him not to.

3. He said he _____ the next day.

4. I would _____ if only I had known.

5. I wonder if she _____ tomorrow.

6. He _____ his mother every Sunday.

7. Do you think I will disturb her if I _____ tomorrow?

Talk Talk Talk  23

(Peter's office)

(Peters Büro)

P. Hello, is Mr Burnes there, please? He's out? Oh, I'm speaking to Mrs Burnes? It's Peter Brückner from ARGO here. How are you? Could you ask your husband to phone me when he gets back, please? No, wait a minute, **don't bother** – I'll call him on his mobile. **I'm sorry to have bothered you**. Goodbye... Hello, Geoff Burnes? Hi, it's Peter Brückner here. I thought I'd call you first just to **put you in the picture** regarding a **policy change** here. Since you're working on a

P. Hallo, ist Mr Burnes zu sprechen? Er ist außer Haus? Oh, spreche ich mit Mrs Burnes? Hier spricht Peter Brückner von ARGO. Wie geht es Ihnen? Könnten Sie Ihren Mann bitten, dass er mich zurückruft, wenn er wieder nach Hause kommt? Nein, warten Sie, **machen Sie sich keine Mühe** – ich rufe ihn einfach auf seinem Handy an. **Bitte entschuldigen Sie die Störung**. Auf Wiederhören ... Hallo, Geoff Burnes? Hi, hier spricht Peter Brückner. Ich dachte

contract right now, I thought you should know what's going on.
If you get around to discussing a contract with Metropolitan Newspapers, would you mention that ARGO will assign a computer specialist to install the software and stay on the job just as long as it takes **to break the system in**?

mir, ich rufe Sie erst einmal an, um Sie über eine kleine **Änderung unserer Geschäftspraktik ins Bild zu setzen**. Da Sie gerade an einem Vertragsabschluss arbeiten, dachte ich mir, Sie sollten wissen, was vor sich geht. Falls Sie über einen Vertragsabschluss mit Metropolitan Newspapers verhandeln sollten, würden Sie dann bitte auch erwähnen, dass ARGO einen Computerspezialisten abstellen wird, der die Software installiert und so lange dabei bleibt, wie es dauert, um **das System in Betrieb zu nehmen**?

G. Sure, it's a good idea. But do we have the **manpower**?

G. Sicher. Das ist eine gute Idee. Aber haben wir dazu genug **Leute**?

P. Mr Morgan assures me that we'll make sure we have the staff to do the job.

P. Mr Morgan hat mir versichert, dass wir dafür sorgen werden, genug Personal zu haben, um diese Aufgabe zu bewältigen.

G. I called him a couple of days ago to report on the Metropolitan Newspapers assignment. I'm getting nowhere fast.

G. Ich habe ihn vor ein paar Tagen angerufen, um ihm einen Bericht über die Verhandlungen mit Metropolitan Newspapers abzugeben. So schnell werde ich da wohl nicht weiterkommen.

P. What seems to be the trouble?

P. Wo liegt denn das Problem?

G. There's a lot of scepticism that I can't **break down**. At first, they were **all ears**. But then there was

G. Sie haben eine Menge Zweifel, die ich nicht **zerstreuen** kann. Zuerst waren Sie **ganz Ohr**. Aber dann gab

a change at the top and I can't get near the new governor.

es einen Wechsel in der Führungsspitze und ich komme einfach nicht an den neuen Governor heran.

P. Governor?

P. Governor?

G. The boss – the Managing Editor. He just doesn't seem to talk my language.

G. Den Boss – den Herausgeber. Er und ich – wir scheinen einfach nicht dieselbe Sprache zu sprechen.

P. You have other assignments, don't you?

P. Sie haben doch noch andere Aufgaben, oder?

G. You bet! I'm busy with the accounting program and at least there I can report some progress.

G. Na, **darauf können Sie wetten**! Ich bin sehr aktiv, was das Buchhaltungsprogramm angeht und wenigstens da kann ich einige Erfolge melden.

P. Then **back off** the Metropolitan Newspapers assignment for now. I'll have a chat with Mr Morgan about it.

P. Dann **stellen Sie** die Verhandlungen mit Metropolitan Newspapers fürs Erste **zurück**. Ich werde mich mit Mr Morgan darüber unterhalten.

G. I'd be glad to. Call me and tell me what he says.

G. Aber gern. Rufen Sie mich an, und erzählen Sie mir, was er darüber sagt.

P. I'll do that. Expect a call from me tomorrow morning at the latest. Will you be at home?

P. Das mache ich. Sie können spätestens morgen früh mit einem Anruf von mir rechnen. Werden Sie da zu Hause sein?

G. If I'm not, try me on my mobile, or leave a message with my wife.

G. Falls nicht, versuchen Sie es einfach auf dem Handy oder hinterlassen Sie meiner Frau eine Nachricht.

Exercise 47

Sie erstatten James Morgan einen Bericht über Ihr Telefonat mit
Geoff Burnes. Wählen Sie Ihre Worte sorgfältig und unterstreichen
Sie jeweils den passendsten Begriff!

Hi / Good morning , Mr Morgan!
I called / found Geoff Burnes and informed him of / talked about
the new sales initiative you have decided on / dreamt up .
He finds the idea of considerable use / very interesting . But he
would wish for / appreciate more information. Will you be calling /
buzzing him?
Or shall we put it in words / in writing and send it by fax / put it in
the fax machine ?
He's impatient / waiting for a reply. Shall I telephone / call him
back?

Talk Talk Talk

(Peter's office. Melissa enters.)

M. Good morning, Peter. How are
you getting along in **the hot seat**?

P. I'm tempted to say it's not so
bad. I've run into my first difficulty.

M. Already?

(Peters Büro. Melissa tritt ein.)

M. Guten Morgen, Peter. Na, wie
ist es, **im Rampenlicht zu arbeiten**?

P. Ich bin fast versucht zu sagen, es
ist gar nicht so schlimm. Ich bin auf
mein erstes Problem gestoßen.

M. Schon?

P. I called Geoff Burnes, and I've had to **take him off one job**. Mr Morgan isn't around so I can't **clear it** with him, but I feel we have to act quickly here if we want to secure that Metropolitan Newspapers contract.

P. Ich habe gerade Geoff Burnes angerufen und ihn von einem **Auftrag abgezogen**. Mr Morgan ist nicht im Büro, also kann ich die Sache nicht mit ihm **abklären**, aber ich habe das Gefühl, dass wir schnell handeln müssen, wenn wir diesen Vertrag mit Metropolitan Newspapers noch unter Dach und Fach bringen wollen.

M. What's Geoff doing wrong?

M. Was macht Geoff denn falsch?

P. Seems to be a personality problem. He can't **establish any rapport with** the man who'll decide for Metropolitan, the new **managing editor**.

P. Das scheint ein Problem mit der persönlichen Chemie zu sein. Er kann keinen **Draht zu** dem Mann **finden**, der jetzt für Metropolitan die Entscheidungen trifft, dem neuen **Herausgeber**.

M. Geoff's a good **sales rep**, but he can be abrasive. He's got enough **on his plate** anyway, hasn't he?

M. Geoff ist ein guter **Außendienstmitarbeiter**, aber er hat seine Ecken und Kanten. Jedenfalls hat er **schon genug am Hals**, oder?

P. Exactly. I told him to concentrate on the accounting system contracts. But I honestly don't know what to do about Metropolitan. Steve's on a **business trip** to the West Country, and Mr Morgan's off for the next three days. Shall I call him at home?

P. Ganz genau. Ich habe ihm gesagt, er soll sich besser auf die Verträge mit unserem Buchhaltungssystem konzentrieren. Aber ehrlich gesagt habe ich keine Ahnung, was wir mit Metropolitan anfangen sollen. Steve ist auf **Geschäftsreise** im Südwesten Englands. Und Mr Morgan hat die nächsten drei Tage frei. Ob ich ihn zu Hause anrufen sollte?

M. At your peril, Peter! He's playing golf and he hates to be disturbed then. You can't reach him anyway – mobile phones are banned on the golf course.

P. Then what shall I do?

M. You're his **stand-in**, Peter. It's your decision. But, if I were you, I'd take over the Metropolitan assignment myself. Give the Managing Editor a call. He can hardly refuse to take it. In Geoff's vocabulary, **get your foot in the door**! There's the telephone! Now **do your stuff**!

M. Auf eigenes Risiko, Peter! Er spielt Golf und hasst es, dabei gestört zu werden. Sie können ihn sowieso nicht erreichen – Handys sind auf dem Golfplatz nicht zugelassen.

P. Was soll ich dann tun?

M. Sie sind seine **Vertretung**, Peter. Es ist Ihre Entscheidung. Aber an Ihrer Stelle würde ich mich selbst um den Metropolitan-Vertrag kümmern. Rufen Sie den Herausgeber an. Er kann sich kaum weigern, Ihren Anruf entgegenzunehmen. Wie Geoff sagen würde: **Versuchen Sie, einen Fuß in die Tür zu bekommen!** Da steht das Telefon! **Tun Sie, was Sie tun müssen!**

Exercise 48

Peter arbeitet allein an Lucys Schreibtisch, während sie Mittagspause macht. Das Telefon klingelt, Peter nimmt ab. Können Sie ihm helfen, den Anruf zu bewältigen, indem Sie die richtigen Wörter oder Ausdrücke unterstreichen?

Hello, ARGO Limited! Can I help you? You'd like to speak to / address / talk at Mr Blackman? I'll see if he's in the house / in / at work .

I'm sorry, there's no response / reply / call back . He must be out / away / not at work . Or perhaps he's in another office. Shall I try another number / line / contact or would you like to wait on / hang up / hold ? You could leave a word / statement / message with me, if you must / like / desire . Right, I'll tell him to respond / get back / call back . Could you please give me your address / extension / number ?

Exercise 49

Finden Sie einfache Verben mit vergleichbarer Bedeutung!

to use the telephone

_____

to be connected with somebody on the telephone

_____

to wait while the operator tries to reach a number

_____

to end a telephone conversation

_____

to respond to the ringing of a telephone

_____

Talk Talk Talk  24

(Peter's office)

P. Hello! **Is that** Metropolitan News-papers? Could you put me through to the Managing Editor's Secretary, please? The line is busy. I'll wait, then... **The line is still engaged? Then I'll call back later. What time would you suggest?** Good, perhaps you would be good enough to tell Mr Fothergill I called. It's Peter Brückner from ARGO Limited. I'm calling concerning the software program we presented to Mr Fothergill. He'll know all about it. Just inform Mr Fothergill that I shall be calling back in an hour or two. Thank you!

(Peters Büro)

P. Hallo! **Bin ich verbunden** mit Metropolitan Newspapers? Könn-ten Sie mich bitte mit der Sekretärin des Herausgebers verbinden? Die Leitung ist besetzt. Schön, ich warte ... **Die Leitung ist immer noch besetzt? Dann rufe ich später noch einmal an. Welche Uhrzeit würden Sie denn vor-schlagen?** Gut, vielleicht sind Sie so nett und richten Mr Fothergill aus, dass ich angerufen habe. Mein Name ist Peter Brückner von ARGO Limited. Ich rufe wegen der Software an, die wir Mr Fothergill schon einmal vorgestellt haben. Er weiß schon Bescheid. Bitte richten Sie Mr Fothergill nur aus, dass ich in ein oder zwei Stunden noch ein-mal zurückrufe. Vielen Dank!

Dos and Don'ts – A matter of form...

If the person you wish to speak to is otherwise engaged or out of the office and you have to leave a message, it's good form to give his or her secretary or representative an idea of the purpose of your call. When you finally succeed in reaching the person you wish to contact, he or she will be prepared for the call and will probably be better informed on the subject you wish to discuss. You'll save valuable time – and give a businesslike impression!

ⓘ Kundenbetreuung

Talk Talk Talk 25

(Peter's office)

(Peters Büro)

P. Hello, Peter Brückner here. Mr Fothergill? **That's very kind of you indeed to call back personally.** I was about to call you. I hope your secretary told you the purpose of my call. Good. **I really am very concerned** that you are having doubts about our Quick-Ed copy-editing program. We have decided to assign a computer expert from our technical staff to accompany clients closely through installation and familiarization. The details are slightly complicated to explain on the telephone, but I would be happy to fax you our memorandum...

P. Hallo, Peter Brückner hier. Mr Fothergill? **Es ist sehr nett von Ihnen, persönlich zurückzurufen.** Ich wollte Sie gerade selbst anrufen. Ich hoffe, Ihre Sekretärin hat Ihnen gesagt, warum ich angerufen habe. Gut. **Ich bin wirklich sehr bestürzt** darüber, dass Sie Zweifel an unserer Quick-Ed Redaktionssoftware haben. Wir haben uns dazu entschlossen, jedem Kunden einen Computerexperten unserer technischen Abteilung zur Seite zu stellen, bis die Installation abgeschlossen ist und die Käufer mit dem Umgang vertraut sind. Die Details sind am Telefon etwas schwer zu erklären, aber ich faxe Ihnen gerne unser Memorandum ...

Exercise 50

Sie müssen anhand kurzer Aufzeichnungen, die Sie bei einer Besprechung gemacht haben, eine Aktennotiz erstellen. Wie sieht die endgültige Fassung der Notiz aus?

Quick-Ed program. Who interested? Installation. Who responsible? Advantages, drawbacks, complaints? Decisions: install at Metropolitan Newspapers, assign Ken Allington, chief computer analyst, to supervise installation/familiarization. Length of assignment? Depends on difficulties of acquainting Metropolitan staff with system. Costs/pricing? Subject of negotiations with Metropolitan. Next meeting: Tuesday 24 August.

Talk Talk Talk 26

(Peter's office)

P. Hello! Peter Brückner speaking. Mr Fothergill? Did you get my fax? Good. Do you have any questions? You want to see me personally? When? Oh dear, I'll have to clear this with Mr Morgan and Mr Burnes. You don't want anything to do with Mr Burnes? Well, this is all very delicate. But I'll certainly have to speak to Mr Morgan. He's back on Monday. I can let you have a definite reply on Tuesday. Can I call you then? Good, until Tuesday, then...

(Peters Büro)

P. Hallo, hier Peter Brückner. Mr Fothergill? Haben Sie mein Fax bekommen? Gut. Haben Sie Fragen dazu? Sie würden mich gern persönlich sprechen? Wann? Meine Güte, das muss ich erst mit Mr Morgan und Mr Burnes abklären. Sie wollen mit Mr Burnes nichts zu tun haben? Tja, das ist eine heikle Situation. Aber ich werde auf jeden Fall mit Mr Morgan sprechen müssen. Er ist Montag wieder im Büro. Ich kann Ihnen am Dienstag eine verbindliche Antwort geben. Kann ich Sie dann wieder anrufen? Gut, dann bis Dienstag ...

(Melissa enters.)
Melissa, that was Fothergill from Metropolitan. He wants to talk to me personally about that Quick-Ed offer.

(Melissa tritt ein.)
Melissa, das war Fothergill von Metropolitan. Er möchte mit mir persönlich über unser Quick-Ed-Angebot sprechen.

M. That will mean a trip to Nottingham – a **venture into the field**.

M. Das bedeutet eine Geschäftsreise nach Nottingham – ein **Außendiensteinsatz**.

P. I know, and I'm not too happy about the prospect!

P. Ich weiß, und ich bin nicht begeistert über diese Aussicht!

Exercise 51

Sie müssen selbst die Vorbereitungen für eine Geschäftsreise treffen. Als Erstes müssen Sie ein Hotelzimmer buchen. Wie gehen Sie es an? Unterstreichen Sie die richtige Variante.

Hello, is that the Hotel Astoria? I would like / request a room for the night of 24 August. Yes, a single. You only have doubles / two-person rooms ? What is the extra charge for single use / occupancy of a double room? That's fine. I plan to arrive / turn up on the afternoon of 24 August.
Is dinner included in the room fee / rate ? Then I would like to reserve / take a table for myself and a business colleague. Does the hotel claim / have a bar? And what other facilities / attractions does the hotel have?

Exercise 52

Als Nächstes müssen Sie ein Auto mieten. Unterstreichen Sie die richtige Variante.

Hello, is that Star Hire? I would like to have / hire a car for two days, 24 and 25 August. Group two, please. What is your price / rate for that group? Does that include / exclude tax and insurance? It's inclusive / including ? Then please go ahead / carry on and reserve / keep a group two car for me for those two days. I'd like to collect / drive off the car at 11 AM. Should I supply you with confirmation / details ? Then I'll buzz / call if I'm delayed. Otherwise, I will be there on time / in time .

Talk Talk Talk  27

(Peter's office)

P. Steve? Oh, thank goodness I've managed to reach you. Fothergill of Metropolitan Newspapers wants to meet me personally to discuss the Quick-Ed program. He doesn't want to deal with Burnes, apparently.

S. Well, I can understand that. Burnes may not **be his cup of tea**. I'd go myself, but I have a lot still to do down here. How soon does Fothergill want to meet you?

(Peters Büro)

P. Steve? Oh, Gott sei Dank, endlich erreiche ich Sie. Fothergill von Metropolitan Newspapers will mich persönlich treffen, um über unser Quick-Ed-Programm zu reden. Offensichtlich will er auf keinen Fall mit Burnes verhandeln.

S. Tja, ich kann das verstehen. Burnes und er liegen **nicht auf einer Wellenlänge**. Ich würde ja selbst gehen, aber ich habe hier einfach zu viel zu tun. Wie bald will Fothergill Sie denn sehen?

P. Right away, he told me on the phone. Should I go up to Nottingham?

S. I don't think we've got any alternative. Get Lucy to **make the arrangements**. Good luck! You'll be okay.

P. Well, I'll do my best, but don't expect any miracles! Lucy, I have to make a business trip to Nottingham. Could you help me with the arrangements? Could you call and reserve a hotel for me, and also a hire car?

L. Certainly, Peter. You look a bit nervous – let me make you a nice cup of tea and then you leave all the arrangements to me.

P. That's very kind of you, Lucy. I have to make a few calls myself and it would help if you could get me a hotel room and a car.

P. Am besten sofort, hat er mir am Telefon gesagt. Soll ich nach Nottingham fahren?

S. Ich glaube nicht, dass uns eine Wahl bleibt. Lassen Sie von Lucy alle **Vorbereitungen treffen**. Viel Glück! Sie schaffen das schon.

P. Ich tue mein Bestes, aber erwarten Sie keine Wunder! Lucy, ich muss auf eine Geschäftsreise nach Nottingham. Könnten Sie mir bei den Vorbereitungen helfen? Könnten Sie anrufen und mir ein Hotelzimmer und einen Wagen mieten?

L. Aber sicher, Peter. Sie sehen ein wenig nervös aus – lassen Sie mich Ihnen ein schönes Tässchen Tee kochen und überlassen Sie mir alle Vorbereitungen.

P. Das ist sehr nett von Ihnen, Lucy. Ich muss selbst ein paar Anrufe erledigen und es würde mir sehr helfen, wenn Sie sich um ein Hotel und einen Wagen kümmern würden.

 **Vocabulary**

accounts	Rechnungsstelle
to assign sb. to sth.	jmd. zu etw. abstellen
at your peril	auf eigene Gefahr
to back off	zurückstellen

to be sb.'s cup of tea	auf einer Wellenlänge liegen; gut miteinander auskommen
bean-counters	Erbsenzähler (abfällig)
to break a system in	ein System in Betrieb nehmen
to break down	*hier:* zerstreuen, aus der Welt schaffen
Do your stuff!	*hier:* Tun Sie, was Sie tun müssen!
expenses	Kosten
to get down to business	zum Geschäft kommen
the hot seat	im Rampenlicht
in a jiffy	im Handumdrehen
into the field	in der Praxis
to make arrangements	Vorbereitungen treffen
managing editor	Herausgeber
manpower	Arbeitskraft/-kräfte; Mitarbeiter
manufacturers	Hersteller
on the double	in Nullkommanichts
pager/beeper	Pager/Piepser
payment agreement	Zahlungsbedingungen
projection	Prognose
to put sb. in the picture	jmd. ins Bild setzen, auf den neuesten Stand bringen
round-up	Zusammenstellung
sales representative	Außendienstmitarbeiter
to settle for	sich zufriedengeben mit
stand-in	Vertretung
to take sb. off a job	jmd. von etw. abziehen
to talk through	einweisen; erklären
to tally	zusammen-, abrechnen; übereinstimmen

On a business trip | Auf Geschäftsreise

Here we go

Peter begibt sich auf Geschäftsreise. Er wird auf eigene Faust ein Verkaufsprojekt in Nottingham übernehmen. Trotz mangelnder Erfahrung gelingt es Peter mit großem persönlichen Einsatz zu einem erfolgreichen Abschluss zu kommen. Mr Morgan, Steve und vor allem Melissa sind stolz auf ihn und gratulieren. Und zu guter Letzt gibt Melissa noch ihr bestgehütetes Geheimnis preis ...

Talk Talk Talk

(Peter's office, Melissa enters.)

M. Well, Peter, you're off on your Nottingham trip today. How do you feel?

P. Nervous! Everything is **arranged**, though. I've called to **confirm** my meeting with Fothergill, and I've called to confirm my hotel room. The car is waiting to be picked up.

M. When do you expect to be back?

(Peters Büro, Melissa tritt ein.)

M. Nun, Peter, heute steht Ihre Reise nach Nottingham an. Wie fühlen Sie sich?

P. Nervös! Obwohl alles **durch-geplant** ist. Ich habe noch einmal angerufen, um meinen Termin mit Fothergill **bestätigen** zu lassen. Dasselbe gilt für meine Zimmer-reservierung. Das Auto steht abhol-bereit.

M. Was glauben Sie, wann Sie wieder zurück sind?

P. The day after tomorrow. But I'll call to tell you when to expect me.

M. Well, I wish you all the luck in the world!

P. Thanks, Melissa. That's kind of you. I'll probably need it.

M. Nonsense, you'll be all right. You know ARGO inside-out now. You'll be able to **manage** Fothergill.

P. It's not really Fothergill I'm so worried about. It's the Quick-Ed system – I haven't had a lot of time to **acquaint myself** with it, unfortunately.

M. But you'll have Duncan Wood from technical support to help you, I hear.

P. Yes, he's coming along tomorrow, after my first meeting with Fothergill. I've been trying to reach him on the phone, just to confirm the arrangements. You could really do me a favour if you tried to get him for me and ask him to call me at the hotel.

P. Übermorgen. Aber ich rufe an und sage Bescheid, wann Sie wieder mit mir rechnen können.

M. Tja, dann wünsche ich Ihnen alles erdenklich Gute!

P. Danke, Melissa. Sehr nett von Ihnen. Ich werde es wahrscheinlich brauchen.

M. Blödsinn, Sie schaffen das schon. Sie kennen ARGO jetzt in- und auswendig. Sie werden mit Fothergill schon **zurechtkommen**.

P. Es ist nicht einmal Fothergill, um den ich mir Sorgen mache – eher das Quick-Ed-System – ich hatte leider nicht viel Zeit, um mich damit **vertraut zu machen**.

M. Aber Sie haben doch Duncan Wood von der Technischen Unterstützung dabei, damit er Ihnen helfen kann, habe ich gehört.

P. Ja, er kommt morgen dazu, nach meinem ersten Treffen mit Fothergill. Ich habe schon versucht, ihn telefonisch zu erreichen, um unsere Abmachungen zu bestätigen. Sie könnten mir wirklich einen großen Gefallen tun, wenn Sie versuchen würden, ihn zu erreichen und ihn zu bitten, mich im Hotel anzurufen.

M. Certainly, Peter. Anything else I can do?

M. Sicher, Peter. Kann ich sonst noch etwas tun?

P. Just **cross your fingers** for me!

P. Drücken Sie mir die Daumen!

Exercise 53

Peter ruft im Hotel an, um zu sagen, dass er spät ankommen wird.
Wie verläuft das Gespräch?

Hello, is that the Hotel Astoria? Could you _____ me with the reception desk, please? Reception desk? I'm _____ to say I shall be late arriving this evening. I asked my office to _____ a message with you, but they said they had difficulty _____ to you. Your telephone has been _____ order all day? No wonder my office couldn't _____ you. They thought the line was constantly _____. The _____ sounds all right now. Does my room have a _____? I will need to _____ a lot of calls while I am staying at the hotel. Does my room have a direct _____? Can a caller from outside _____ straight through, without going _____ the switchboard?
I need to reserve a table in your restaurant, so could you please _____ to the restaurant manager? Hello, is that the restaurant? I'm _____ to the beer cellar? But I asked to be _____ to the restaurant. Can you _____ me, please?
The line is _____? Then I'll _____.
But please _____ to the restaurant as soon as you can.
I'm already running very late.

Background information

Hotel practice. Hotels in Britain – and particularly in the United States – often require a credit card number when a room is booked. Always state the approximate time you expect to be arriving and call to inform the reception desk if you are delayed. Rooms not claimed after 6 p.m. can legally be relet by the hotel unless prior arrangements have been made. Rooms booked but not claimed can be charged at the full rate – deducted from the credit card account of the "no-show".

Talk Talk Talk 28

(Car-hire company office)

P. Good morning! My office **has booked** a group two car for me for two days.

Agent May I have your name, sir?

P. Brückner. Peter Brückner from ARGO Limited. My secretary called to make the booking.

Agent Here we are! May I see your **driving licence**, sir, and some form of other identification?

P. Here is my driving licence and my passport.

(Im Büro der Autovermietung)

P. Guten Morgen! Mein Büro hat einen Wagen der Kategorie Zwei für zwei Tage für mich **gebucht**.

Schalterangestellter Sagen Sie mir bitte noch Ihren Namen, Sir?

P. Brückner. Peter Brückner von ARGO Limited. Meine Sekretärin hat den Wagen gebucht.

Schalterangestellter Da haben wir es ja! Dürfte ich bitte noch Ihren **Führerschein** und ein anderes Dokument sehen, das Ihre Identität bestätigt, Sir?

P. Hier sind mein Führerschein und mein Ausweis.

Agent Ah, you're German, sir! But your documents are European – they're fine. No problem. Just let me enter the details in the computer. There we are. The car is outside waiting for you, sir. Have a good journey...

Schalterangestellter Ah, Sie kommen aus Deutschland, Sir! Aber Sie haben EU-Dokumente – damit gibt es keine Probleme. Lassen Sie mich nur rasch die Details in den Computer tippen. Das war es schon. Der Wagen wartet draußen schon auf Sie, Sir. Gute Reise ...

P. Oh, would you do me a favour and call my office to tell them I have picked the car up. I'm in such a hurry I really don't have the time. Here's the number. Ask for Miss Lucy Scott. She is the secretary who called you to make the reservation.

P. Oh, könnten Sie mir wohl einen Gefallen tun und in meinem Büro anrufen und Bescheid geben, dass ich den Wagen abgeholt habe? Ich bin so in Eile, dass ich wirklich keine Zeit mehr habe. Hier ist die Nummer. Fragen Sie einfach nach Miss Lucy Scott. Sie ist die Sekretärin, die bei Ihnen angerufen und die Buchung gemacht hat.

Agent Certainly, sir. Happy to help. All part of the service!

Schalterangestellter Natürlich, Sir. Sehr gern. Das gehört alles zum Service!

Exercise 54

Welches Wort passt in die Lücken?

1. Could I please _____ a message for Mr Morgan?
   a. make
   b. give
   c. leave
   d. send

2. Can I tell him who's _____?
   a. speaking
   b. calling
   c. talking
   d. there

3. Would you _____ Miss Walker that I'll call back.
   a. mention
   b. message
   c. tell
   d. instruct

4. I'll _____ the message to her.
   a. transmit
   b. give
   c. send
   d. hand

5. You can reach me _____ the number I gave you.
   a. with
   b. during
   c. on
   d. under

Talk Talk Talk

(In the ARGO office, James Morgan enters.)

(Im Büro von ARGO, James Morgan tritt ein.)

L. Good heavens, Mr Morgan. We weren't expecting you back until next week!

L. Meine Güte, Mr Morgan. Wir hatten Sie vor nächster Woche gar nicht zurückerwartet!

J. The weather turned very nasty, Lucy, so I packed up and came home. I hate playing golf in the rain. Is everything all right? Are Melissa and Peter in?

J. Das Wetter wurde so schlecht, dass ich einfach meine Sachen gepackt habe und nach Hause gefahren bin, Lucy. Ich hasse es, Golf im Regen zu spielen. Ist hier alles in Ordnung? Sind Melissa und Peter da?

L. Miss Walker is, but Mr Brückner is on his way to Nottingham.

L. Miss Walker schon, aber Mr Brückner ist auf dem Weg nach Nottingham.

J. Nottingham?

J. Nottingham?

M. (enters) My, Mr Morgan! We didn't expect you until next week!

M. (tritt ein) Na so was, Mr Morgan! Wir hatten Sie vor nächster Woche gar nicht zurück erwartet!

J. Good morning, Melissa. I would have called, but I didn't have my mobile with me. I never carry it on golfing trips, as you know. What's this about Peter being on his way to Nottingham?

J. Guten Morgen, Melissa. Ich hätte ja angerufen, aber ich hatte mein Handy nicht dabei. Ich nehme es nie zum Golfspielen mit, wie Sie ja wissen. Was hat es damit auf sich, dass Peter auf dem Weg nach Nottingham ist?

M. He had to make a very **important decision** in a hurry, and he didn't want to break into your golfing holiday. He wouldn't have been able **to get hold of** you, anyway.

M. Er musste in großer Eile eine **wichtige Entscheidung** treffen und er wollte Sie nicht während Ihres Golfurlaubs stören. Er hätte Sie ja sowieso **nicht erreicht**.

J. Well, that's true enough. Now come into my office and tell me what all this is about...

J. Tja, das stimmt allerdings. Kommen Sie doch mit in mein Büro und erklären Sie mir, was überhaupt los ist ...

Exercise 55

Füllen Sie die Lücken mit den passenden Begriffen!

getting through   reach (2x)   connection   spend   chat   engaged

out of order   on (2x)   got through to   talks   tell   postpone   say

I tried to _____ you yesterday, but your phone seemed
to be _____. I'm calling today to _____
that we shall be able to come to dinner, after all. James managed to
_____ his parents and _____ them that we
have to _____ our visit until next week. We had terrible
trouble _____. When my mother is _____
the phone she _____ for hours. The line was constantly
_____. No sooner had we _____ her and had
a short _____ with her than she was _____
the phone again to a neighbour. I keep telling her she should
_____ less time on the phone, but she then says that's her
main _____ with the outside world.

Talk Talk Talk

(James Morgan's office)	(James Morgans Büro)
J. Lucy! Do you have the number of Peter's hotel?	**J.** Lucy! Haben Sie die Nummer von Peters Hotel?
L. Yes, shall I call it for you?	**L.** Ja, soll ich für Sie dort anrufen?

J. Yes, please!

J. Ja, bitte!

L. I **have** the Hotel Astoria **on the line**.

L. Ich **habe** das Hotel Astoria **in der Leitung**.

J. Is that the reception? Good. Could you put me through to Mr Brückner's room, please? He hasn't arrived yet? Then could I leave a message for him, please? He should phone me at the office or at home. James Morgan is the name. **Please make sure he gets the message**. It is very important. Thank you!

J. Ist dort die Rezeption? Gut. Bitte verbinden Sie mich mit dem Zimmer von Peter Brückner. Er ist noch nicht angekommen? Könnte ich dann bitte eine Nachricht für ihn hinterlassen? Er soll mich im Büro oder zu Hause anrufen. Mein Name ist James Morgan. **Bitte sorgen Sie dafür, dass er diese Nachricht bekommt.** Es ist wirklich sehr wichtig. Vielen Dank!

(Melissa enters.)
M. I **couldn't help** overhearing your call. I hope Peter did the right thing.

(Melissa tritt ein.)
M. Ich kam nicht darum herum, Ihr Gespräch mitzuhören. Ich hoffe, Peter hat das Richtige getan.

J. Of course! He showed great initiative. I just want to call him to help him prepare for tomorrow's meeting with Fothergill.

J. Natürlich! Er hat eine großartige Initiative an den Tag gelegt. Ich wollte nur mit ihm telefonieren, um ihm dabei zu helfen, sich auf das morgige Treffen mit Fothergill vorzubereiten.

M. He did seem very nervous.

M. Er schien ziemlich nervös zu sein.

J. And that's just what he shouldn't be at a meeting like this. If I can do it on the phone, I'd like to try and **boost his confidence**.

J. Und genau das sollte er bei so einem Meeting nicht sein. Wenn es über das Telefon überhaupt möglich ist, würde ich **sein Selbstvertrauen** gern etwas **aufbauen**.

M. Well, you're certainly the person to do that, James.

J. Frankly, I think you're better equipped. He seems to have **taken a real shine to** you, Melissa!

M. Oh, God – there's my phone. **Saved by the bell!**

M. Tja, wenn das jemand kann, dann sicherlich Sie, James.

J. Ehrlich gesagt glaube ich, dass Sie dafür besser geeignet sind. Er scheint **einen Narren an Ihnen gefressen zu haben**, Melissa!

M. Oh, Gott – mein Telefon klingelt. **Rettung in letzter Sekunde!**

Exercise 56

Setzen Sie in den folgenden Sätzen die richtige Präposition ein!

in   on   off   up   at   through   down

1. She has been _____ the phone for a very long time. When she's finally _____ the phone, could you please put me _____.

2. Would you like to hang _____? As soon as she has hung _____ I'll try and get her _____ the line.

3. His new phone line is finally _____ and running. Now he's rarely _____ the phone, his line is constantly engaged.

4. Would you like to hold _____? Mr Morgan is still _____ the phone. When he hangs _____ I'll tell him you are waiting _____ the other line.

5. _____ the start of our phone conversation I didn't realize who you were.

6. Can you really feed all that information _____ the line. Wouldn't it be easier to put it _____ an email?

🚗 Auf Geschäftsreise

Talk Talk Talk 29

(Peter's hotel)

P. Hello, Mr Morgan? You asked me to call. I would have called you anyway, but I've just arrived at the hotel.

J. That's all right, Peter. I just wanted to talk to you about tomorrow's meeting with Fothergill.

P. I hope you didn't mind my going ahead and travelling up here. It did appear to be an urgent matter.

J. You're right. You did the right thing. I just want to make sure you are **adequately briefed**.

P. I have all the information with me, and I shall spend this evening **swotting up** on it.

J. If you have any questions at all, call me at any time – either on my home number or on my mobile.

(Peters Hotel)

P. Hallo, Mr Morgan? Sie haben mich gebeten, Sie zurückzurufen. Ich hätte auf jeden Fall noch angerufen, aber ich bin gerade erst im Hotel angekommen.

J. Schon in Ordnung, Peter. Ich wollte nur mit Ihnen über das morgige Treffen mit Fothergill reden.

P. Ich hoffe, Sie haben nichts dagegen, dass ich auf eigene Faust hier hochgefahren bin. Es schien mir eine sehr dringende Angelegenheit gewesen zu sein.

J. Sie haben völlig Recht. Sie haben genau das Richtige getan. Ich wollte nur sicher gehen, dass Sie **angemessen vorbereitet** sind.

P. Ich habe alle nötigen Informationen mitgenommen und ich werde den Abend damit verbringen, sie zu **büffeln**.

J. Wenn Sie noch irgendwelche Fragen haben, rufen Sie mich jederzeit an – entweder zu Hause oder auf meinem Handy.

Exercise 57

Welche Wörter passen in die Lücken?

reserve | sure | give | book | vacancy | arrive | call | give | tell

delayed | reserved | available

I'm calling to _____ a room for the night of 24 August. Do you

have a _____?

Yes, we have one single and one double still _____.

Could I _____ the single room?

Certainly, in whose name should I _____ the room?

Brückner. Peter Brückner.

When do you expect to _____?

I'm leaving London within the next hour and expect to _____ at

the hotel by six o'clock.

We shall reserve the room for you until seven, just to be _____.

If you are _____, please _____ and inform us.

Certainly. Could I also _____ a table in the restaurant for two

people?

What time would you like the table _____?

Eight o'clock. My business partner might _____ a little later than

that. If he calls you could you _____ him a message.

Certainly. What shall we _____ him?

That I have _____ a table in the restaurant for eight o'clock.

Talk Talk Talk  30

(Peter's hotel)

P. Hello, Mr Morgan? I'm sorry to disturb you, but I have one or two questions concerning tomorrow's meeting.

J. Go ahead!

P. I've established that the Metropolitan Newspapers's main newsroom has more than twenty terminals. Will the system support so many?

J. No problem.

P. I presume the quoted price is for one system, but Metropolitan is a fairly large group, as you know. Do we offer **discounted prices for larger orders**?

J. Peter, I shall be **overjoyed** if we just get one system installed first of all. Concentrate on that initial order. Fothergill will just be **sounding you out** at first. If he likes the system the hard business negotiations will follow. **Stick to** the quoted price for **now**.

(Peters Hotel)

P. Hallo, Mr Morgan? Es tut mir leid, Sie zu stören, aber ich habe ein oder zwei Fragen bezüglich des Meetings morgen.

J. Schießen Sie los!

P. Ich habe in Erfahrung gebracht, dass in der Hauptredaktion von Metropolitan Newspapers mehr als zwanzig Terminals im Einsatz sind. Unterstützt unser System so viele Computer?

J. Kein Problem.

P. Ich vermute, dass sich der angegebene Preis auf ein System bezieht, aber Metropolitan ist eine ziemlich große Gruppe, wie Sie ja wissen. Gewähren wir **für größere Abnahmen Mengenrabatt**?

J. Peter, ich werde **heilfroh** sein, wenn Sie es schaffen, zunächst einmal ein System installieren zu lassen. Konzentrieren Sie sich auf diese erste Bestellung. Fothergill will Sie zunächst **aushorchen**. Wenn ihm das System gefällt, werden noch harte Preisverhandlungen folgen. Halten **Sie zunächst mal** am alten Preis **fest**.

P. He asked me to call tonight to confirm the time of tomorrow's meeting. May I call you back if he has any questions I can't answer?

P. Er hat mich darum gebeten, heute Abend noch einmal durchzurufen, um den Termin des morgigen Meetings zu bestätigen. Kann ich Sie zurückrufen, falls er noch irgendwelche Fragen hat, die ich nicht beantworten kann?

J. I'm right by the phone – call at any time. But relax – and enjoy your evening.

J. Ich werde in der Nähe des Telefons bleiben – rufen Sie jederzeit an. Aber entspannen Sie sich – und genießen Sie Ihren Abend.

P. Thank you, Mr Morgan. After supper, I'll be watching television. There's a Mafia film on that I wanted to see.

P. Vielen Dank, Mr Morgan. Nach dem Abendessen werde ich noch etwas fernsehen – es läuft ein Mafiafilm, den ich gerne sehen würde.

J. Well, I hope that's the right choice under the circumstances!

J. Tja, ich hoffe, unter den gegebenen Umständen ist das eine gute Wahl!

Exercise 58

Füllen Sie die Lücken mit den passenden Wörtern!

rate   called   arriving   served   delayed   asked   reserve   call

I _____ yesterday and asked if the hotel had a double room free for the night of 4 April. I _____ if the room had a telephone and a television set. I then said I would like to _____ the room. I said I would be _____ between 5 p.m. and 6 p.m.,

and that if I were _____ I would _____ to advise the hotel
of my late arrival. I asked if the room _____ included breakfast
and whether full English breakfast or continental was _____.
I told the reception clerk I liked to start the day on a full English breakfast because I often missed out on lunch.

Background information

If you like to start the day with a good breakfast, make sure you ask your chosen hotel at the time of your reservation what you can expect for your first meal of the day. London hotels in particular are switching more and more to so-called "continental breakfasts" – meaning French-style, not the extensive buffet travellers can expect in many other European countries such as Germany. Many hotels which serve "continental" breakfast offer additional dishes, but charge for them. The further you penetrate into the British countryside, the greater your chance of finding the "great English breakfast". Bed-and-breakfast establishments almost invariably serve what the English call "the works" – meaning a full breakfast that often features local specialities such as "black pudding" (a form of "blood sausage") or kippers (smoked haddock).

Talk Talk Talk  31

(Astoria Hotel, Peter's room)

(Astoria Hotel, Peters Zimmer)

P. Hello! Yes, Peter Brückner speaking. Mr Meadows has arrived? Good, would you please tell him I'll be right down? Ask him to wait for me in the bar.

P. Hallo! Ja, hier spricht Peter Brückner. Ist Mr Meadows schon angekommen? Gut, würden Sie ihm bitte ausrichten, dass ich sofort herunterkomme? Bitten Sie ihn, an der Bar auf mich zu warten.

(Astoria Hotel bar)

P. Hello, Mr Meadows? I'm Peter Brückner from ARGO. I'm very pleased to meet you.

Mr M. How do you do, Mr Brückner?

P. What are you drinking? Will you join me in a sherry before we go in to eat?

Mr M. That would be nice.

P. I hope you didn't mind my calling you **out of the blue** like that. I had very little notice of my trip to Nottingham.

Mr M. Not at all. I'm very glad to help where I can.

P. Before joining Metropolitan Newspapers you were at the Middlesex Echo, am I right?

Mr M. Yes. I was Executive News Editor there. Now, as you know, I'm Group Editor at Metropolitan.

P. During your time at the Middlesex Echo you **became acquainted** with our Quick-Ed editing system.

(Hotelbar des Astoria)

P. Mr Meadows? Ich bin Peter Brückner von ARGO. Ich freue mich, Sie kennenzulernen.

Mr M. Wie geht es Ihnen, Mr Brückner?

P. Was möchten Sie gerne trinken? Trinken Sie mit mir einen Sherry, bevor wir etwas essen?

Mr M. Aber gern.

P. Ich hoffe, Sie hatten nichts dagegen, dass ich Sie einfach so **ohne Vorwarnung** angerufen habe. Ich bin sehr kurzfristig zu meiner Reise nach Nottingham aufgebrochen.

Mr M. Ganz und gar nicht. Ich freue mich, helfen zu können, wo ich nur kann.

P. Bevor Sie zu Metropolitan Newspapers gegangen sind, waren Sie beim Middlesex Echo, stimmt's?

Mr M. Ja, ich war dort Nachrichtenredakteur. Jetzt bin ich, wie Sie sicher wissen, Leitender Redakteur bei Metropolitan.

P. Während Ihrer Zeit beim Middlesex Echo konnten Sie sich doch schon mit unserem Quick-Ed-Redaktionssystem **vertraut machen**.

🚗 Auf Geschäftsreise

Mr M. Indeed. **I was very impressed by** it.

P. I shall be meeting Mr Fothergill tomorrow. Does he know about your enthusiasm for Quick-Ed?

Mr M. I haven't really had the chance to talk to him about it yet.

P. Will you be at tomorrow's meeting?

Mr M. No, I have to visit one of our publishing offices in Newcastle.

P. That's bad news. But you could really do me a big favour if you **get to** speak to Mr Fothergill on your return.

Mr M. What about?

P. Just tell him what you told me – that you are impressed by Quick-Ed.

Mr M. Certainly, there's no problem there.

P. Then come, let's go and eat.

Mr M. In der Tat. Und **ich war sehr beeindruckt** davon.

P. Ich werde morgen Mr Fothergill treffen. Weiß er, wie begeistert Sie von Quick-Ed sind?

Mr M. Ich hatte bis jetzt noch nicht die Möglichkeit, mit ihm darüber zu reden.

P. Werden Sie beim Meeting morgen dabei sein?

Mr M. Nein, ich muss eine unserer Zweigstellen in Newcastle besuchen.

P. Das sind ja schlechte Neuigkeiten. Aber Sie könnten mir wirklich einen großen Gefallen tun, wenn sie **dazu kämen**, nach Ihrer Rückkehr mit Mr Fothergill zu reden.

Mr M. Und worüber?

P. Sagen Sie ihm einfach, was Sie mir gesagt haben – dass Sie von Quick-Ed sehr beeindruckt sind.

Mr M. Natürlich, da sehe ich kein Problem.

P. Dann kommen Sie, lassen Sie uns etwas essen.

Exercise 59

„To get" ist ein überbeanspruchtes Verb der englischen Sprache.
Finden Sie dafür elegantere Ersatzformen in den folgenden Sätzen!

| performed | obtain | persuade | understand | recover from |
| caught |

1. I think I can **get** him to sign.   _____
2. I **got on** well in the examinations.   _____
3. I **got** the flu while visiting London.   _____
4. If you **get** more than sixty pounds
   for that antique, I will be surprised. _____
5. I don't think he'll ever **get over**
   her death.   _____
6. He didn't **get** the joke. He has no
   sense of humour!   _____

False friends

The handy but overworked little verb "to get" entices many Germans into an embarrassing misuse. "To get" is translated in German by "bekommen". English has a very similiar verb: to become. Frequently, "become" is incorrectly used instead of "get" to translate "bekommen" – the common meaning of "to become" is to pass from one state or condition to another: "He became ill after eating that awful meal." This misuse can lead to awkward or even embarrassing misconstructions. "I became a dog on my birthday" is not exactly what is meant when the speaker is relating what he or she received as a birthday present!

🚗 Auf Geschäftsreise

Talk Talk Talk

(Metropolitan Newspapers head office)

(Hauptbüro von Metropolitan Newspapers)

P. Good morning! **I have an appointment to see** Mr Fothergill.

P. Guten Morgen! **Ich habe einen Termin mit** Mr Fothergill.

Receptionist What name shall I give?

Empfangsdame Wen darf ich melden?

P. Brückner. Peter Brückner from ARGO Limited.

P. Brückner. Peter Brückner von ARGO Limited.

R. Just one moment, please. I'll try to reach Mr Fothergill. – Hello, Miss Stanton. I have a Mr Brückner here to see Mr Fothergill. You'll **be right down**. I'll tell him, then. Mr Fothergill's secretary is on her way down. She'll take you to Mr Fothergill's office.

R. Einen Moment, bitte. Ich versuche, Mr Fothergill zu erreichen. – Hallo, Miss Stanton. Ich habe hier einen Mr Brückner für Mr Fothergill. Sie **kommen gleich herunter**. Ich werde es ihm sagen. Mr Fothergills Sekretärin ist auf dem Weg nach unten. Sie wird Sie in Mr Fothergills Büro bringen.

P. Thank you very much.

P. Haben Sie vielen Dank.

Miss S. Good morning! I'm Mr Fothergill's secretary. If you come with me, I'll take you to his office now.

Miss S. Guten Morgen! Ich bin Mr Fothergills Sekretärin. Wenn Sie mich bitte begleiten würden, ich führe Sie in sein Büro.

P. Thank you very much. I'm sorry I'm slightly late. I had some problems getting here because of an accident on the main road.

P. Vielen Dank. Tut mir leid, wenn ich ein wenig zu spät bin. Ich hatte Probleme bei der Anfahrt wegen eines Unfalls auf der Hauptstraße.

Miss S. That's quite all right. Mr Fothergill was late, anyway, getting to the office this morning. Apparently, he had a lot to do on the way.

Miss S. Das ist schon in Ordnung. Mr Fothergill ist heute ohnehin etwas später ins Büro gekommen. Offensichtlich hatte er auf dem Weg hierher sehr viel zu tun.

Exercise 60

Ein anderes überbeanspruchtes Verb des Englischen ist „to do". Finden Sie auch hierfür elegantere Ersatzformen in den folgenden Sätzen.

| covered | performed | that's enough | exhausted | complete (2x) |

1. **That will do**, Johnny!
   Now behave yourself! _____
2. I don't know if I can **do** it in the required time. _____
3. If you **do** the task correctly you'll get top marks! _____
4. That was quite a climb – I'm completely **done in**! _____
5. I think I **did** well in the exam.
6. The train **did** the distance in record time. _____

Talk Talk Talk  32

(Mr Fothergill's office)

Mr F. Come in, come in! How do you do, Mr Brückner? I'm very pleased to meet you!

P. How do you do, Mr Fothergill? Thank you for this opportunity to meet you.

Mr F. A **face-to-face** meeting is much more satisfactory than a phone call – that's my philosophy. Your people are always calling me up and trying to explain what you have to offer in a few minutes on the phone. You're the first to offer to travel up here to describe the system to me in person.

P. It's a pleasure, Mr Fothergill. We believe the system is so good that no effort can be spared in making its benefits known.

Mr F. Well, young man, you've got two hours to do that. Miss Stanton! Can you bring in some coffee, please? And now **down to business**...

(Mr Fothergills Büro)

Mr F. Hereinspaziert! Wie geht es Ihnen, Herr Brückner? Ich freue mich, Sie kennenzulernen!

P. Wie geht es Ihnen, Mr Fothergill? Danke, dass Sie mir die Möglichkeit geben, mich mit Ihnen zu treffen.

Mr F. Ein **persönliches** Gespräch ist doch viel angenehmer als diese Telefoniererei – das ist meine Philosophie. Ihre Leute rufen mich andauernd an und versuchen, mir in ein paar Minuten am Telefon zu erklären, was sie mir anzubieten haben. Sie sind der Erste, der mir angeboten hat, hier hochzufahren und mir das System persönlich vorzustellen.

P. Ist mir ein Vergnügen, Mr Fothergill. Wir sind davon überzeugt, dass unser System so gut ist, dass keine Mühe ausgelassen werden sollte, um seine Vorzüge bekannt zu machen.

Mr F. Tja, junger Mann, dafür haben Sie jetzt zwei Stunden Zeit. Miss Stanton! Können Sie uns bitte einen Kaffee bringen! Und jetzt **kommen wir zur Sache** ...

Exercise 61

Peter beginnt mit seiner Präsentation. Helfen Sie ihm bei der Wahl der richtigen Worte!

| explaining | understand | install | put | functions | start | contain |

| load | play | ranging | straightforward |

Let me begin by _____ how the system _____. There are just two DVDs to _____. They _____ the entire software. You can _____ them in any drive. The discs contain individual files, _____ from rules to styles. Let's _____ with the first one. We'll _____ it and then _____ with it. You'll then _____ how _____ the system is.

Talk Talk Talk 🔊 33

(Hotel Astoria, Peter's room)

P. Good morning! Peter Brückner.

R. This is the reception. I have a call for you. **I'm putting the caller through now ...**

P. Hello! Brückner here!

J. Good morning, Peter. It's James Morgan here. I'm just calling to find out how you got on yesterday.

(Hotel Astoria, Peters Zimmer)

P. Guten Morgen! Peter Brückner.

R. Hier ist die Rezeption. Wir haben ein Gespräch für Sie. **Ich stelle den Anrufer gleich durch ...**

P. Hallo! Brückner!

J. Guten Morgen, Peter! Hier spricht James Morgan. Ich rufe nur an, um zu fragen, wie es gestern gelaufen ist.

P. Well, **the presentation went very well**, I think. In fact, Fothergill had allowed just two hours for the presentation and demonstration, but it actually went on all day and I've had to extend my stay here by another night. I called Lucy and asked her to inform you. I hope she did.

J. Yes, indeed. That's fine. So what's your **general impression**?

P. I think they're interested, but I feel Fothergill will need some time to think it over.

J. Yes, he gives me the impression of being a very careful type who doesn't like to give up too easily in a **business negotiation**. Now, you have had a very tiring time – stay over another night and have a look around Nottingham. It's an interesting city, and don't miss out on a trip to Sherwood Forest. I'll be expecting you in the office the day after tomorrow...

P. Nun ja, **die Präsentation lief sehr gut**. Tatsache ist, Fothergill wollte mir zunächst nur zwei Stunden für die Präsentation und die Vorführung geben, aber dann dauerte es den ganzen Tag. Ich musste meinen Aufenthalt hier um eine weitere Nacht verlängern. Ich habe Lucy angerufen und sie gebeten, Sie zu informieren. Ich hoffe, das hat sie getan.

J. Ja, das hat sie. Sehr schön. Und, wie ist Ihr **Gesamteindruck**?

P. Ich glaube, sie sind interessiert, aber Fothergill wird vermutlich noch etwas Zeit brauchen, um darüber nachzudenken.

J. Ja, er macht wirklich den Eindruck, als wäre er ein sehr vorsichtiger Mensch, der in einer **geschäftlichen Verhandlung** nur ungern zu früh nachgibt. Aber hören Sie – das war eine sehr anstrengende Zeit für Sie – bleiben Sie doch noch eine weitere Nacht und schauen Sie sich Nottingham an. Eine sehr interessante Stadt – und lassen Sie sich einen Ausflug in den Sherwood Forest nicht entgehen. Ich erwarte Sie dann übermorgen zurück im Büro ...

Exercise 62

Auch „to give" ist ein überbeanspruchtes Wort im Englischen.
Geben Sie in den folgenden Sätzen Alternativen an!

| quit | disclose | avoided | relinquished | surrender | hinted | call |

1. I **gave** him **a wide berth** when I
   saw him in the street. I can't
   stand the man.   _____

2. **Give me a call** when you
   get home.   _____

3. I **gave up** all claim to the
   property.   _____

4. You know you're beaten! **Give in**! _____

5. I **gave up** my job at the Exchange
   after Lewis and Company **gave**
   me the hint that I could expect _____
   to earn much more there.   _____

6. Please don't **give away** what I've
   just told you!   _____

Auf Geschäftsreise

Talk Talk Talk

(The front office of ARGO Limited)

L. Oh, good morning, Peter! Did you have a good trip?

P. Well, I don't really know. I think it **went well** enough.

(James Morgan, Melissa and Steve all enter together.)

J. Where's the champagne, Lucy?

L. I'll get it right now, Mr Morgan. How many glasses?

J. Five – no six, Chip deserves some bubbly, too. Chip!

C. Yes, Mr Morgan, right here. Champagne? Whose birthday is it?

J. No birthday, Chip, but still a very **good reason to celebrate**.

P. Celebrate?

J. We've just **landed** the most promising order of the year.

(Empfangsbüro von ARGO Limited)

L. Oh, guten Morgen, Peter! Hatten Sie eine angenehme Reise?

P. Na ja, ich weiß nicht genau. Ich glaube, es lief **gut genug**.

(James Morgan, Melissa und Steve treten gemeinsam ein.)

J. Wo ist der Champagner, Lucy?

L. Ich hole ihn sofort, Mr Morgan. Wie viele Gläser?

J. Fünf – nein, sechs. Chip hat sich auch etwas Schampus verdient. Chip!

C. Ja, Mr Morgan, bin schon da. Champagner? Wer hat denn Geburtstag?

J. Kein Geburtstag, Chip, aber wir haben trotzdem einen sehr **guten Grund zum Feiern.**

P. Feiern?

J. Wir haben gerade den vielversprechensten Auftrag des Jahres **unter Dach und Fach gebracht.**

M. Oh, come on, Mr Morgan. **Put him out of his misery!**

M. Oh, nun kommen Sie schon, Mr Morgan. **Lassen Sie ihn doch nicht länger zappeln!**

J. Fothergill called me last night and said he'd decided to install Quick-ed in two of his newspapers, with an option to buy, at a small discount, for the rest of his group.

J. Fothergill hat mich gestern Abend angerufen und mir gesagt, dass er sich dazu entschlossen hat, Quick-Ed in zwei seiner Zeitungen zu installieren – mit der Option, sie für einen kleinen Rabatt auch für den Rest seiner Verlagsgruppe zu kaufen.

P. Good heavens! He didn't seem that convinced when I left him.

P. Meine Güte! Er schien nicht so überzeugt zu sein, als ich ihn verlassen habe.

J. Fothergill is a cautious man, as I told you on the phone, Peter. But he liked your style. And he liked the product you demonstrated so ably. Well done.

J. Fothergill ist ein vorsichtiger Mann, wie ich Ihnen schon am Telefon sagte, Peter. Aber er mochte Ihren Stil. Und er mochte das Produkt, das Sie ihm so gekonnt vorgeführt haben. Gut gemacht.

S. You've become our star salesman, Peter. Must have been my training!

S. Sie sind jetzt unser Starverkäufer, Peter. Das muss an meinem Training liegen!

J. Well, we'll drink to that, Steve.

J. Schön, darauf sollten wir trinken, Steve.

M. Ja, lasst uns anstoßen. Ein toller Erfolg, lieber Peter!

M. Ja, lasst uns anstoßen! Ein toller Erfolg, lieber Peter!

P. Bitte? You speak German?

P. Bitte? Sie sprechen Deutsch?

S. Melissa is as secretive as old Fothergill. I've just discovered why she could never join us in an after-work drink. She was studying German at night-school – every night!

M. And last night was the end of the course. So tonight I'm inviting you two to dinner.

S. But no German please, Melissa!

S. Melissa ist genau so geheimnistuerisch wie der alte Fothergill. Ich habe gerade herausgefunden, warum Sie nie mitgekommen ist, wenn wir einen Feierabend-Drink zu uns genommen haben. Sie hat an einer Abendschule Deutsch gelernt – jeden Abend!

M. Und letzten Abend war die letzte Unterrichtsstunde. Also lade ich Sie beide heute Abend zum Essen ein.

S. Aber bitte kein Deutsch, Melissa!

 Vocabulary

to acquaint oneself with	sich vertraut machen mit
adequately briefed	angemessen vorbereitet/ eingewiesen
to be right down	gleich herunterkommen
to become acquainted with sth.	vertraut werden mit
to book	buchen
to boost sb.'s confidence	Selbstvertrauen aufbauen (umgangssprachlich)
business negotiation	geschäftliche Verhandlung
can't help	nicht umhinkommen
to cross one's fingers	Daumen drücken
discounted prices for larger orders	Mengenrabatt
driving license	Führerschein
face to face	persönlich
general impression	Gesamteindruck
to get down to business	zur Sache/zum Geschäftlichen kommen
to get hold of	erreichen
to get to	dazu kommen
to go well	gut laufen
to have an appointment to see sb.	einen Termin mit jdm. haben
to have sb. on the line	jmd. in der Leitung haben
head office	Hauptbüro
to land (an order)	(einen Auftrag) an Land ziehen
to manage	schaffen/in der Lage sein/ etw. in den Griff bekommen
out of the blue	ohne Vorwarnung/ „aus heiterem Himmel"
overjoyed	überglücklich
to put a caller through	einen Anrufer durchstellen
to put sb. out of his/her misery	jmd. nicht mehr länger zappeln lassen
Saved by the bell!	Rettung in letzter Sekunde

to sound out	aushorchen, ausfragen
to stick to	bei etw. bleiben
to swot up	büffeln, sich intensiv mit etw. beschäftigen
to take a shine to sth./sb.	einen Narren gefressen haben an etw./jmd.
What name shall I give?	Wen darf ich melden?

 # Letter of application |
Bewerbungsschreiben

Here we go

Nach Peters Rückkehr von einer weiteren Geschäftsreise nach Manchester, erfährt er, dass ARGO Limited auf der Suche nach einem neuen Mitarbeiter für die Marketingabteilung ist und aus diesem Grund eine Stellenanzeige in einer Zeitung geschaltet hat. Schnell treffen die ersten Bewerbungen bei der Firma ein und müssen nun sorgfältig geprüft und ausgewertet werden.

Talk Talk Talk

(Peter enters the office.)

L. Well, hello, Peter! Did you have a successful journey to Manchester?

P. I don't know yet if it was successful, Lucy. But the trip itself was fine.

L. Mr Morgan is waiting for you.

(Peter enters Morgan's office.)

J. Good morning, Peter. How did the trip to Manchester go?

(Peter betritt das Büro.)

L. Na so was, hallo, Peter. **War Ihre Reise** nach Manchester **erfolgreich**?

P. Ich weiß noch nicht, ob sie erfolgreich war, Lucy. Aber die Fahrt selbst lief sehr gut.

L. Mr Morgan wartet schon auf Sie.

(Peter betritt Morgans Büro.)

J. Guten Morgen, Peter. Wie lief Ihr Ausflug nach Manchester?

P. I think it's too early to say, Mr Morgan. But the **presentation went well enough** and certainly **they showed great interest**. As you know, we have some **stiff** competition there.

J. I agree, we can't expect **immediate results** with this assignment. I think we'll have to sit patiently by and just wait for a **decision**...

P. Ich glaube, es ist noch zu früh, um etwas sagen zu können, Mr Morgan. Aber die **Präsentation verlief zufriedenstellend** und **sie haben großes Interesse gezeigt**. Wie Sie ja wissen, haben wir dort **harte** Konkurrenz.

J. Das sehe ich auch so, wir können bei diesem Auftrag keine **sofortigen Ergebnisse** erwarten. Ich denke, wir müssen einfach geduldig ausharren und auf eine **Entscheidung** warten ...

Exercise 63

Im letzten Gespräch verwendete James Morgan die Begriffe „immediate" und „patiently". „Patient" und „immediate" sind Adjektive, die das Nomen näher bestimmen, „immediately" und „patiently" hingegen sind Adverbien, die das Verb näher bestimmen. Setzen Sie im folgenden Text entweder das richtige Adverb oder das richtige Adjektiv ein!

1. Thank you for waiting so patient _____ for a reply to your letter.

2. I would be grateful for immediate _____ action in this important matter.

3. We have been full _____ employed in searching for the causes of the delay.

4. Would you please make sure we are informed prompt _____.

5. Our company expects complete _____ compliance with the terms of the licence agreement.

6. The delay in deliveries cannot necessary _____ be blamed on our department.

7. Their despatch department is usual _____ very prompt _____ in attending to our orders.

Talk Talk Talk  34

(James Morgan's office)

J. Peter, Melissa might have told you that **an opening** has arisen in the **Marketing Department**, and **we are advertising the post**. I'd like you to take over the **initial selection** process.

P. Certainly, but what does that **entail**?

J. First of all, careful reading of the **applications**. With the employment situation as it is, we are expecting

(James Morgans Büro)

J. Peter, Melissa hat Ihnen ja vielleicht schon gesagt, dass sich **eine freie Stelle** in der **Marketingabteilung** ergeben hat und wir **für diese Stelle annoncieren**. Ich hätte gerne, dass Sie den **ersten Auswahlprozess** übernehmen.

P. Sicher, was **gehört dazu**?

J. Zunächst einmal das sorgfältige Lesen der **Bewerbungen**. Bei der derzeitigen Situation auf dem

quite a number. There are already some on file, so please take those into consideration, too. When you have **sorted out a rough shortlist of candidates** let's then get together with Melissa and narrow down the selection process.

Arbeitsmarkt erwarten wir eine ganze Menge davon. Wir haben bereits ein paar Bewerbungen in den Akten, also berücksichtigen Sie diese bitte auch. Wenn Sie **eine erste Auswahl der Bewerber zusammengestellt** haben, schließen Sie sich mit Melissa zusammen und grenzen die Auswahl weiter ein.

P. What should I be looking for?

P. Nach was soll ich denn Ausschau halten?

J. This is a trainee position. We are looking for a young person who has just completed university or Technical College, preferably with a **degree in economics** or another **business-related discipline**. Melissa will be wanting somebody with marketing potential, with a **forceful personality** – and that sometimes is evident from the first page of a letter of application.

J. Es geht um eine Position als Trainee. Wir suchen nach einem jungen Menschen, der gerade die Universität oder die Technische Hochschule abgeschlossen hat, am besten mit einem Abschluss in **Wirtschaftswissenschaft** oder einem anderen **wirtschaftlichen Ausbildungsfach**. Melissa wird jemanden mit Talent zum Marketing haben wollen, jemanden mit einer **ausgeprägten Persönlichkeit** – und so etwas wird manchmal schon auf der ersten Seite eines Bewerbungsanschreibens ersichtlich.

P. I'm not awfully sure just how forceful Melissa expects a trainee to be!

P. Ich bin mir nicht sicher, wie viel Persönlichkeit Melissa bei einem Trainee wirklich erwartet!

Exercise 64

Suchen Sie in den folgenden Sätzen nach der richtigen Präposition:

1. If you're passing the library on the way to work could you look
   _____ for me and collect anything they have on Adam Smith.
2. Just look _____ yourself! You look as if you've been dragged
   _____ a hedge backwards!
3. If you're in the neighbourhood tomorrow, drop _____ and
   we'll have tea.
4. Could you look this _____ in your dictionary for me?
5. They are real snobs. They look _____ on anyone they feel is
   below their own social rank.
6. The problem with kids today is they have nobody to look
   _____ to. That's what my dad says.
7. We'll certainly look _____ this matter and see if we can find
   the cause of the problem.

Background information

And **look** here! There are some phrases to note, too!

Look here!	Now just look here, you can't tell me what to do.
Look sharp!	Look sharp, hurry up! Breakfast is in ten minutes!
Look lively!	Get a move on! We haven't got all day, you know!
To look daggers	He looked daggers at me – he was obviously very annoyed.

Talk Talk Talk
(James Morgan's office)

J. Here are the first applications, Peter. Go through them and make a first selection.

P. Righto (returns to his office). Lucy, be a dear and make me some tea, please. I shall be **tied down** in my office for some time. Now, let's look at these letters...

(James Morgans Büro)

J. Hier sind die ersten Bewerbungen, Peter. Sehen Sie sie durch und treffen Sie eine Vorauswahl.

P. Klaro (geht in sein Büro zurück). Lucy, seien Sie bitte ein Schatz und kochen Sie mir einen Tee. Ich werde eine Weile in meinem Büro **eingebunden** sein. Gut, dann schauen wir uns mal diese Briefe an ...

 Dear Sirs,

Having read your advertisement offering a position in your marketing department, I feel I might be just the person you are looking for. Although I **broke off** my university studies after one semester, I later gathered practical experience in marketing in the shoe department of Holly and Brights, **the major department chain**. After five years in this department, I feel the time has come **to move on to something more demanding**. Possibilities at Holly and Brights are limited, so I am looking for a position in a completely different area of business. I do have some experience of computer technology, having just invested in a PC.

My colleagues at Holly and Bright will testify to my cheerful and helpful disposition. If you need any further information, please write to me "poste restante" at Herne Bay post office because I am in the process of moving address. From 1 July, I can be contacted c/o Miss Judy O'Connell, at 35 Cedar Drive, Herne Bay.

I hope to hear from you soon.

Yours sincerely,

Bill Boulton

P. Well, I think we can forget that one, for a start. What else is in the postbag?

P. Tja, ich denke, den können wir schon mal vergessen. Was haben wir denn sonst noch im Postsack?

 Dear Sirs,

Further to your advertisement in the Morning Echo, I would like to add my humble name to the list of those you will be interviewing for the vacancy in your marketing department. Perhaps I cannot claim the qualifications required and am a little too advanced in age (52) to hope for a post as trainee, but in my long career with J.P. Engineering I have always been ready to learn something new. You might have read reports that J.P. Engineering is preparing for **retrenchments,** and I feel that for my own security I must begin to look around for alternative employment.
I would therefore be very pleased if you could consider my application for the vacancy in your company. I can promise loyalty, hard work and a willingness to learn new technologies – even those related to the computer age, which I'm afraid has passed me by!

Your loyal and obedient servant,

Henry J. Jobson

Background information
"Poste restante" (French for "letters remaining") describes the department in British post offices where letters can be sent and then collected personally by the "addressee". Addressee? That's the person to whom the letter is sent.
"c/o" is short for "care of". It is added to the address when the letter is to be delivered into the care of somebody other than the addressee:
Mr John Ripton
c/o Mrs Jane Simpson
The Oaks
Bramley

Dos and Don'ts – A matter of form...

"Your loyal and obediant servant"? You will very rarely encounter this archaic way of signing off a formal letter. Variations include: "Your loyal and dutiful servant!" Charming and genteel as they sound, resist any temptation to use them!

Exercise 65

Let's take a break ...

„Break" als Verb oder Nomen ist oft in umgangssprachlichen Ausdrücken zu finden. Setzen Sie in den folgenden Sätzen die passende Form (inkl. Phrasal Verbs) ein:

1. I'm tired. Let's take a _____.
2. Jim and Jane aren't going out together any more. They
   _____ up.
3. Police are investigating a _____ at the local bank.
4. Police were called in to _____ the demonstration.
5. I'll have to get a new car. Mine is constantly _____.
6. The right wing of the party _____ from the mainstream before the last election.
7. The ship was _____ for scrap.
8. An epidemic of measles has _____ in the north of the country.

Talk Talk Talk  35

(Peter's office. James Morgan enters.)

J. So how's it going, Peter? Have you found our ideal candidate yet?

P. I've only been through two letters so far, and they certainly don't qualify.

J. Mind if I look?

P. Not at all, help yourself!

(James Morgan reads the letters.)

J. You know what dismays me, Peter? Some people seem incapable of reading an advertisement correctly. We were very clear indeed in stating our **requirements**. I just can't see how anybody could fail to understand. I'm just unable to explain it.

P. I think the letters were written from a position of despair. Boulton is obviously bored with his department store job, and Jobson fears he'll be out of a job before long.

(Peters Büro. James Morgan tritt ein.)

J. Wie läuft es, Peter? Haben Sie schon unseren Traumkandidaten gefunden?

P. Ich habe bis jetzt erst zwei Briefe durch und sie haben sich beide ganz sicher nicht qualifiziert.

J. Was dagegen, wenn ich mal einen Blick darauf werfe?

P. Überhaupt nicht, nur zu!

(James Morgan liest die Briefe.)

J. Wissen Sie, was ich wirklich erschreckend finde, Peter? Einige Leute scheinen nicht in der Lage zu sein, eine Anzeige korrekt zu lesen. Wir haben unsere **Anforderungen** klar ausgedrückt. Es ist mir schleierhaft, wie jemand sie missverstehen kann. Ich kann so etwas einfach nicht erklären.

P. Ich denke, diese Briefe wurden aus der Verzweiflung heraus geschrieben. Boulton ist in seinem Kaufhausjob offensichtlich gelangweilt und Jobson fürchtet, dass er bald ohne Arbeit dastehen wird.

J. But that's no reason to regard us as an escape route...

J. Aber das ist noch kein Grund, uns als letzten Ausweg zu miss-brauchen ...

Background information

"Incapable" or "unable"? Both words mean that someone is not able to do something, but "incapable" has a negative connotation and is usually translated into German as "unfähig". "He is quite incapable of assuming the position of managing director" means he does not have the skills and abilities that are necessary to take on a senior leadership position. Another example: "Is she totally incapable of doing that job properly?" As you can see, "incapable" is used with "of" and the -ing form of the verb. On the other hand, "unable" always takes the infinitive.

Exercise 66

Vervollständigen Sie folgende Sätze!

1. I regret we are unable accept _____ your kind invitation to dinner.

2. She is totally incapable tell _____ him that she wants a divorce.

3. Are you incapable read _____ the small print on the sales agreement?

4. I am afraid we are unable deliver _____ by the date you mention.

5. He appears to be incapable be _____ on time for any appointment.

Talk Talk Talk

P. Do we have a **standard response to unsuccessful applicants**?

J. Yes, Lucy can help you there. But in the case of these two applicants I think a personal letter might be kinder. See what you can do!

P. I'll do my best, but I don't have much experience of this sort of thing...

P. Haben wir ein **standardisiertes Absageschreiben für abgelehnte Kandidaten**?

J. Ja, Lucy kann Ihnen da helfen. Aber ich denke, im Fall dieser beiden Bewerber wäre ein persönlicher Brief freundlicher. Schauen Sie doch mal, was Sie machen können!

P. Ich versuche mein Bestes, aber ich habe nicht viel Erfahrung in solchen Dingen ...

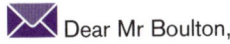 Dear Mr Boulton,

Thank you for your letter responding to our advertisement in the Morning Echo. **I regret to inform you that your impressive professional experience does not completely match the requirements of the position we are seeking to fill.**
Thank you, nonetheless, for your interest. I wish you every success in your present career.

Yours sincerely,

Peter Brückner
Assistant Managing Director
ARGO Limited

Talk Talk Talk

(James Morgan's office. Peter enters.)

P. Do you think this reply will do?

J. (reads it) I think that's very **well worded**. I don't see the point of being too **offhand**. A personal touch can't do any harm. You can use the same wording in the second letter.

P. I'll give them to Lucy to type and then get **stuck into** the others...

(James Morgans Büro. Peter tritt ein.)

P. Glauben Sie, dass diese Antwort angemessen ist?

J. (liest den Brief) Ich finde, er ist sehr gut **formuliert**. Ich sehe keinen Grund dafür, zu **unpersönlich** zu sein. Ein persönlicher Touch kann nicht schaden. Sie können dieselbe Formulierung beim zweiten Brief verwenden.

P. Ich werde sie Lucy zum Abtippen geben und mich dann in die anderen **vertiefen** ...

Exercise 67

Ein Lebenslauf ist einer der wichtigsten Teile einer Bewerbung. Der englische Begriff dafür, „CV", steht kurz für den lateinischen Ausdruck „Curriculum Vitae". Suchen Sie im folgenden Lebenslauf die fehlenden Verben und setzen Sie sie in die korrekte Zeit!

return   organize   gain   take (2x)   join   leave   employ   enrol
feel   be   attend   complete   include   study   be born   travel
maintain

Name: John Tatterell

I _____ in Plymouth, Devon, on 22 May, 1968. After

_____ Plymouth Grammar School for six years, I _____

with A-level passes in English, French and Social Studies.

I _____ one year off and _____ extensively

in North and South America. On _____ to Britain in

1987, I _____ for a course in business studies at Hen-

don Technical College. After _____ the course in 1989,

I _____ Jackson and Tucker Limited as a management

trainee. During my time there, I _____ experience in all

departments of the company, and at present I _____ as

assistant to the Marketing Director. My French _____

still fluent, and I _____ German and Spanish in my spare

time. My duties at Jackson and Tucker _____

contact with foreign clients and _____ participation in

trade fairs in mainland Europe. This work _____ me to

Milan, Munich, Stockholm and Copenhagen, and I _____

very much at home in an international arena.

(Peter reads the next letter.)   (Peter liest den nächsten Brief.)

 Dear Sirs,

I would be grateful if you considered my application for the position
your company has advertised in the Morning Echo. As you will see from
the **accompanying CV**, I have just left university with a Master's degree in
Business Administration and am looking for a post which would allow me
to **put into practice** what I have learnt over the past five years. With my

background in computer studies, a company such as yours would offer the ideal opportunity for me. One year of my degree course was **devoted to** marketing and market research, and **I would be very happy to have the chance to work in the kind of area your advertisement describes**. I am available under the above address and telephone number to provide additional information, and of course I am available at any time to attend a personal interview.

Yours faithfully,

Roger Fenton

Talk Talk Talk

(James Morgan's office)

(James Morgans Büro)

P. Mr Morgan, this letter here sounds promising.

P. Mr Morgan, dieser Brief hier klingt vielversprechend.

J. Let's have a look! (He reads the letter.) You're right. The young man seems to have the qualifications we are looking for. **Some practical experience** would be desirable, but he would certainly get that here. Where's his CV?

J. Schauen wir mal! (Er liest den Brief.) Sie haben Recht. Dieser junge Mann scheint genau die Qualifikationen zu haben, die wir suchen. Ein paar **praktische Erfahrungen** wären zwar wünschenswert gewesen, aber die wird er hier schon noch bekommen. Wo ist sein Lebenslauf?

✉ CV – Roger Fenton.

Born: 20 February 1975 in Carlisle.

Education:
Primary: St. Christopher's Preparatory School, Carlisle.

Secondary: Carlisle Grammar School.
Certificates: 6 GSCEs (English Language, English Literature, History, Biology, Economics, French). 3 A-levels: (English, Economics, Business Studies).
Higher education: University of York. (BA in Economics, American Studies); London School of Economics (MBA).

Additional studies and work experience: One year (1998 – 99) exchange student at Yale University, USA Six months' (1995) practical experience in the Marketing Division of Santos Holdings, London.

References can be obtained from Professor Hamilton Harding of the University of York and Dr Jonathan Digby-Smith, Managing Director, Santos Holdings.

Talk Talk Talk

J. Quite impressive. Reads well, even though I do prefer a **written CV** instead of one in this **tabular form**. It makes it more difficult to assess the person behind the facts. But, of course, we'll be inviting him for an interview. Young Fenton certainly **falls into** the shortlist category. Have you already **made up a file**, Peter?

P. Well, this is the first application that qualifies, so I'll create a file right now and put the letter in it. What about a reply to the application?

J. Recht eindrucksvoll. Liest sich sehr gut, obwohl ich einen **ausformulierten Lebenslauf** einem in dieser **tabellarischen Form** vorziehe. So ist es schwieriger, den Menschen hinter den Daten einzuschätzen. Aber natürlich werden wir ihn zu einem Gespräch einladen. Unser junger Mr Fenton **fällt** ganz sicher **in** die Vorauswahl. Haben Sie bereits **einen Ordner angelegt**, Peter?

P. Na ja, das ist die erste Bewerbung, die sich qualifiziert, also werde ich sofort einen Ordner anlegen und den Brief einfügen. Wie sieht es mit einer Antwort auf die Bewerbung aus?

J. I think we can send out a standard reply to applicants we shall be inviting for an interview. I'll leave that to you...

J. Ich denke, wir können an die Bewerber, die wir zu einem Gespräch einladen, einen Standardbrief schicken. Das überlasse ich Ihnen ...

Exercise 68

„Impression", „impressive", „impressively" oder „to impress"?
Finden Sie die richtige Form (inklusive Präposition) für folgende Sätze:

1. I was very _____ his performance.

2. I didn't find his performance as _____ as the last time I saw him in the concert hall.

3. The new system has been functioning most _____ since its installation.

4. What kind of _____ did she leave _____ you?

5. That's a very _____ motorbike you've got there.

6. Were you really _____ what she said?

7. I find it very difficult _____ him with the facts.

8. Did you think our presentation left _____ the audience?

9. I thought he spoke _____ about a difficult subject.

10. They said they were very _____ what he had to say.

(Peter dictates…)   (Peter diktiert …)

 Dear Mr Fenton,

We acknowledge receipt of your application for the position which has become available in our Marketing Department, and **we have pleasure in inviting you for an interview** at a date yet to be set. Interviews will, however, be held during the last two weeks of July. If for any reason you are unable to come to London during this time, please let us know in good time and we shall endeavour to organize our schedule to match yours.

Yours sincerely,

Peter Brückner
Assistant Managing Director
ARGO Limited

I look forward to hearing from you soon.

(Peter opens another letter.)   (Peter öffnet einen weiteren Brief.)

 Dear Sirs,

My attention was caught by your company's insertion in the Morning Echo, advertising the vacancy in your Marketing Department. **I would be very grateful if you considered my application for the post.** For the past three years I have been employed by the Robinson public relations agency, mostly writing advertising copy (cf. accompanying CV). I would now like very much to make the change to the purely business sector and, in particular, the hi-tech field. For that reason, I would be very interested indeed in working for a company such as yours.
I look forward to hearing from you soon.

Yours faithfully,

Nigel Branson

Nigel Branson's CV:

Nigel John Branson.

Born 12 October 1975 in Huddersfield, Yorkshire. Educated at St. Christopher's Preparatory School and Huddersfield Grammar School, leaving in 1993 with 7 GSCEs and 3 A-levels (English, History and Geography). Four years study (1993-97) at the University of Sussex, Brighton, graduating with BA (2:1 classification). In September 1997 joined Robinson Public Relations, London, as copywriter.

Background information

The word **"acknowledge"** has several meanings in the business English vocabulary. In the above letter, it is used to register receipt of the job application: "We acknowledge receipt of your letter of...".
In business letters, it is a common substitute for: "Thank you for your letter of..."

Other uses are seen in the following examples:
1. We acknowledge your company's complaints and will do all we can to rectify the situation (agree to the truth of).
2. The lawyers acknowledged the deed and added it to the file (gave it legal validity, accepted it as valid).
3. The accountant acknowledged his responsibility for the mistake in the annual report (admitted his guilt).
4. We acknowledge your efforts to correct the mistake (we express appreciation).
5. They acknowledged our presence at the concert (took notice of).
6. We acknowledge Mr Hoskins as the responsible officer in this case (recognize his authority).

The abbreviations **CF** and **cf.** have very different meanings in business English:

1. CF – "carried forward" – used in financial statements when a sum or figure is "carried forward" from one column or page to another.
2. cf. – (as used in the above letter) "compare" (from the Latin imperative "confer"). In Nigel Branson's letter, he uses the abbreviation to draw attention to the fact that his summarized career is dealt with in more detail in an accompanying CV.

Exercise 69

Das Wort „acknowledge" hat viele Synonyme, z. B.: accept, admit, allow, avow, certify, concede, confess, confirm, grant, own, profess, recognize.
Finden Sie in den folgenden Sätzen die korrekten Synonyme für dieses Wort!

1. Could your lawyer please acknowledge the validity of the will?

   _____

2. I acknowledge total responsibility for the errors in the report.

   _____

3. We acknowledge receipt of your letter of 12 March.

   _____

4. The company acknowledged our authority to act in this matter.

   _____

5. He acknowledged our presence at the meeting but still ignored us.

   _____

Talk Talk Talk

(Peter's office, Melissa enters.)   (Peters Büro, Melissa tritt ein.)

M. Hope I'm not disturbing, but I was just passing the door and **curiosity got the better of me**. Have you found anyone promising?

M. Ich hoffe, ich störe nicht, aber ich kam gerade an Ihrer Tür vorbei und **konnte der Neugier nicht widerstehen**. Haben Sie schon jemand Vielversprechenden entdeckt?

P. Well, yes and no – at least we've got the start of a shortlist of candidates. When are you joining the selection panel?

P. Tja, ja und nein – wenigstens konnten wir schon eine Vorauswahl treffen. Wann werden Sie zur Bewerberauswahl dazukommen?

M. I'll be there at the interviews. I'm leaving the hard work to you. But there are rewards – come on, it's my round at the Nag's Head...

M. Ich werde bei den Vorstellungsgesprächen dabei sein. Ich überlasse Ihnen die Knochenarbeit. Aber Sie sollen auch belohnt werden – kommen Sie, ich spendiere eine Runde im Nag's Head ...

(The Nag's Head pub)   (Im Nag's Head)

M. Cheers, Peter! How many possibles have you got so far?

M. Prost, Peter! Wie viele mögliche Kandidaten haben Sie bis jetzt?

P. Just two, really, although a couple more are on file. They **wrote enquiring** about employment possibilities before we inserted the advertisement.

P. Erst zwei, obwohl wir noch ein paar in den Akten haben. Sie haben **Initiativbewerbungen** an uns geschickt, bevor wir die Stellenanzeige aufgegeben hatten.

M. And how many more applications have you got to read?

M. Und wie viele Bewerbungen müssen Sie noch lesen?

P. About half a dozen, I believe. James wants to **narrow** the shortlist **down** to no more than six, anyway.

P. Etwa ein halbes Dutzend, schätze ich. James möchte die Liste der Vorauswahl auf nicht mehr als sechs Bewerber **einschränken**.

M. Well, **keep me posted** – I'll be working with the person we choose for the job.

M. Na gut, **halten Sie mich auf dem Laufenden** – ich werde schließlich mit dem ausgewählten Bewerber zusammenarbeiten.

P. Don't worry – you can take over the selection process right now, if you want.

P. Keine Sorge – Sie können das Auswahlverfahren sofort übernehmen, wenn Sie wollen.

M. No thanks, Peter – that's your job!

M. Nein, vielen Dank, Peter – das ist Ihr Job!

Exercise 70

„Who", „whom" oder „whose"?

Füllen Sie die Lücken mit der korrekten Form!

1. With _____ were you talking so long on the telephone?

2. To _____ address did you send that letter?

3. _____ did you talk to for so long on the phone last night?

4. Have you yet decided _____ should head the company next year?

5. I never realized _____ she really was.

6. _____ would you like to accompany you to the dinner?

7. _____ name is to appear at the top of the letter?

Talk Talk Talk 36

(Peter's office, Steve enters.)

S. Hi, Peter! Are you still **head-hunting**?

P. Hi, Steve! I haven't seen you for a while. Have you been **away**?

S. I had to do the usual round of the sales posts. One of the guys had heard there was a place in marketing. He wants to get out of sales and would be interested in something else within the company. I told him to get an application in.

P. I'm working through them right now. But this position is for a young career-starter, you know.

S. Never too late to start, Peter old chap!

(Peters Büro, Steve tritt ein.)

S. Hi, Peter! Immer noch beim **"Head-hunting"**?

P. Hi, Steve! Lange nicht gesehen. Waren Sie **außerhalb** unterwegs?

S. Ich habe die übliche Tour bei unseren Verkaufsstellen gemacht. Einer von den Kollegen hat gehört, dass es eine Stelle im Marketing gibt. Er möchte aus dem Verkauf heraus und ist an einer Anstellung in der Firma selbst interessiert. Ich habe ihm gesagt, er soll eine Bewerbung einreichen.

P. Ich arbeite mich gerade durch. Aber diese Position ist für einen jungen Berufseinsteiger gedacht, wissen Sie.

S. Es ist nie zu spät einzusteigen, Peter, alter Freund!

Background information

Head-hunting
In this highly competitive professional world, more and more companies are engaging specialist firms to hunt specifically for the employees they need. The practice is called "head-hunting".

Exercise 71

„Interest, interested, interesting" ...

Vervollständigen Sie die folgenden Sätze mit den passenden Wörtern (und den Präpositionen, wenn nötig)!

1. The company found this proposal _____ particular _____.

2. The company found this proposal particularly _____.

3. The company is particularly _____ this proposal.

4. The company's _____ has been caught _____ the proposal.

5. She made an _____ impression on us.

6. Would a brochure _____ your company?

7. Would a brochure be of _____ your company?

8. They sat through the whole lecture. They were very _____.

9. They sat through the whole lecture. They found it very _____.

10. Are you really _____ what he has to say?

11. The suggestion aroused much _____.

Talk Talk Talk

(Peter's office, Peter takes a fax from the machine.)

(Peters Büro, Peter nimmt ein Fax aus dem Gerät.)

P. Well, Steve's man lost no time...

P. Na so was, Steves Bekannter hat keine Zeit verloren …

 Dear Mr Brückner,

Mr Blackman informs me that a position has become vacant in ARGO's Marketing Department, and I would be grateful if you were able to consider my application. Although I have been employed in sales at ARGO for the past five years, I feel that in that time I have acquired skills which could benefit the company in a wider area. After five years in sales, I must confess that I would like to move on and gain further experience within the company.

My full details and work record are, of course, on file, so I shall not bother you with a CV, **but if you require any further information I am only too ready to supply it.**
I hope for a favourable response.

Yours sincerely,

Dale Spinks

Background information

The expression **"only too"** is found frequently in business correspondence. It is a slightly archaic form, which can just as easily – only too easily – be substituted by "very":

a) I shall be only too (very) pleased to comply with your wishes.
b) We shall be only too (very) ready for your comments.
c) We shall be only too (very) delighted to see you next Tuesday.
d) They were only too (very) glad to see the company fail.
e) He was only too (very) glad to call off the meeting.

Exercise 72

Vervollständigen Sie folgende Sätze mit „only" oder „only too":

1. I wanted to meet her before she left. Why did she refuse?

_____

2. They should be pleased they didn't take up that offer.

_____

3. I'm grateful for the help you gave me.

_____

4. It's not the anger it causes, but also the pain.

_____

5. We've two miles to go before we get home.

_____

Talk Talk Talk  37

(Peter's office, Chip, the courier, enters.)

P. Hello, Chip! What can I do for you?

C. This package from Dickens and Jolly is for you – they asked me to deliver it personally. Oh, Mr Brückner, I hear there's a vacancy in the Marketing Department.

(Peters Büro, Chip, der Kurier, tritt ein.)

P. Hallo, Chip! Was kann ich für dich tun?

C. Dieses Paket ist für Sie, von Dickens und Jolly – sie haben mich gebeten, es persönlich abzugeben. Oh, Mr Brückner, ich habe gehört, dass es eine freie Stelle in der Marketingabteilung gibt.

P. Oh, no, Chip, not you, too!

P. Oh, nein, Chip, nicht du auch noch!

C. Good lord, you wouldn't catch me wanting to work there **for all the tea in China**! I like my freedom. **Whizzing about** the place on a motorbike is my idea of a job. I wouldn't last a morning in an office with Miss Walker. That woman and me would be a real mistake!

C. Um Himmels Willen, **nicht für alles Geld der Welt** möchte ich hier arbeiten! Ich mag meine Freiheit und mit dem Motorrad **herumzufahren** ist meine Vorstellung von einem Traumjob. Ich würde es keinen Vormittag zusammen in einem Büro mit Miss Walker aushalten. Diese Dame und ich – das würde nicht gut gehen!

P. Chip, if you were as fast on your motorbike as you are with words, we'd have the most efficient courier service in London. But just watch what you have to say about Miss Walker, you cheeky rascal!

P. Chip, wenn du mit deinem Motorrad so schnell wärst wie mit deinem Mundwerk, wärst du der effektivste Kurierservice in London. Aber sei vorsichtig, was du über Miss Walker sagst, du Frechdachs!

C. Hey, you're not so bad with words yourself! At least, for a German!

C. Hey, Sie können aber auch gut mit Worten umgehen! Wenigstens für einen Deutschen!

P. Out with you, before I find something to chuck at you...

P. Raus mit dir, bevor ich etwas finde, dass ich nach dir werfen kann ...

False friends

"**Aktuelle** Stellenangebote" translates as "**current** vacancies". In English, "actual" means something real, not imagined. In many cases, the English for "aktuell" is "up to date": "The file is up to date". Hyphens are used when the adjective precedes the noun: "an up-to-date file".

Exercise 73

Finden Sie die passenden Wörter zu den Umschreibungen. Sie fangen alle mit der Vorsilbe „mis-" an!

misspend   miscellany   misanthrope   mishap   mispronounce

misshapen   misdirect

1. To pronounce a word incorrectly. _____
2. Bad luck strikes you if you experience this. _____
3. Someone who doesn't like people and avoids society. _____
4. A word for something that is not the correct shape. _____
5. Give out money wastefully and you... _____
6. A mixture or medley of anything _____
7. Give somebody the wrong instructions or advice and you... _____

📚 Vocabulary

addressee	Adressat
to advertise a post	eine Stelle annoncieren
away	außerhalb (einer Firma etc.)
to be tied down	in etw. eingebunden sein
to break off	aufhören/abbrechen
(a) business-related discipline	wirtschaftliches Ausbildungsfach
Curiosity got the better of me.	Ich konnte der Neugier nicht widerstehen.

degree in economics	Abschluss in Wirtschaftswissenschaft
devoted	gewidmet
discipline	*hier:* Fachgebiet
to entail	beinhalten/nach sich ziehen
to fall into (an area)	hineinfallen (im Sinne von „dazugehören")
for all the tea in China	(Redewendung) etwa: Für alles Geld der Welt
forceful	*hier:* ausgeprägt (Charakter)
to get stuck into sth.	sich in etw. vertiefen/„hineinknien"
initial(ly)	anfänglich
to keep sb. posted	auf dem Laufenden halten/ informieren
to make up a file	einen Ordner anlegen
to narrow down	eingrenzen
offhand	unpersönlich
opening vacancy	freie Stelle
to put into practice	in die Praxis umsetzen
requirements	Anforderungen
retrenchment	Einschränkung/Kürzung; Kosten- reduzierung
to sort out	aussortieren
stiff	steif/*hier:* rauh, umkämpft
tabular	tabellarisch
well worded	wohlformuliert
to whizz about	umhersausen

The conference | Die Konferenz

Here we go

Nach einem Urlaub in New York nimmt Peter an einer Konferenz über Informationstechnologie teil, bei der er zahlreiche wichtige Kontakte knüpft und die Bekanntschaft eines Ministers macht, der die Veranstaltung eröffnet.

Talk Talk Talk  38

P. Hello, Beryl. Can you find the time this afternoon to come to my office and **fill me in** on this conference I shall be attending?

P. Hallo Beryl. Haben Sie heute Nachmittag Zeit, um in mein Büro zu kommen und mich über die Konferenz zu **informieren**, an der ich teilnehmen soll?

B. Certainly, Peter. I'll be there in ten minutes. Just let me **deal with** this piece of work on my desk. I'll send Chip around with **the relevant papers** so you can start to read up on it ...

B. Selbstverständlich, Peter. Ich werde in zehn Minuten da sein. Lassen Sie mich nur das bisschen Arbeit auf meinem Tisch **erledigen**. Ich schicke Chip mit den **nötigen Papieren** vorbei, damit Sie anfangen können, sich einzulesen ...

P. Chip! Hello there! How are you? How's work going?

P. Chip! Hallo! Guten Tag! Wie geht's? Was macht die Arbeit?

C. Fine, thanks, Mr Brückner.

C. Danke gut, Mr Brückner.

P. So what have you got there for me?

P. Was hast du mir denn mitgebracht?

👥 Die Konferenz

C. Ms Platt sent these papers round for you. She says take a butcher's at them and she'll be here in a jiffy. She's on her way up the apples and pears right now – I can hear her.

P. Now, **come off it**, Chip. I know you're just having me on with all that cockney slang…

C. Ms Platt lässt Ihnen diese Papiere hier zukommen. Sie möchte, dass Sie einen Blick darauf werfen; sie wird in ein paar Minuten hier sein. Sie steigt gerade die Treppe herauf – ich kann sie hören.

P. Jetzt **hör' auf** damit, Chip. Ich weiß, du nimmst mich auf den Arm mit diesem ganzen Cockney-Slang …

Background information

We were introduced to some of Chip's cockney rhyming slang.
Do you know the meaning of a butcher's? It's short for butcher's hook – which conveniently rhymes with "look". So a butcher's is a "look" – "Are those your holiday snaps? Give me a butcher's!"

Other very expressive cockney slang expressions include "Burton-on-Trent" for "rent", trouble-and-strife for "wife" and several based on the use of "apples": apples and pears ("stairs"), apple pie ("sky") and apple pips ("lips").

It used to be said that a true cockney had to be born within the sound of the bells of Bow Church in the east end of London, but that's no longer the case. You'll now hear many Londoners from as far afield as the western suburbs calling themselves cockneys.

Exercise 74

Finden Sie Alternativen für den Ausdruck „done"!

1. The meal was delicious. The joint of beef was **done** to perfection.

_____

2. I'm not very good at chess. Now you've taken my queen **I'm done for**.

_____

3. The team was **done** in after that exhausting game.

_____

4. In polite company it's **not done** to eat peas off the blade of your knife, you know!

_____

Talk Talk Talk
(Peter's office)

(Peters Büro)

P. Come in, Beryl. I've only had a chance to **take a brief glance at** these papers – in fact, all I know at the moment is that this **conference is devoted** to advances in information technology and that it lasts four days. I'm glad **it's being held** here in London. I've done enough travelling for a while.

P. Kommen Sie herein, Beryl. Ich konnte bisher nur einen **kurzen Blick** auf die Papiere **werfen** – ich weiß im Augenblick lediglich, dass die **Konferenz** den Fortschritten der Informationstechnologie **gewidmet ist** und vier Tage dauert. Ich bin froh, dass sie hier in London **abgehalten wird**. Ich bin für eine Zeit lang genug gereist.

B. Yes, in fact that's why Mr Morgan has **registered** ARGO to attend. He doesn't want you back in Glasgow until the new year, so the conference **fits nicely** into your schedule.

B. Ja, genau deshalb hat Mr Morgan ARGO zur Teilnahme **angemeldet**. Er möchte nicht, dass Sie vor Neujahr nach Glasgow zurückgehen, deshalb **passt** die Konferenz **gut** in Ihren Terminkalender.

P. Let's have a look at the programme. There are some interesting **speakers**, I see – including some from abroad.

P. Gehen wir das Programm durch. Wie ich sehe, gibt es einige interessante **Referenten** – inklusive einiger aus dem Ausland.

B. That's also what interests Mr Morgan. Apparently, about sixty percent of the participants will be from abroad. It will be a very **international forum**. Mr Morgan believes it will be an ideal opportunity for us to **expand our network of contacts** and at the same time tap into new ideas and advances. He'll be attending some sessions himself, but he wants you to **see it through** from beginning to end.

B. Das ist es auch, was Mr Morgan interessiert. Offensichtlich werden ungefähr sechzig Prozent aus dem Ausland kommen. Es wird ein wirklich **internationales Forum** sein. Mr Morgan glaubt, es wird eine ideale Gelegenheit für uns sein, **unser Netz von Kontakten** zu **erweitern** und zur gleichen Zeit auf neue Ideen und Fortschritte zu stoßen. An einigen Veranstaltungen wird er selbst teilnehmen, aber er möchte, dass Sie von Anfang bis Ende **dabei sind**.

P. I'll be glad to, of course. I see a minister is **opening the conference** and that the first **session** will be addressed by Professor Karl Schlüter of York University. He was one of my teachers in Hamburg – a very clever man and an excellent speaker...

P. Das mache ich natürlich gerne. Ich sehe, dass ein Minister **die Konferenz eröffnet** und die **Sitzung** von Professor Karl Schlüter von der Universität York geleitet wird. Er war in Hamburg einer meiner Lehrer – ein sehr kluger Mann und ein exzellenter Redner ...

False friends

The word **"devoted"** has subtle shades of meaning which often present difficulties for non-native English speakers. Peter has mastered one meaning with no problem – noting that the conference he is to attend will be "devoted" to the subject of information technology. The conference will **concern itself** entirely **with** this subject, the four days will be **dedicated** to the topic. The word also has a very religious sense, describing the act of dedicating oneself to a sacred cause or God – "She became a nun and devoted herself to God." But it also has a more mundane meaning, describing in sometimes exaggerated form an intense liking or love – "He's devoted to his family", "I'm devoted to my favourite band".

Background information

Beryl tells Peter the conference **"fits nicely"** into his schedule, meaning there's room for it in Peter's working week. This is a very common use of **"fit"** – others include:

a good fit	well-tailored, (in carpentry) well made
to fit in (with)	to be in harmony or accord (with), to accommodate oneself
fitting	suitable, appropriate
in fits and starts	in an erratic manner
fit to be tied	extremely irritated or angry
fit to burst	replete, full of food; helpless with laughter
fit to kill	in an extravagant or striking manner

Exercise 75

Füllen Sie die Lücken mit der korrekten Wendung mit „fit"!

1. I think there's something wrong with the car – the engine is going _____.

2. No more for me thanks. It was delicious, but I'm _____.

3. I don't really mind what we do. I'll just _____ with the rest.

4. Where are you off to tonight? You look _____.

5. I'm so damned angry I'm _____.

6. You look very smart in that new outfit, it's a very _____.

7. I find it very _____ that Susan should be taking over the company founded by her father.

8. Do your plans _____ with ours?

Talk Talk Talk

(ARGO offices, four days later)

B. Now, do you have everything, Peter? You know where the con-ference venue is?

P. I certainly hope so, Beryl. I'd be in trouble if I didn't, wouldn't I?

(ARGO-Büros, vier Tage später)

B. Haben Sie jetzt alles, Peter? Sie wissen, wo der **Konferenzort** ist?

P. Das hoffe ich doch, Beryl. Ich wäre in Schwierigkeiten, wenn ich das nicht täte, stimmt's?

B. Nothing would surprise me after the Glasgow mix-up.

P. But Steve's not organizing it, thank goodness.

B. That's another reason why you're going, and not Steve. Mr Morgan wants nothing to go wrong.

P. That sounds a bit intimidating, Beryl.

B. Don't worry, we're all expecting you to **come through with flying colours**. Now, here's your accreditation and your pass, two copies of the conference **programme** an **advance copy** of the minister's speech. The invitations to the ARGO cocktail party are still being printed, but I'll send Chip around with them this afternoon. So, off you go. All the best – toi, toi, toi, as you say. I love that expression. You see, Peter, we're learning from you, too.

P. Thanks, Beryl. Just remind me once again of the best way of getting there. I don't want to take a taxi in this traffic.

B. Nach dem Durcheinander in Glasgow würde mich nichts überraschen.

P. Aber Gott sei Dank wird das Ganze nicht von Steve organisiert.

B. Das ist ein weiterer Grund, warum Sie gehen und nicht Steve. Mr Morgan will nicht, dass etwas schiefgeht.

P. Beryl, das klingt ein bisschen einschüchternd.

B. Keine Bange, wir erwarten alle, dass Sie **mit fliegenden Fahnen durchkommen**. Nun, hier ist Ihre Akkreditierung und Ihr Pass, zwei Kopien des Konferenz**programms**, eine **Vorabkopie** der Rede des Ministers. Die Einladungen für die ARGO-Cocktailparty werden noch gedruckt, aber ich schicke Chip heute Nachmittag damit vorbei. So, los geht's. Alles Gute – toi, toi, toi, wie Sie sagen. Ich liebe diesen Ausdruck. Sie sehen, Peter, wir lernen auch von Ihnen.

P. Danke, Beryl. Sagen Sie mir doch noch einmal, wie ich am besten dort hinkomme. Ich möchte bei diesem Verkehr kein Taxi nehmen.

B. Take the Central line to Oxford Circus, and then it's two stops on the Piccadilly line. The hotel is right opposite the tube station… Oh, Peter! Haven't you forgotten something?

P. Beryl?

B. Your umbrella – it's raining cats and dogs outside…

B. Nehmen Sie die Central Line zum Oxford Circus und dann zwei Haltestellen mit der Piccadilly-Linie. Das Hotel ist genau gegenüber der U-Bahn-Station … Oh, Peter! Haben Sie nicht etwas vergessen?

P. Beryl?

B. Ihren Regenschirm – draußen regnet es in Strömen …

Exercise 76

Füllen Sie die Lücken, indem Sie die Verben in die korrekte Zeitform bringen!

1. I would have won that contract if the company `submit` _____ the tender in time.

2. We would have come if we `receive` _____ the invitation.

3. Dave would be in very big trouble if the boss `know` _____ about his mistake.

4. His explanation would appear `be` _____ satisfactory.

5. The team would have won if they `try` _____ harder from the start of the game.

6. I wouldn't worry if I `be` _____ you.

Talk Talk Talk  39

(Lansdown Hotel, central London)

P. Good morning! I'm here for the **conference on information technology**. Is this the **information desk**?

Receptionist Yes, it is. **Are you accredited?**

P. Yes, my name is Brückner. Peter Brückner, from ARGO Limited.

R. Let me see. Yes, here's your name on the list. Let me give you this **information pack**, these meal vouchers and two **name tags**. The conference **is taking place** in the Regency Room. Coffee and afternoon tea are served in the foyer, and lunch is in the main dining room. The Regency Room is that way.

P. Thank you. I'm a little early. Is the room already open?

R. Yes, you can go in now and take any place that pleases you.

(Regency Room)
P. Ah, you're also an **early customer**, I see. Is this place taken?

(Lansdown Hotel, Zentrum Londons)

P. Guten Morgen! Ich bin wegen der **Informationstechnologie-Konferenz** hier. Ist das der **Informationsschalter?**

Empfangsdame Ja, das ist er. **Sind Sie akkreditiert?**

P. Ja, mein Name ist Brückner. Peter Brückner, von ARGO Limited.

R. Lassen Sie mich nachsehen. Ja, Ihr Name steht hier auf der Liste. Nehmen Sie bitte dieses **Infopaket**, diese Essensgutscheine und zwei **Namensschilder**. Die Konferenz **findet** im Regency Room **statt**. Kaffee und Nachmittagstee werden im Foyer serviert und Mittagessen gibt es im großen Speisesaal. Zum Regency Room geht es da entlang.

P. Danke. Ich bin ein bisschen früh dran. Ist der Raum bereits geöffnet?

R. Ja, Sie können jetzt hineingehen und Platz nehmen, wo Sie möchten.

(Regency Room)
P. Ah, ich sehe, Sie sind auch ein **Überpünktlicher**. Ist dieser Platz besetzt?

Roy Noble No, I'd be glad if you took it. I'm feeling a bit isolated in this vast room. I thought the conference started at nine thirty, so I'm **a good half hour early**.

Roy Noble Nein, es würde mich freuen, wenn Sie Platz nehmen würden. Ich fühle mich etwas verloren in diesem riesigen Raum. Ich dachte, die Konferenz würde um neun Uhr dreißig beginnen, also bin ich eine **gute halbe Stunde zu früh dran**.

P. I was surprised how quickly I got here. The London transport system isn't as bad as many people **make out**.

P. Ich war erstaunt, wie schnell ich hierher gekommen bin. Das Londoner Verkehrssystem ist nicht so schlecht, wie manche Leute **behaupten**.

R. You're not from London?

R. Sie kommen nicht aus London?

P. No, I work for a **London-based company**, but I'm German. Peter Brückner from ARGO Limited.

P. Nein, ich arbeite für eine **Firma mit Sitz in London**, aber ich bin Deutscher. Peter Brückner von ARGO Limited.

R. ARGO? I've heard of the company. My name is Roy Noble, of Noble Electronics. We **deal** mostly **in semiconductors**… Business isn't too good at the moment because of the **slump** in the **new technology area**. How are you faring?

R. ARGO? Ich habe von dieser Firma gehört. Mein Name ist Roy Noble, von Noble Electronics. Wir **handeln** hauptsächlich **mit Halbleitern** … Das Geschäft läuft im Moment nicht allzu gut wegen der **Wirtschaftskrise** auf dem **Gebiet der Neuen Technologien**. Wie **geht es bei Ihnen?**

P. Actually, not bad at all. We're even **expanding** at the moment.

P. Gar nicht schlecht zurzeit. Wir sind sogar auf **Expansionskurs**.

R. How have you managed that?

R. Wie schaffen Sie das?

P. I think one reason is **diversification**. We have spread our activities over a wide area. When one **sector weakens**, we can **switch our attention** to a stronger or **more promising** one.

P. Ich glaube, ein Grund lautet **Diversifikation**. Wir haben unsere Aktivitäten auf ein weites Gebiet ausgebreitet. Wenn ein **Sektor schwächer wird**, können wir unsere **Aufmerksamkeit** auf einen stärkeren oder **vielversprechenderen** verlagern.

R. I'd like to hear more – but it looks as if we're about to get under way...

R. Ich würde gerne mehr erfahren – aber es sieht so aus, als würden wir gleich loslegen …

Background information
Don't be shy …
Legendary English reserve is cast aside in **networking** and **business dealings**. Peter has an empty room in which to find a seat, but wisely chooses to place himself next to another early arrival and to **engage him** immediately **in conversation**. Since they are attending the same conference, they obviously have much in common. Each has nothing to lose, and everything to gain, by overcoming any natural reserve and making direct contact.

Exercise 77

Unterstreichen Sie den jeweils passenden Begriff!

1. We'll have to stay here for the night, I don't think the storm is going to let with / down / up / against .

2. That mail order company really let us up / down / in / over – they promised delivery within three days, but we're still waiting for the parcel.

3. If that's John at the door, can you let him up / down / in / out ?

4. We're giving Sue a surprise party on her fortieth birthday – please don't let up / in / on / down .

5. Can't we let Mike in / on / in on / up on the secret?

6. The police could find no evidence against the arrested man, so they let him on / go / run / up .

Talk Talk Talk

R. Well, I found the minister's speech very interesting. He obviously has **a good grasp of** the subject. It always surprises me how quickly ministers **get to grips with** the speciality they have been assigned… Well, perhaps there is a future for us as Ministers of Information Technology or some such department! Another coffee? The break lasts half an hour...

Session chairman Roy! I'd like you to meet the minister. Minister, Roy Noble here is an example of the **new entrepreneurship** abroad in Europe.

R. Nun, ich fand die Rede des Ministers sehr interessant, er hat das Thema offensichtlich **gut im Griff**. Es erstaunt mich immer, wie schnell sich Minister **mit** den speziellen Themen **auseinandersetzen**, die ihnen übertragen wurden … Nun, vielleicht gibt es für uns eine Zukunft als Minister für Informationstechnologie oder in einem ähnlichen Ministerium! Noch einen Kaffee? Die Pause dauert eine halbe Stunde ...

Konferenzleiter Roy! Ich möchte Ihnen den Herrn Minister vorstellen. Herr Minister, Roy Noble hier ist ein Beispiel **neuen Unternehmertums** drüben in Europa.

R. How do you do, sir? Mr Brückner and I were just talking about your most interesting **address** to the conference.

R. Guten Tag, Sir. Herr Brückner und ich haben uns gerade über Ihre höchst interessante **Ansprache** an die Konferenz unterhalten.

Minister Mr Brückner? Sie sind Deutscher? Es freut mich sehr, Sie kennenzulernen – but, please, spare me the **embarrassment** of having to delve deeper into my inadequate **knowledge** of your language and tell me what brings a German such as yourself to London and to a conference such as this.

Minister Herr Brückner? Sie sind Deutscher? Es freut mich sehr, Sie kennenzulernen – aber bitte, ersparen Sie mir die **Peinlichkeit**, tiefer in meinen unzulänglichen **Kenntnissen** Ihrer Sprache zu graben und erzählen Sie mir, was einen Deutschen wie Sie nach London und zu einer Konferenz wie dieser hier führt.

P. I'm afraid the coffee break isn't long enough, minister. It's a long story.

P. Ich fürchte, die Kaffeepause ist nicht lang genug, Herr Minister. Das ist eine lange Geschichte.

M. Then do **join** my party for lunch. We're table number one, isn't that so, Leo?

M. Dann **schließen** Sie sich zu Mittag meiner Gesellschaft an. Wir haben Tisch Nummer 1, nicht wahr, Leo?

False friends

Be careful in distinguishing between the verbs **"assign"** and **"resign"**. Assign is a transitive verb with the chief meaning of **giving responsibility** to somebody – "I assigned her the job of maintaining contact with branch offices". Resign is used mainly in an intransitive sense, where it means to **relinquish** (or quit) a position – "After losing the vote of confidence, the prime minister resigned".

👥 Die Konferenz

Talk Talk Talk

(Lansdown Hotel dining room)

(Lansdown Hotel, Speisesaal)

R. Where's table number one? Ah, there!

R. Wo ist Tisch Nummer 1? Ah, dort!

P. May we join you, as you kindly suggested, minister?

P. Dürfen wir uns zu Ihnen setzen, wie Sie so freundlich vorschlugen, Herr Minister?

M. Certainly, certainly. Do sit down. And how did you find the professor's contribution?

M. Sicher, sicher. Nehmen Sie Platz. Und wie fanden Sie den Beitrag des Professors?

P. Very interesting indeed.

P. Wirklich sehr interessant.

R. Same here. And some very interesting points were raised in the discussion afterwards.

R. Das meine ich auch. Und es wurden einige interessante Punkte in der Diskussion danach aufgebracht.

M. I thought so, too. It's encouraging to hear so many new ideas and new interpretations of what we – I speak for myself, of course – often take for granted. New technology is forcing us to appraise old approaches. We just have to break out of timeworn practices and join the drive forwards or get left behind. This really is a revolution. Is this the way you see things in Germany, Mr Brückner?

M. Das fand ich auch. Es ist ermutigend, so viele neue Ideen und neue Interpretationen davon zu hören, was wir – ich spreche natürlich für mich selbst – oft als gegeben hinnehmen. Die Neuen Technologien zwingen uns, alte Errungenschaften abzuschätzen. Wir müssen einfach aus ausgedienten Praktiken ausbrechen und uns dem Vorstoß anschließen oder wir werden hinterherhinken. Das ist wirklich eine Revolution. Sehen Sie in Deutschland die Dinge auch auf diese Weise, Mr Brückner?

P. I think so, minister. I can really speak only for my own company.

M. And that is?

P. ARGO Limited.

M. Very **far-sighted**, I'm sure. Very impressive. Tell me more about this ARGO...

P. Ich denke schon, Herr Minister. Ich kann wirklich nur für meine eigene Firma sprechen.

M. Und das ist?

P. ARGO Limited.

M. Sicherlich sehr **weitsichtig**. Sehr beeindruckend. Erzählen Sie mir mehr von dieser ARGO ...

Background information

The government minister tells Peter many new technological advances are **taken for granted** – meaning they are accepted without much further thought or appreciation. We have already met several expressions using **"take"** – and now here are some more:

to take into account	to include in an assessment
to take a dim (or poor) view of something	to disapprove
to take charge	to assume control or custody
to take heart	to gain courage or confidence
to take hold	to grasp, to seize
to take sb.'s name in vain	to use somebody's name without respect
to take note (of sth.)	to commit to memory
to take stock (of sth.)	to make an assessment or valuation
to take the biscuit	to be the most extrem case ever
to take sb. to task	to criticize, to call to account

Exercise 78

Füllen Sie die Lücken mit dem passenden Ausdruck, der das Wort „take" enthält!

1. The company made record profits last year. That _____.
2. _____ this advice. You'll find it very useful in the future.
3. Let's sit down with cool heads and _____ the situation.
4. The staff have _____ from the good news coming from head office.
5. The board members were very dissatisfied with the performance of the chairman and severely _____.
6. The site manager _____ workers arriving late and leaving early.

Talk Talk Talk

M. Well, it's time for the **second session** to start, and it's time for me to be off. I'd like to stay, but there's work at the Ministry.

P. I'm very happy to have met you, and thank you very much for your patience in listening to my **description** of what we do and what we plan.

M. Nun, es ist Zeit für die **zweite Sitzung** und es ist Zeit für mich zu gehen. Ich würde gerne bleiben, aber ich habe im Ministerium zu tun.

P. Es war mir eine große Freude, Sie kennenzulernen und ich danke Ihnen sehr herzlich für Ihre Geduld, mit der Sie meiner **Beschreibung**, was wir tun und was wir vorhaben, zugehört haben.

M. Not at all, Mr Brückner. You didn't do all the talking, by any means. Mr Noble here had a lot to say about his **enterprise**. I have learnt a lot from you both, and I wish you all the very best in your extremely **worthwhile endeavours**.

M. Ich bitte Sie, Mr Brückner. Sie haben gar nicht die ganze Zeit über geredet. Mr Noble hier hatte viel über sein **Unternehmen** zu erzählen. Ich habe viel von Ihnen beiden gelernt und ich wünsche Ihnen das Allerbeste bezüglich Ihres ausgesprochen **lohnenden Bestrebens**.

R. Thank you very much, minister.

R. Vielen Dank, Herr Minister.

P. Yes, thank you very much indeed.

P. Ja, ich danke Ihnen wirklich vielmals.

M. Well then, goodbye. I must be on my way...

M. Also dann, auf Wiedersehen. Ich muss mich auf den Weg machen.

J. Hello, Peter! Ready for the second session, then? I missed **the opening of the conference** and the lunch. There's so much to do back at the office. But I did want to catch the address by the **head** of the British Electronics Association. There's **bound to be** some interesting discussion afterwards.

J. Hallo Peter! Sind Sie denn bereit für die zweite Sitzung? Ich habe die **Eröffnung der Konferenz** und das Mittagessen versäumt. Im Büro ist so viel zu tun. Aber ich wollte den Vortrag des **Vorsitzenden** der British Electronics Association nicht verpassen. Danach gibt es **bestimmt** eine interessante Diskussion.

P. Should I return to the office, do you think?

P. Glauben Sie, ich sollte zum Büro zurückkehren?

J. No, not at all. It's **in good hands** – Beryl and that clever young nephew of hers **are in charge**. And Steve is **looking by** later today.

J. Nein, gar nicht. Es ist **in guten Händen** – Beryl und ihr kluger junger Neffe **kümmern sich darum**. Und Steve **schaut** heute noch **vorbei**.

P. Steve? I thought he was in Glasgow.

J. He's **fairly well wrapped things up** there. He **got moving** for a change – I suspect he couldn't wait to get back to London.

P. Steve? Ich dachte, er wäre in Glasgow.

J. Er hat die **Sachen** dort **ziemlich gut abgewickelt**. Er **hat sich** diesmal **beeilt** – ich vermute, er konnte es nicht abwarten, nach London zurückzukehren.

Background information

From the exchange between the minister and Peter Brückner, it is clear that Peter has not **hogged the conversation**. He also **drew his other table companion**, Roy Noble, **into the discussion** – a wise and diplomatic move, particularly when dealing with politicians!

Exercise 79

Füllen Sie die Lücken mit der passenden Zeitform!

1. I was disappointed to miss _____ her when she called.

2. I am very happy to hear _____ that you recover _____ from that very serious operation.

3. They said they were very relieved to catch _____ us before we board _____ the plane.

4. I was angry for days after hear _____ that he leave _____ that pile of work unfinished.

5. I hoped to meet _____ you, but it be _____ not mean to be.

Talk Talk Talk  40

J. I'm ready for this coffee break. All those **facts and figures** are **scrambling my brain**.

J. Ich kann diese Kaffeepause brauchen. All diese **Fakten und Zahlen schwirren** mir noch **im Kopf herum**.

P. I **recorded** it all, if you'd like to **go over** it later.

P. Ich habe alles **aufgenommen**, falls Sie es später **durchgehen** wollen.

J. Recorded it?

J. Es aufgenommen?

P. This **pocket recorder** here. It's very handy. It **picks up** everything.

P. Dieser **Taschenrekorder** hier. Er ist sehr handlich. Er **nimmt** alles **auf**.

J. Well, I'll be damned! I didn't think of that. Well done!

J. Donnerwetter! Daran habe ich nicht gedacht. Gut gemacht!

P. Will you be staying for the **final session**?

P. Werden Sie bis zur **Abschlusssitzung** bleiben?

J. No, I have to get moving. But, look, do join me for a drink afterwards. You can fill me in on the rest of the **day's proceedings**. I'll wait for you at the office. That is, if you **have** nothing else **in mind**.

J. Nein, ich muss weg. Aber gehen wir danach doch noch auf einen Drink. Sie können mich dann über den Rest des **Tagesverlaufs** informieren. Ich werde im Büro auf Sie warten. Das heißt, wenn Sie nichts anderes **vorhaben**.

P. No, I've **kept my appointment book clear** for the duration of the conference. I'll come straight back to the office after the session ends.

P. Nein, **ich habe** mir für die Dauer der Konferenz **meinen Terminkalender freigehalten**. Ich komme nach Ende der Sitzung direkt ins Büro.

J. And bring that recording with you, if you would. Very useful. Well done, Peter!

J. Und würden Sie die Aufnahme mitbringen? Sehr nützlich. Gut gemacht, Peter!

Background information

The clever businessperson always has a small **digital recorder** at the ready. It's as useful as a **pocket diary** or **calculator** – all of which are now available on most smartphones. But be sure to draw attention to recording equipment in any business encounter and to request permission to use it.

At the ready? That means ready for immediate use. **At hand** – an expression we've already encountered – has the same meaning.
A recorder picks up sounds. There are several other useful expressions using "pick":

to pick and choose	to select with care
to pick (at sth.)	to nag, to criticize repeatedly
to pick on sb.	to single out for criticism or special attention
to pick one's way	to proceed slowly and carefully
to pick out	to discern, to make out
to pick up	to buy or acquire casually or by chance; to learn; to catch (a disease or a cold); to catch sight of; to resume or continue; to improve; to increase (speed or strength)
to pick up on sth.	to notice, to become aware of something

Exercise 80

Füllen Sie die Lücken mit den passenden Wendungen, die das Wort "pick" enthalten!

1. Why _____ her? The whole department was to blame, if you ask me.

2. Did you _____ the signals his speech was sending out?

   Yes, I did. The message was unmistakable.

3. Can you _____ the outline of the mountains, over there on the horizon?

4. The nice thing about this new shop is that you can _____ at leisure.

5. How do you like this picture I _____ in the antique shop in High Street?

6. They _____ along the rough path as if it were a minefield.

Talk Talk Talk 41

(ARGO offices)

L. Peter? I have a call for you from the **Ministry of Overseas Trade**.

P. The Ministry of Overseas Trade? Are you sure, Lucy?

(ARGO-Büros)

L. Peter? Ich habe ein Gespräch für Sie vom **Außenhandelsministerium**.

P. Das Außenhandelsministerium? Sind Sie sicher, Lucy?

👥 Die Konferenz

L. They **asked to speak to** Mr Brückner. I have a Mr Carter on the line. Shall I **put** him **through**?

L. Sie **wollten mit** Mr Brückner **sprechen**. Ich habe einen Mr Carter in der Leitung. Soll ich ihn **durchstellen**?

P. Yes, of course, Lucy. Hello? Peter Brückner here.

P. Ja natürlich, Lucy. Hallo? Hier ist Peter Brückner.

Mr C. Mr Brückner. The minister has asked me to call you and ask if you would be kind enough to find the time to **attend a meeting** at the Ministry next Tuesday. He is **meeting with a delegation** from the World Trade Organization and would value your presence.

Mr C. Mr Brückner. Der Minister hat mich gebeten, Sie anzurufen und zu fragen, ob Sie so nett wären, sich nächsten Dienstag die Zeit zu nehmen, um **an einer Besprechung** im Ministerium **teilzunehmen**. Er **trifft sich** mit einer **Delegation** der Welthandelsorganisation und hätte Sie gerne dabei.

P. Me? What can I contribute?

P. Ich? Was kann ich beisteuern?

Mr C. The minister only asked if you would agree to attend. He didn't tell me what role he envisaged for you. But he did suggest that if you could find the time you and I should get together before next Tuesday to **look at the agenda**. Would Friday be all right?

Mr C. Der Minister fragte nur, ob Sie einverstanden wären, teilzunehmen. Er sagte mir nicht, welche Rolle er Ihnen zugedacht hat. Aber er hat vorgeschlagen, dass, falls Sie Zeit hätten, wir beide uns vor nächstem Dienstag treffen sollten, um **die Tagesordnung durchzugehen**. Würde Ihnen Freitag passen?

P. Just let me look in my **diary**. Ah, the conference is over on Thursday. Yes, Friday would be fine. When and where?

P. Lassen Sie mich kurz in meinem **Terminkalender** nachsehen. Ah, die Konferenz ist am Donnerstag vorbei. Ja, Freitag wäre schön. Wann und wo?

Mr C. Here at the Ministry, at eleven? Just ask for me at reception and they'll arrange to show you up.

Mr C. Hier im Ministerium, um elf Uhr? Fragen Sie einfach an der Rezeption nach mir und man wird Ihnen den Weg zeigen.

P. I'll be there. Goodbye.
Ah, James – you've just missed a most interesting conversation. The Ministry of Overseas Trade wants me to **participate in a meeting** there next week. I accepted, of course – I hope that's all right.

P. Ich werde da sein. Auf Wiederhören.
Ah, James – Sie haben ein äußerst interessantes Gespräch verpasst. Das Außenhandelsministerium möchte, dass ich dort nächste Woche **an einer Besprechung teilnehme.** Ich habe natürlich zugesagt – ich hoffe, das ist in Ordnung.

J. Well, I hope we're not going to lose you to the government now. But, no, **in all seriousness – go for it**! You obviously made quite an impression on the minister...

J. Nun, ich hoffe, wir verlieren Sie jetzt nicht an die Regierung. Aber, nein, **ganz im Ernst – gehen Sie hin**! Sie haben offensichtlich einen sehr positiven Eindruck auf den Minister gemacht ...

False friends

"Show up" has two very different meanings.
If you cause embarrassment to somebody you show him or her up. But if you show somebody up to a room or an office you guide them there, you show them the way.

Exercise 81

Vervollständigen Sie! Einige Begriffe wiederholen sich.

free   calling   on the line   help   reach   line   wait   speak   call

have   put through   rang off   discuss   hold   busy   waiting

engaged   hello   call back

Lucy _____, ARGO here. Can I _____ you?

Mr T. Thatcher of North End Electronics here. I'd like to

_____ to Mr Morgan please.

L. I'll see if he's _____. Just _____ a

moment, please. Mr Morgan? I _____ a Mr Thatcher of

North End Electronics _____. Shall I _____

him _____?

J. No, Lucy. I'm very busy at the moment. He's _____

about sales, so _____ him _____ Steve.

L. Hello, Mr Thatcher? Mr Morgan is _____ on another

_____ at the moment. He has asked me to _____

you _____ Mr Blackman. Sorry to keep you _____.

I'll _____ you _____ right away. Oh dear! Mr

Blackman's _____ is _____. Would you like

to _____? His line should be _____ very soon.

Mr T. No. I have a _____ waiting for me on another

_____. I'll _____ back.

J. Hello Lucy? Is Thatcher still _____? I've just remem-

bered something I wanted to _____ with him. Can you

_____ him _____?

L. No, Mr Morgan. He _____. He says he'll _____ later.

J. Lucy, this is rather important. Do you think you could _____ his number for me?

L. Well, he said something about having a _____ on an-other _____. But I'll try to _____ him for you.

Background information

Let's show you now some everyday expressions employing the word "show":

show business (showbiz)	the entertainment industry (principally the theatre and films)
showcase	a favourable setting in which something is displayed
showdown	a decisive confrontation or contest
showing	performance, appearance, presentation
showman	a person with the ability of projecting or presenting himself (also herself) effectively
to show off	to display or exhibit proudly; to seek to attract attention by extravagant or foolish behaviour
to show one's hand	to disclose one's intentions
showpiece	an oustanding example of put on display
to show the door	to eject, to tell, to leave the building or a project

🧑‍🤝‍🧑 Die Konferenz

 **Vocabulary**

address	Ansprache
advance copy	Vorabkopie
to ask to speak to sb.	mit jmd. sprechen wollen
to attend a meeting	an einer Besprechung teilnehmen
to be accredited	akkreditiert sein
to be bound to be	bestimmt/sicher sein
to be in charge (of sth.)	zuständig sein für, sich kümmern um
to be on one's way	auf dem Weg sein, wegmüssen
to come off it	mit etw. aufhören
to come through with flying colours	mit fliegenden Fahnen durchkommen/Erfolg haben
conference on information technology	Informationstechnologie-Konferenz
conference venue	Konferenzort
contribution	*hier:* (Rede-)Beitrag
day's proceedings	Tagesverlauf
to deal in semiconductors	mit Halbleitern handeln
to deal with sth.	etw. erledigen
description	Beschreibung
diary	Terminkalender
diversification	Diversifikation/breiteres Angebot
early customer	früh dran sein, ein „Überpünktlicher"
embarrassment	Peinlichkeit, Verlegenheit
enterprise	Unternehmen
to expand one's network of contacts	das Netz von Kontakten erweitern
facts and figures	Fakten und Zahlen
fairly well	ziemlich gut
to fare	ergehen
to fill sb. in	jmd. informieren
final session	Abschlusssitzung
to fit nicely	gut passen
to get to grips with sth.	sich mit (etw.) auseinandersetzen
Go for it!	Gehen Sie hin!/Machen Sie das!

to go over	durchgehen
to have a good grasp of sth.	etw. gut im Griff haben
to have in mind	vorhaben
head	*hier:* Vorsitzende(r)
I'm very happy to have met you.	Es war mir eine große Freude, Sie kennenzulernen!
in all seriousness	ganz im Ernst
in good hands	in guten Händen
information desk	Informationsschalter
information pack	Infopaket
international forum	internationales Forum
to join sb.	sich zu jmd. setzen
to keep one's appointment book clear	seinen Terminkalender freihalten
knowledge	Kenntnisse
London-based company	Firma mit Sitz in London
to look at the agenda	die Tagesordnung durchgehen
to look by	vorbeischauen
to make out	*hier:* behaupten
to meet with a delegation	sich mit einer Delegation treffen
Ministry of Overseas Trade	Außenhandelsministerium
name tag	Namensschild
new entrepreneurship	neues Unternehmertum
new technology sector	Gebiet der Neuen Technologien
to open a conference	eine Konferenz eröffnen
opening of a conference	Konferenzeröffnung
to participate in a meeting	an einer Besprechung teilnehmen
to pick up	*hier:* aufnehmen
pocket recorder	Taschenrekorder
programme	Programm
promising	vielversprechend
to put sb. through	jmd. durchstellen
to raise (a point)	*hier:* etw. aufbringen (z. B. Diskussionspunkte)
to record	aufnehmen, aufzeichnen
to register	(sich) anmelden, registrieren

relevant papers	nötige Papiere
to scramble the brain	im Kopf herumschwirren
sector	Sektor, Gebiet, Branche
to see sth. through	bei etw. dabei sein
session	Sitzung
slump	*hier:* Wirtschaftskrise
speaker	Referent, Redner
to switch one's attention to sth.	Aufmerksamkeit verlagern
to take a brief glance at	einen kurzen Blick werfen auf
to take place	stattfinden
time-worn	ausgedient
to weaken	schwächen
to work for	arbeiten für
worthwhile endeavours	lohnendes Bestreben/Bemühungen
to wrap things up	Sachen abwickeln

International relations | Internationale Beziehungen

Here we go

Peter hat eine interessante Besprechung im Außenhandelsministerium und nimmt dann an einer Ministerkonferenz teil, wobei er den Minister erneut trifft und einige nützliche Anleitungen in internationalen Geschäftspraktiken sammelt. Er begegnet auch Archie Atherton-Smythe, den er während seines Urlaubs in New York kennengelernt hat, und der ihn zu einer Wochenendparty in seinem Haus auf dem Land einlädt ...

Talk Talk Talk

(Ministry of Overseas Trade, London)

(Außenhandelsministerium, London)

P. Good morning! I **have an appointment** with Mr Carter.

P. Guten Morgen! Ich **habe eine Verabredung** mit Mr Carter.

Receptionist Just one moment. Let's see. Your name, please?

Empfangsdame Einen Moment bitte. Lassen Sie uns mal sehen. Ihr Name, bitte?

P. Brückner. Peter Brückner from ARGO Limited.

P. Brückner. Peter Brückner, von ARGO Limited.

R. Mr Brückner. Yes, here we are. Would you be so kind as to **sign the book** on this page. Here is a

R. Mr Brückner. Ja, hier steht es. Wären Sie so nett und würden hier **im Buch unterschreiben**. Hier ist

visitor's pass. Mr Carter's office is room 315 on the third floor. The lift is over there, on your right.

ein **Besucherausweis**. Mr Carters Büro ist Zimmer 315 im dritten Stock. Der Fahrstuhl ist dort hinten rechts.

P. Thank you... (on the third floor) Is this Mr Carter's office?

P. Danke ... (im dritten Stock) Ist das Mr Carters Büro?

Secretary Yes, it is. You must be Mr Brückner. Mr Carter is expecting you. Go right in please...

Sekretärin Ja, das ist es. Sie müssen Mr Brückner sein. Mr Carter erwartet Sie. Gehen Sie gleich hinein ...

P. Mr Carter? I'm Peter Brückner.

P. Mr Carter? Ich bin Peter Brückner.

Mr C. Delighted to meet you. Please come in and sit down. Mollie, fetch Mr Brückner and me some coffee, please. Now, Mr Brückner, let me describe what the Minister **has in mind** for you. That is, if you would be so good as to agree to attend our conference next week...

Mr C. Freut mich, Sie kennenzulernen. Bitte treten Sie ein und nehmen Sie Platz. Mollie, bringen Sie Mr Brückner und mir bitte Kaffee. Nun, Mr Brückner, lassen Sie mich beschreiben, was der Minister mit Ihnen **im Sinn hat**. Das heißt, wenn Sie so nett wären und an unserer Konferenz nächste Woche teilnehmen ...

Dos and Don'ts – A matter of form...

The British say that punctuality is the politeness of princes. Always be just a little early for business appointments. When meeting friends, it is usual to arrive at the agreed time – not earlier. Many people make a habit of being "fashionably late" for social gatherings.

Exercise 82

Füllen Sie die Lücken mit der korrekten Form von „must" oder „might"!

1. That _____ be our bus coming now. It's the number 29, isn't it?

2. The company _____ surely be on the way to recovery by now. Its first quarter results were very good indeed.

3. You _____ be very tired after that long journey.

4. I _____ be interested in investing in your company if you can support your optimism with convincing evidence of potential improvement.

5. They _____ be interested in buying the house after Mr Jenning's convincing sales talk.

6. You _____ be the new sales manager by all accounts.

Talk Talk Talk 42

Mr C. At **multinational conferences** such as this one, the minister likes to find people from within the British business community who have **foreign experience** or **foreign experts** who are working here in Britain. You belong to the latter category.

Mr C. Bei **multinationalen Konferenzen** wie dieser trifft der Minister gerne Leute aus der britischen Geschäftswelt, die über **Aus-landserfahrung** verfügen oder **Auslandsexperten**, die hier in England arbeiten. Sie gehören zur letzteren Kategorie.

P. But my experience in the **international arena** is very limited.

P. Aber meine Erfahrung auf der **internationalen Bühne** ist sehr begrenzt.

Mr C. That doesn't matter. You are a kind of bridge between the British business environment and Europe – I mean, of course, mainland Europe! The minister has also invited business people with **practical knowledge** of **dealing in American, Asian and African markets**.

Mr C. Das macht nichts. Sie bilden eine Art Brücke zwischen dem britischen Geschäftsumfeld und Europa – ich meine natürlich das europäische Festland! Der Minister hat ebenso Geschäftsleute mit **praktischen Handelserfahrungen auf amerikanischen, asiatischen und afrikanischen Märkten eingeladen**.

P. Are there differences?

P. Gibt es da Unterschiede?

Mr C. Huge ones. I'm told you have just returned from America. Didn't you notice any **differences in approach** between your contacts here and those you made over there?

Mr C. Riesige. Ich hörte, Sie kommen gerade aus Amerika zurück. Sind Ihnen keine **Unterschiede in der Handlungsweise** zwischen Ihren Kontakten hier und denen, die Sie dort gemacht haben, aufgefallen?

P. Well, yes, I suppose I did. I found American business people even more informal than the British.

P. Nun ja, ich denke schon. Ich fand amerikanische Geschäftsleute sogar noch zwangloser als die britischen.

Mr C. Exactly, although I think at our government level we are not that – what do the Americans say? – **laid back**!

Mr C. Genau, obwohl ich glaube, dass wir in Regierungskreisen nicht so – wie sagen die Amerikaner? – **relaxed** sind!

Background information

1. Many British people – even at an official level – still talk about Europe as if their country isn't part of the continent. The **"Continent"** is exactly that: the land mass across the English Channel ("We're off to the Continent on holiday tomorrow!"). The words "Europe" and "Continent" to signify Europe without the British Isles are so ingrained in the English language that their use does not necessarily signal opposition to concepts of a united Europe. In the same way, the United States is "across the pond" – the other side of the Atlantic Ocean!

2. Mr Carter uses an uncharacteristic slang expression here in describing the Americans – **laid-back**, meaning in this context "relaxed". Lately, the expression has also come to mean "lazy" or "indifferent" – but Mr Carter is obviously not describing Americans in this way. There are several expressions employing **"laid"** or **"lay"**, including:

laid up	ill, disabled by injury
to lay money on sth.	to wager, to make a bet
layabout	a workshy person who lives off the State or family members
to lay aside	to put aside for future use, to store
to lay down arms	to surrender, to give up
to lay off	to discharge (workers, usually in the long term)
to lay on	to plan, to arrange, to organize
to lay sth. on the table	to put an item on the agenda

Exercise 83

Wählen Sie den passenden Ausdruck mit „lay" oder „laid"!

1. They _____ when the opposing troops approached.

2. He caught a very nasty virus on his holiday in Africa and has been _____ for two months.

3. The government has drawn up new legislation, which will be _____ next week.

4. She is very worried about her son, who seems to have become a real _____.

5. The party was a great success; the Smiths _____ a magnificent feast.

False friends
Lay or lie?

The correct use of the verbs **"lay"** and **"lie"** has been debated for many years, and even the most eminent philologists can't agree among themselves. You're best advised to stay out of the argument and to remember just one basic rule: "lay" is normally a transitive verb (commanding an object) and "lie" an intransitive one (where no object is required). The difference is best seen in sentences such as:

"Lay down your weapon and lie on the floor!"

"I only wanted to lie down for ten minutes but I'd scarcely laid my head on the pillow than I slipped into a deep slumber."

This exercise is good for the back: lie out straight on the floor, lay a heavy book on your feet and then raise your legs twenty times!

Talk Talk Talk 43

Mr C. Ah, coffee! Thank you, Mollie. How do you take yours, Mr Schröder?

P. Brückner. The name's Brückner. Black, no sugar, please, Mr Carter.

Mr C. Ah, dear me, I'm so sorry. I'm not so good with German names. Now, if you were Chinese I'd have no problem.

P. You've **worked in China**?

Mr C. No, but I've had a lot of **dealings** with the Chinese, and I studied Mandarin at university.

P. Then you must be quite the expert.

Mr C. You know, you can study all you like in the classroom, but it's practical experience that counts. Take the Chinese. I came out of university quite fluent in Mandarin, but I hadn't a clue how to speak effectively to Chinese visitors. And this applies to all Asian countries, you know.

Mr C. Ah, Kaffee! Danke sehr, Mollie. Wie trinken Sie Ihren, Mr Schröder?

P. Brückner. Mein Name ist Brückner. Schwarz, ohne Zucker bitte, Mr Carter.

Mr C. Ach du meine Güte, entschuldigen Sie. Ich tue mich schwer mit deutschen Namen. Nun, wenn Sie Chinese wären, hätte ich kein Problem.

P. Sie haben **in China gearbeitet**?

Mr C. Nein, aber ich habe viele **Verhandlungen** mit Chinesen geführt und ich habe an der Universität Mandarin studiert.

P. Dann müssen Sie ein ziemlicher Experte sein.

Mr C. Wissen Sie, Sie können im Klassenzimmer studieren, was Sie wollen, aber es ist die praktische Erfahrung, die zählt. Nehmen Sie zum Beispiel die Chinesen. Ich habe die Universität mit ziemlich fließendem Mandarin verlassen, aber ich hatte keine Ahnung, wie ich wirklich mit den chinesischen Besuchern sprechen sollte. Und das gilt für alle asiatischen Länder, wissen Sie.

P. How do you mean exactly?

Mr C. You must **approach a meeting** with Chinese people in a very specific way. Remember, the Chinese, and of course the Japanese – but also other Asian peoples – **hate to lose face**, so confrontation, impatience and particularly anger are to be avoided **at all costs**. This can be very frustrating for a Westerner, who might be misled by polite smiles and expressions of enthusiasm or agreement that a deal has been sealed. Not a bit! It takes great patience and knowledge of the Asian character to achieve success in that **difficult market**.

P. How interesting. I have read similar assessments, but it's most interesting to hear this expressed at ministerial level.

Mr C. Don't mistake my comments for prejudice. Not a bit! In fact, I'm a great admirer of the **Asian business ethic**.

P. Wie meinen Sie das genau?

Mr C. Sie müssen **an eine Verhandlung** mit Chinesen auf eine ganz bestimmte Art **herangehen**. Denken Sie daran, dass die Chinesen, und natürlich die Japaner – aber auch andere asiatische Völker – **es hassen, ihr Gesicht zu verlieren**, also müssen Konfrontationen, Ungeduld und besonders Ärger **um jeden Preis** vermieden werden. Das kann für einen Abendländer sehr frustrierend sein, der durch höfliches Lächeln und Ausdrücke der Begeisterung oder Zustimmung zu dem falschen Schluss kommen könnte, dass die Vereinbarung besiegelt worden ist. Kein bisschen! Es erfordert große Geduld und gute Kenntnisse des asiatischen Charakters, um auf diesem **schwierigen Markt** Erfolg zu erzielen.

P. Wie interessant. Ich habe über ähnliche Einschätzungen gelesen, aber es ist höchst interessant, das auf ministerialer Ebene ausgedrückt zu hören.

Mr C. Verwechseln Sie meine Kommentare nicht mit Vorurteilen. Kein bisschen! Tatsächlich bin ich ein großer Bewunderer der **asiatischen Geschäftsethik**.

False friends

Mr Carter tells Peter he's "so sorry" that he's **"not so good"** with German names. He's not using a comparative form here – "so" in this context means **"very"**. And if something is so-so it's neither good nor bad, it's average. Peter tells Mr Carter he must be **"quite the expert"** after studying Mandarin at university – here also, the word "quite" has acquired the meaning of "very" – "You must be very much an expert". Note that when Mr Carter says he left university "quite" fluent in Mandarin, he is being modest about his ability, which in fact is "quite" impressive. But be careful! "Quite" can have the meaning of "moderately" or "reasonably", depending on the context and even on the inflection of the word. Peter tells Mr Carter that what he has had to say was **"most interesting"** – "most" here is not part of any comparative but also means "very". Said with sarcasm, of course, it can also mean the complete opposite.

Exercise 84

Schreiben Sie die folgenden Sätze um, ohne „quite" und „most" zu verwenden!

1. I didn't think the speaker was that good. His address to the forum, in fact, was quite dull.

   _____

2. He thinks he's quite the expert, but he doesn't really know that much.

   _____

3. I'm most obliged to you for your assistance, which has been quite beyond the bonds of friendship.

   _____

Talk Talk Talk  44

P. I am very interested in what you have to say because I believe ARGO is planning to **break into** the Asian market, difficult though it will be.

Mr C. Oh, there are other tips I could give you then, if we had the time. I'll pass on just one more most important one: in any encounter with an Asian businessperson, first **present your business card**. It's expected and appreciated. From then on in, you're on your own. Just remember to be polite and deferential at all times. Never, ever show impatience, irritation or anger. That will get you nowhere.

P. Will there be many participants from Asia at the conference?

Mr C. Oh yes, quite a few. I don't know if you class Russia as Asia, but Moscow is sending a very **high-level delegation**.

P. And how would you describe the best way of **doing business with Russians**?

P. Ich habe großes Interesse an dem, was Sie zu sagen haben, da ich glaube, dass ARGO plant, **in den asiatischen Markt einzudringen**, so schwer das auch sein wird.

Mr C. Oh, da könnte ich Ihnen noch weitere Tipps geben, wenn wir Zeit dazu hätten. Ich werde nur noch zu einem weiteren sehr wichtigen kommen: Bei jeder Begegnung mit einem asiatischen Geschäftsmann **überreichen Sie** zuerst **Ihre Visitenkarte**. Das wird erwartet und begrüßt. Von da an sind Sie auf sich selbst gestellt, solange Sie daran denken, die ganze Zeit über höflich und ehrerbietig zu sein. Zeigen Sie niemals Ungeduld, Gereiztheit oder Ärger. Das wird zu nichts führen.

P. Werden viele Teilnehmer aus Asien bei der Konferenz dabei sein?

Mr C. Oh ja, eine ganze Menge. Ich weiß nicht, ob Sie Russland zu Asien zählen, aber Moskau schickt eine **hochkarätige Delegation**.

P. Und was ist Ihrer Meinung nach die beste Art, **mit Russen Geschäfte zu machen**?

Mr C. Forget the past – you're dealing with a completely new generation and a totally new set of standards. Being a German, you would have no difficulty dealing with Russians. They are **highly motivated**, **innovative** and **progressive** business people.
But let's take a look now at the agenda. I don't want to take up more of your time than necessary. You must be a very busy man...

Mr C. Vergessen Sie die Vergangenheit – Sie verhandeln mit einer völlig neuen Generation und ganz neuen Grundsätzen. Als Deutscher hätten Sie keine Schwierigkeit, mit Russen zu verhandeln. Sie sind **hoch motivierte**, **innovative** und **progressive** Geschäftsleute.
Aber lassen Sie uns jetzt einen Blick auf die Tagesordnung werfen. Ich möchte nicht mehr von Ihrer Zeit in Anspruch nehmen als nötig. Sie müssen ein sehr beschäftigter Mann sein ...

Background information

There are undeniably differences to be observed in **business dealings** with people from distinct regions of the world, such as Asia. But **clichés** and, of course, **prejudices** should be avoided at all costs. A **correct appearance**, **politeness** and **consideration for a competitor's point of view** are invariably sufficient in any business situation. And, of course, business cards – not only in encounters with Asian business people.

False friends

Visitenkarte? The term "visiting card" is not generally used in the world of work. Historically, these were used to announce formal visits by important people. However, business cards are sometimes called by another name: calling cards.

Exercise 85

Füllen Sie die Lücken mit „ever" oder „never"!

1. Did you _____ see that film I recommended?

2. Have you _____ been to Paris? I can hardly believe it.

3. Did you _____ see such a thing in your life?

4. Well, I _____ ! I _____ expected to see the Smiths at this party.

5. She says that she's happier than _____ before now that she's married.

6. I'm _____ so pleased to see Tom as when he's sober.

Talk Talk Talk

(Peter's office)

P. Hello Lucy, how are you? **Any messages for me?**

L. Yes, a Mr Atherton-Smith called.

P. Atherton-Smythe? Good old Archie? What did he say?

L. He'll **call back** later this afternoon.

(Peters Büro)

P. Hallo Lucy, wie geht es Ihnen? **Irgendwelche Nachrichten für mich?**

L. Ja, ein Mr Atherton-Smith hat angerufen.

P. Atherton-Smythe? Der gute alte Archie? Was hat er gesagt?

L. Er wird im Laufe des Nachmittags **noch einmal anrufen**.

P. He didn't **leave a number**?

P. Hat er keine **Nummer hinterlassen**?

L. No, he said he was **running from one appointment to another** and didn't know where he'd be when you got back. He also said that unfortunately, he wasn't available on his mobile these days either.

L. Nein, er sagte, er würde **von einer Verabredung zur nächsten rasen** und wüsste nicht, wo er sein würde, wenn Sie zurückkommen. Er sagte auch, dass er zurzeit leider auch nicht auf seinem Handy erreichbar ist.

P. OK, I'll wait for his call... Well, hello, Steve! Long time no see, as you say. How are you? How's life?

P. In Ordnung, ich werde auf seinen Anruf warten ... Ja, hallo Steve! Lange nicht gesehen, wie man sagt. Wie geht es Ihnen? Was macht das Leben?

S. Peter! Hi! Good to see you again. How was New York? James has really put me through it. It seems the company just can't keep up with business now and we've really got to get down to some hard slogging. It's **all hands to the wheel. What are you up to** at the moment? Okay, you can tell me over a beer.
Lucy, when Mr Morgan comes back, tell him Peter here and I are having a late lunch or an early cocktail hour – I don't mind which.

S. Peter! Hi! Schön, Sie wieder zu sehen. Wie war New York? James hat mich wirklich hart rangenommen. Es scheint, als könnte die Firma gerade nicht mit dem Geschäft mithalten und wir müssen wirklich hart schuften. Es heißt **alle Mann ans Ruder. Woran arbeiten Sie** gerade? In Ordnung, das können Sie mir bei einem Drink erzählen.
Lucy, wenn Mr Morgan zurückkommt, sagen Sie ihm, Peter und ich nehmen ein spätes Mittagessen oder einen frühen Cocktail ein – egal was.

L. And Mr what's-his-name, Mr Brückner?

L. Und Mr „Wie-hieß-er-noch-mal", Mr Brückner?

P. Atherton-Smythe, Lucy. If he calls, tell him we're at the Bleke Street wine bar if he happens to be in the area anytime in the next hour or so.

S. So who exactly is this Atherton-Smythe fellow, Peter?

P. Archie? I met him in New York. He was there on business. We got along well with each other as soon as we started talking.

S. Oh, right. And did you happen to meet any other nice people over there?

P. Yes, Steve. Actually, Archie introduced me to a nice young lady called Janet…

P. Atherton-Smythe, Lucy. Wenn er anruft, sagen Sie ihm bitte, wir sind im Weinlokal in der Bleke Street, falls er in der nächsten Stunde oder so zufällig in der Gegend ist.

S. Wer ist denn dieser Atherton-Smythe, Peter?

P. Archie? Ich habe ihn in New York kennengelernt. Er war geschäftlich dort und wir sind ins Gespräch gekommen und haben uns auf Anhieb gut verstanden.

S. Aha. Und haben Sie vielleicht sonst noch nette Bekanntschaften gemacht?

P. Ja Steve. Tatsächlich hat mich Archie einer netten jungen Dame vorgestellt, Janet …

Background information

Rumour plays as big a role in British life as anywhere else, and the English language has at least three very expressive ways of describing how this information – or, often, misinformation – is passed on:

A little bird told me she's got a new boyfriend.
That new company is on the verge of bankruptcy – I heard it on the grapevine.
I heard on the bush telegraph that Charles and Mary are splitting up.
People who pass on information secretively in this way are called "rumourmongers".

Exercise 86

**Füllen Sie die Lücken unter Verwendung der Präpositionen „up"
und „down" sowie – wenn nötig – der korrekten Verbform!**

1. I don't know what Pete get _____ last night, but this
   morning he looks very tired indeed.
2. When it come _____ to it, all that matters to John is
   good health and a happy home life.
3. Mary is really _____ heart after being jilted so suddenly
   like that.
4. I like your suggestion, it suits me _____ the ground.
5. The boss is very much _____ that new employee, he
   doesn't like him at all.
6. You have presented us with a very difficult problem here. I can't
   remember ever be _____ anything so complicated.

Talk Talk Talk  45

(The Bleeke Street wine bar)	(Das Weinlokal in der Bleeke Street)
S. Shall we **split** a bottle of that excellent Nuits Saint George?	**S.** Sollen wir uns eine Flasche dieses exzellenten Nuits St. George **teilen**?
P. Fine by me, Steve.	**P. Gerne**, Steve.
S. James Morgan obviously has plans for you, my friend. You'll be	**S.** James Morgan hat offensichtlich Pläne mit Ihnen, mein Freund. Über

in government before long, **mark my words**.

P. You forget two important things, Steve. I'm German. And I'm not at all interested in politics. ARGO is my life at the moment.

S. And is no one likely to be sharing that life soon?

P. Like who?

S. Janet? Or Melissa? Or someone else entirely?

P. Melissa? Well…

P. Hi, Archie! How good to see you again! You **got the message** I left at the office? Come, join us in a glass of this excellent wine. Steve, this is the Archie I've been telling you about. Archie, **this is my colleague** and good friend Steve Blackman.

A. **I'm very pleased to make your acquaintance.** Any friend of Peter's is a friend of mine. Have you settled back into life in Britain

kurz oder lang werden Sie in der Regierung sitzen, **denken Sie an meine Worte**.

P. Steve, Sie vergessen zwei wichtige Dinge. Ich bin Deutscher. Und ich bin überhaupt nicht an Politik interessiert. ARGO ist derzeit mein Leben.

S. Und wird niemand dieses Leben bald teilen?

P. Wer könnte das denn sein?

S. Janet? Oder Melissa? Oder jemand ganz anderes?

P. Melissa? Na ja, …

P. Hi, Archie! Wie schön, Sie wiederzusehen! Sie haben die **Nachricht bekommen**, die ich im Büro hinterlassen habe? Kommen Sie, leisten Sie uns Gesellschaft bei einem Glas dieses ausgezeichneten Weins. Steve, das ist der Archie, von dem ich Ihnen erzählt habe. Archie, **dies** ist **mein Kollege** und guter Freund Steve Blackman.

A. **Sehr erfreut, Ihre Bekanntschaft zu machen.** Jeder Freund von Peter ist auch ein Freund von mir. Peter, haben Sie sich nach

after your holidays in New York, Peter?

P. No problem, Archie. I think I'm a European at heart.

A. Well, I certainly am. I like the Americans, and I like and admire their country, but I just can't keep up with their pace of life. I **ran for cover** immediately after I got back and made for my place in Buckinghamshire. Been there for the past few days. Peter, that's the real reason I called you. I'm having a house party next weekend. **Can you make it?** Your friend, too, of course, if he cares to.

S. That's very kind of you, but I have to return to Glasgow **at the double** now Peter's **back in harness**.

P. Of course I'd like to come, Archie. But first let's talk about how you got on in New York. **I hope the trip was worth it for you and your company**...

dem Urlaub in New York wieder eingelebt in das britische Leben?

P. Kein Problem, Archie. Ich glaube ich bin ein waschechter Europäer.

A. Nun, das bin ich sicherlich. Ich mag die Amerikaner und ich mag und bewundere ihr Land, aber ich kann einfach nicht mit ihrem Lebensrhythmus mithalten. Ich **brachte mich** sofort **in Sicherheit**, als ich zurück war und machte mich auf den Weg zu meinem Haus in Buckinghamshire. Dort bin ich die letzten paar Tage gewesen. Peter, das ist der eigentliche Grund, weshalb ich Sie angerufen hatte. Nächstes Wochenende gebe ich eine Hausparty. **Können Sie das einrichten?** Ihr Freund ist natürlich auch eingeladen, wenn er möchte.

S. Das ist sehr nett von Ihnen, aber ich muss jetzt **doppelt so schnell** nach Glasgow zurückkehren, jetzt wo Peter **wieder in der Tretmühle** ist.

P. Ich komme natürlich gerne, Archie. Aber zuerst einmal lassen Sie uns darüber sprechen, wie es Ihnen in New York ergangen ist. **Ich hoffe, die Reise hat sich für Sie und Ihre Firma gelohnt** ...

Background information

1. The British probably conclude more business deals in social encounters than in the formal surroundings of offices. One economics researcher has estimated that deals worth nearly one billion pounds sterling a year are made on British golf courses alone! Restaurants, bars and clubs also witness big business at work within their walls. And it's certain that Archie's country house party will be more than just an occasion for sampling bottles from his wine cellar!

2. Steve jokes that Peter has a future in politics, adding: "Mark my words". There are several everyday expressions using "mark", some of them especially useful in business situations:

to lose one's mark	to miss the chance of doing business
to make one's mark	to make a favourable impression
to mark down	to reduce the price
markdown	the amount by which a retail price is reduced
markup	the amount added to the cost of a product in order to reach a profitable retail price; the gross profit
to mark time	to remain stationary but in readiness (from the military term describing the action of marching on the spot without advancing)
on the mark	accurate
on your marks	under starter's orders in a race: "On your marks, get set, go!"
up to the mark	up to standard, satisfactory (usually used in the negative)

Exercise 87

Füllen Sie die Lücken mit der richtigen Wendung mit "mark"!

1. She quickly _____ in the office and won rapid promotion.
2. Your calculation of the _____ on that new product was very accurate – right _____.
3. His work performance has not been very satisfactory lately, he's not been at all _____.
4. The runners are _____, and they're off!
5. After an impressive run of success, the company appears to have ground to a standstill. It is just _____.
6. They could so easily have sealed that deal but by holding out for a higher price they _____.

Talk Talk Talk  46

(Ministry of Overseas Trade)

(Außenhandelsministerium)

Mr C. Ah, Mr Brückner! Welcome, welcome! How good to see you again. This way, please. The minister is **receiving guests** in the **conference room**... Minister, this is Mr Brückner – but I'm sure you remember him.

Mr C. Ah, Mr Brückner! Willkommen, willkommen! Wie schön, Sie wiederzusehen. Bitte hier entlang. Der Minister **empfängt** gerade die **Gäste** im **Konferenzraum** ... Herr Minister, das ist Mr Brückner – aber ich bin sicher, Sie erinnern sich an ihn.

M. Yes, indeed. Thank you so much for agreeing to attend, Mr

M. Ja, in der Tat. Vielen Dank, dass Sie sich bereit erklärt haben,

Brückner. **I value your participation highly.**

P. I'm honoured to have been invited, Minister.

M. We'll be getting under way shortly, but please **let me introduce you to** the president of the Central and South American Trade Organization, Rodrigo Jaime de Calares. Señor Jaime, **may I introduce** Mr Peter Brückner from ARGO Limited. Mr Brückner is a **shining example** of what we were just talking about – the necessity **of cross-border**, practical integration of **non-national business acumen**. Mr Brückner, you see, is German but working for a British concern which is now expanding into the North American market. He is a living example of one of the **chief items on our agenda** here. I hope you don't mind being described in those terms, Mr Brückner?

P. Well, I'm not sure if I grasped the full meaning of the role you have given me, but I have complete faith in your judgment, of course, minister.

beizuwohnen, Mr Brückner. **Ich schätze Ihre Teilnahme sehr.**

P. Es ist mir eine Ehre, eingeladen worden zu sein, Herr Minister.

M. Nun, wir werden in Kürze beginnen, doch **lassen Sie mich Sie** dem Präsidenten der Handelsorganisation von Zentral- und Südamerika, Rodrigo Jaime de Calares, **vorstellen**. Señor Jaime, **darf ich vorstellen**, Peter Brückner von ARGO Limited. Mr Brückner ist ein **leuchtendes Beispiel** dafür, worüber wir gerade gesprochen haben – die Notwendigkeit der **Grenzüberschreitung**, praktische Integration von **nicht-nationalem Geschäftsscharfsinn**. Sehen Sie, Mr Brückner ist Deutscher, arbeitet aber für eine britische Firma, die jetzt auf dem nordamerikanischen Markt expandiert. Er ist ein lebendes Beispiel für einen der **Hauptpunkte auf unserer Tagesordnung** hier. Ich hoffe, es stört Sie nicht, anhand dieser Begriffe beschrieben zu werden, Mr Brückner?

P. Nun, ich bin mir nicht sicher, ob ich die ganze Bedeutung der Rolle, die Sie mir gegeben haben, erfasst habe, aber ich habe natürlich völliges Vertrauen in Ihr Urteilsvermögen, Herr Minister.

M. Then **let me leave you with** Señor Jaime while I prepare for the opening of the conference.

J. Do you know Central or South America, Mr Brückner?

P. Unfortunately not. In fact, I've only just returned from my first visit to North America.

J. I think you'd feel very much at home in my country, Argentina, and anywhere else in the region. We very much **value** the **German style of doing business**.

P. And that is?

J. Hard, direct – but always correct. You say no, you mean no. When you say yes, we know we have a **contract**. In our region, yes can often mean no. We hate to say no – but that is a very bad **trait** in business.

P. Yes – I mean no. Oh dear, Señor Jaime, I think you've confused me a bit there.

M. Dann **lasse ich Sie jetzt mit** Señor Jaime **allein**, während ich mich auf die Eröffnung der Konferenz vorbereite.

J. Kennen Sie Zentral- oder Südamerika, Mr Brückner?

P. Leider nicht. Eigentlich bin ich gerade erst von meinem ersten Besuch in Nordamerika zurückgekehrt.

J. Ich glaube, Sie würden sich in Argentinien, meiner Heimat, sehr wohl fühlen und überall sonst in der Region. Wir **schätzen die deutsche Art, Geschäfte zu machen**, sehr.

P. Und das ist?

J. Hart, direkt – aber immer korrekt. Wenn sie Nein sagen, dann meinen sie auch Nein. Wenn sie Ja sagen, wissen wir, dass wir einen **Vertrag** haben. In unserer Region kann Ja oft Nein bedeuten. Wir hassen es, Nein zu sagen – aber das ist bei Geschäften ein sehr schlechter **Charakterzug**.

P. Ja – ich meine nein. Oh je, Señor Jaime, ich glaube, da haben Sie mich ein bisschen durcheinandergebracht.

J. Another Latin American **tactic** – ah, but **the conference is about to start**. I shall explain everything later, but I am not promising you will understand...

J. Eine weitere lateinamerikanische **Taktik** – ah, aber **die Konferenz fängt gleich an**. Ich werde später alles erklären, aber ich verspreche Ihnen nicht, dass Sie es verstehen werden ...

Background information

In **business dealings** in Spain, Central and South America, don't be caught out by the flamboyant enthusiasm of Spanish farewells. "Hasta pronto" ("See you shortly") does not mean you will be invited back the following day to seal a deal – treat all Spanish forms of farewell ("Hasta entonces", "Hasta luego") as versions of "Auf Wiedersehen" and you won't be disappointed by false hopes.

Exercise 88

Füllen Sie die Lücken mit der korrekten Zeitform der angegebenen Verben!

1. The company recently `set up` _____ a branch office in Glasgow to serve the Scottish market.

2. I `be` _____ in London for several months now, but I still `not have` _____ the time to tour the city's sights.

3. Jane told me she `be` _____ to Paris only once in her life. She `go` _____ when she was a student.

4. He told me he have _____ a terrible time when he go

_____ to Russia last year.

5. They both fall _____ ill with food poisoning after they

 visit _____ that new seafood restaurant on the harbour-

side.

6. He just called to say he fall _____ ill and won't be able

to complete the project he start _____ last month.

Talk Talk Talk  47

(ARGO offices, London)

(ARGO-Büros, London)

J. Peter, how did the foreign trade conference go? I've already had a call from the Ministry to thank us for sending you. The minister appears to have been very pleased by your attendance.

J. Peter, wie ist die Außenhandelskonferenz gelaufen? Ich habe schon einen Anruf vom Ministerium erhalten, um uns zu danken, dass wir Sie geschickt haben. Der Minister scheint von Ihrer Teilnahme sehr erfreut gewesen zu sein.

P. I found it very instructive and felt honoured to meet government representatives and business people from so many different countries. I made what might be a very useful contact for us with the president of the Central and South American Trade Organization.

P. Ich fand sie sehr lehrreich und fühlte mich sehr geehrt, Regierungsverteter und Geschäftsleute aus so vielen verschiedenen Ländern zu treffen. Ich habe einen Kontakt geknüpft, der für uns sehr nützlich sein könnte, mit dem Präsidenten der Handelsorganisation von Zentral- und Südamerika.

J. Good for you! Why don't you take off early for the weekend? You must be **all in** after all this hectic activity.

J. Gut gemacht! Warum gehen Sie nicht frühzeitig ins Wochenende? Sie müssen **ganz erledigt** sein, nach all den hektischen Aktivitäten.

P. I was about to ask you if you would mind if I **took** this afternoon **off**. I've been invited to a friend's place in the country for the weekend.

P. Ich wollte Sie gerade fragen, ob Sie etwas dagegen hätten, wenn ich mir heute Nachmittag **freinehme**. Ich bin über das Wochenende auf den Landsitz eines Freundes eingeladen.

J. By all means, Peter. Where is this place?

J. Aber natürlich, Peter. Wo ist dieser Landsitz?

P. Somewhere in Buckinghamshire. I have to find out first how to get there.

P. Irgendwo in Buckinghamshire. Ich muss erst noch herausfinden, wie man da hinkommt.

J. Lovely county, and I'm sure you'll have a great time. Just the time of year for some shooting. Does your friend shoot?

J. Schöne Grafschaft, und ich bin sicher, Sie werden eine tolle Zeit verbringen. Gerade die richtige Jahreszeit zum Jagen. Jagt Ihr Freund?

P. I don't think so. His hobby seems to be his wine cellar.

P. Das glaube ich nicht. Sein Weinkeller scheint sein Hobby zu sein.

J. You lucky chap – you'll at least be **well stocked** in that quarter...

J. Sie Glückspilz – Sie werden zumindest diesbezüglich **gut versorgt** werden ...

(Walsingham Manor, Buckinghamshire)

(Walsingham Manor, Buckinghamshire)

P. This must be the place. Through these gates, please.

Taxidriver This is quite a manor, guv. Your pal a millionaire or something? Rock star, perhaps?

P. No. He's in **banking**.

A. Peter, my dear boy. Welcome, welcome. Leave the taxi to me. Eight pounds? Here's ten, my good man. Thank you for delivering my good friend safe and sound...

P. Das muss das Haus sein. Durch diese Tore, bitte.

Taxifahrer Ganz schön großer Kasten, Chef! Ist Ihr Freund ein Millionär oder so etwas? Vielleicht Rockstar?

P. Nein, er ist im **Bankwesen** tätig.

A. Peter, mein lieber Junge. Willkommen, willkommen. Überlassen Sie mir das Taxi. Acht Pfund? Hier sind zehn, guter Mann. Danke, dass Sie meinen Freund gut und wohlbehalten hier abgeliefert haben ...

Exercise 89

Unterstreichen Sie die passenden Präpositionen!

1. He took up / on / with / to a very difficult task when he accepted that job.

2. She took him up / on / to / over their first meeting, and now they are married.

3. They didn't perform that job very well and were thoroughly taken to / up / on / over task by the boss.

4. The salesman really took them on / over / with / for a ride by selling them that beaten-up car for three thousand pounds.

5. He feels his abilities aren't being properly recognized and believes he is being taken with / on / for / by granted.

6. I don't think it's very fair to take her name for / in / at / under vain like that.

Talk Talk Talk  48

A. You're just in time for a cocktail before dinner. Most of the other guests are here. Alfred! Take Mr Brückner's coat and hat, please. Alfred is my new butler, but he's rather ancient and slow.

P. A butler! Archie, you do live well.

A. Not as well as my grandfather, who left me this little place and the company. My father, God rest his soul, frittered a lot away at cards and on the racecourse. I'm trying to claw it all back... Ah, here's the man who is helping me. My **financial adviser**, Solomon Gold – his name sums him up, he's **worth his weight in gold** to me. Sol, you old rascal, meet my friend Peter Brückner. Peter, this is Solomon Gold. If you need **advice** in any financial matter turn to him.

A. Sie kommen gerade richtig zu einem Cocktail vor dem Abendessen. Die meisten der anderen Gäste sind hier. Alfred! Nehmen Sie bitte Mr Brückners Mantel und Hut. Alfred ist mein neuer Butler, aber er ist ziemlich alt und langsam.

P. Ein Butler! Archie, Sie leben aber gut.

A. Nicht so gut wie mein Großvater, der mir dieses kleine Haus und die Firma hinterlassen hat. Mein Vater, Gott gebe seiner Seele Frieden, hat eine Menge beim Karten spielen und auf der Rennbahn verplempert. Ich versuche, mir alles zurückzuholen ... Ah, da ist der Mann, der mir dabei hilft. Mein **Finanzberater**, Solomon Gold – sein Name sagt alles, für mich ist er **sein Gewicht in Gold wert**. Sol, Sie alter Schurke, lernen Sie meinen Freund Peter Brückner kennen.

Peter, das ist Solomon Gold. Wenn Sie in irgendeiner finanziellen Angelegenheit **Rat** brauchen, wenden Sie sich an ihn.

S. Oh, I haven't always been so reliable with that advice as I've proved with you, Archie. Peter, I'm delighted to meet you...

S. Oh, ich bin nicht immer so verlässlich mit diesem Rat gewesen, wie ich mich bei Ihnen erwiesen habe, Archie. Peter, es freut mich, Sie kennenzulernen ...

A. And over here, Peter, is James Duvall – do you remember him from New York? The film producer Duvall? He's come to look my little place over as a possible location for that period drama he was telling us about.

A. Und hier drüben, Peter, ist James Duvall – erinnern Sie sich an ihn aus New York? Der Filmproduzent Duvall? Er ist gekommen, um zu sehen, ob mein bescheidenes Zuhause als möglicher Platz für diesen Kostümfilm, von dem er uns erzählt hat, infrage kommt.

J. And to look you over too, Archie. I think I might have a good role for you. Hello, Peter! Good to see you again.

J. Und auch, um bei Ihnen vorbeizuschauen, Archie. Ich glaube, ich hätte da eine gute Rolle für Sie. Hallo Peter! Schön, Sie wiederzusehen.

A. Peter, I've got somebody here who'll make you even more nostalgic. See that pretty girl over there by the fireplace?

A. Peter, es ist jemand hier, der Sie sogar noch nostalgischer stimmen wird. Sehen Sie das hübsche Mädchen da drüben am Kamin?

P. Why yes, but it can't be – can it?

P. Aber ja, aber das kann nicht sein – oder?

A. Janet! Come here, my dear! Look who's come for dinner!

J. Peter!

P. Janet! But how...?

A. Has nothing to do with you, dear boy. Janet has **taken over** the Royal Star Banking **account**. She's in England to **acquaint herself with the operation** and then, because of her near-fluent German, is off to Germany next week to **look at cooperation possibilities** there.

P. Janet, I left New York without clearing up that misunderstanding at Tiffany's.

J. You don't have to explain, Peter. Archie told me the whole story.

P. And now you're off to Germany?

J. To Dresden.

P. I'm going back to Hamburg next week for Christmas and New Year. But I know Dresden very well. My family is originally from Saxony.

A. Janet! Kommen Sie her, meine Liebe! Sehen Sie mal, wer zum Essen kommt!

J. Peter!

P. Janet! Aber wie ...?

A. Hat nichts mit Ihnen zu tun, mein Lieber. Janet hat die Royal Star Banking als **Kunden übernommen**. Sie ist in England, um **sich mit der Operation vertraut** zu **machen**. Und dann fährt sie wegen ihres beinahe fließenden Deutsch nächste Woche nach Deutschland, um sich dort **nach Kooperationsmöglichkeiten umzusehen**.

P. Janet, ich verließ New York, ohne das Missverständnis bei Tiffany's aufzuklären.

J. Sie müssen nichts erklären, Peter. Archie hat mir die ganze Geschichte erzählt.

P. Und jetzt sind Sie auf dem Weg nach Deutschland?

J. Nach Dresden.

P. Ich fahre nächste Woche zu Weihnachten und Neujahr nach Hamburg zurück. Aber ich kenne Dresden sehr gut. Meine Familie kommt ursprünglich aus Sachsen.

J. I'm told Christmas is a lovely time to be there.

J. Man sagt, zu Weihnachten ist es dort sehr schön.

P. Dresden has a wonderful Christmas market. May I show it to you? Dresden is just a few hours from Hamburg by train.

P. Dresden hat einen wunderschönen Weihnachtsmarkt. Darf ich ihn Ihnen zeigen? Dresden ist mit dem Zug nur ein paar Stunden von Hamburg entfernt.

J. This is where we met isn't it, Peter? A train journey!...

J. So haben wir uns kennengelernt, nicht wahr, Peter? Auf einer Bahnfahrt! ...

 **Vocabulary**

account	*hier:* Kunde, auch Bericht, Rechnung, Konto
to acquaint oneself with the operation	sich mit der Operation vertraut machen
agenda	Tagesordnung
all hands to the wheel	alle Mann an die Ruder
to approach a meeting	an eine Verhandlung herangehen
Asian business market	asiatischer Geschäftsmarkt
at all costs	um jeden Preis
attendance	Teilnahme
back in harness	wieder in der Tretmühle
banking	Bankwesen
to be all in	völlig erledigt sein
to be worth (one's) weight in gold	sein Gewicht in Gold wert sein
to break into the Asian market	in den asiatischen Markt eindringen
by all means	aber natürlich
to call back	zurückrufen
Can you make it?	Können Sie das einrichten? (Verabredung)
chief items	Hauptpunkte
conference room	Konferenzraum

contact	Kontakt
cross-border	grenzüberschreitend
to deal in American markets	auf amerikanischen Märkten verhandeln
differences in approach	Unterschiede in der Handlungsweise/Methode
difficult market	schwieriger Markt
to do business with sb.	mit jmd. Geschäfte machen
fine by me	gerne
foreign experience	Auslandserfahrung
foreign expert	Auslandsexperte
to get the message	die Nachricht erhalten
Good for you!	Gut gemacht!
to hang on to	dran bleiben
to hate to lose face	es hassen, das Gesicht zu verlieren
to have an appointment	eine Verabredung haben
high-level delegation	hochkarätige Delegation/Abordnung
highly motivated	hoch motiviert
How did the conference go?	Wie ist die Konferenz gelaufen?
I'm very pleased to make your acquaintance.	Sehr erfreut, Ihre Bekanntschaft zu machen.
initials	Initialen
innovative	innovativ
instructive	lehrreich
international arena	internationaler Schauplatz
laid back	relaxed
to leave a number	eine Nummer hinterlassen
to look at cooperation possibilities	sich nach Kooperationsmöglichkeiten umsehen
to make a useful contact	einen nützlichen Kontakt knüpfen
Mark my words!	Denken Sie an meine Worte!
May I introduce ...	Darf ich vorstellen ...
message	Nachricht
multinational conference	multinationale Konferenz
non-national business acumen	nicht-nationaler Geschäftsscharfsinn
occurrence	Vorfall

practical knowledge	praktische Erfahrung
to present one's business card	seine Visitenkarte überreichen
progressive	progressiv, fortschrittlich
to run for cover	sich in Sicherheit bringen, verstecken
to run from one appointment to another	von einer Verabredung zur nächsten rasen
shining example	leuchtendes Beispiel
to sign the book	im Buch unterschreiben
to split	*hier:* teilen
tactic	Taktik
to take off	*hier:* sich freinehmen
to take over	übernehmen
Tell me another!	Sie können mir viel erzählen!
The conference is about to start.	Die Konferenz fängt gleich an.
This is my colleague.	Dies ist mein Kollege.
trait	Charakterzug
visitor's pass	Besucherausweis
well stocked	gut versorgt
What are you up to?	Woran arbeiten Sie gerade?/Was machen Sie gerade?

At a glance:
Phrases for business
correspondence |
Auf einen Blick:
Formulierungen für die
Geschäftskorrespondenz

Letterhead

Address

Dear Sir or Madam

Dear Mr.../Mrs...

For the attention of (FOA)

Reference (RE)

I am writing in response to your invitation...

This is to inform you that...

I regret to inform you that...

Briefkopf

Anrede

Sehr geehrte Damen und Herren

Sehr geehrte/r Herr .../Frau ...

zu Händen (z. Hd.)

Betreff

Ich schreibe Ihnen als Antwort auf Ihre Einladung ...

Hiermit möchten wir Sie darüber informieren, dass ...

Ich bedauere, Ihnen mitteilen zu müssen, dass ...

Conventional endings

Many thanks for your assistance.

My thanks/Thank you very much for your kind offer.

Please find enclosed ...

Should you require any further information/If you need more information, please do not hesitate to contact us.

Should you have any further queries on the subject, please feel free to call me.

I look forward to hearing from you soon.

I look forward to meeting you in person.

Schlussformeln

Vielen Dank für Ihre Hilfe.

Danke für Ihr freundliches Angebot.

Anbei finden Sie/Als Anlage senden wir Ihnen ...

Sollten Sie noch weitere Informationen benötigen, bitte zögern Sie nicht, uns zu kontaktieren.

Wenn Sie Fragen zu diesem Thema haben, rufen Sie mich bitte an.

Ich freue mich, bald von Ihnen zu hören.

Ich freue mich darauf, Sie persönlich kennenzulernen.

We look forward to your visit.	Wir freuen uns auf Ihren Besuch.
Yours sincerely,	Mit freundlichen Grüßen *(bei persönlicher Anrede)*
Yours faithfully,	Mit freundlichen Grüßen *(bei unpersönlicher Anrede)*
Encl./Encls.	Anlage/n
Enquiry	**Anfrage**
We have seen your advertisement in the (name of journal)	Wir haben Ihre Anzeige/Annonce in ... gesehen
We learned from... that you are manufacturers of...	Wir haben von ... erfahren, dass Sie Hersteller von ... sind.
Please quote your lowest/best prices for...	Bitte nennen Sie uns Ihre günstigsten Preise für ...
Please send us a **quotation** for...	Bitte machen Sie uns ein **Angebot** über ...
Please let us know what your **terms of busines** are.	Bitte nennen Sie uns Ihre **Geschäftsbedingungen**.
We should like to have your illustrated catalogue/brochure and latest price list.	Für die Zusendung Ihres illustrierten Katalogs/einer Broschüre/der gegenwärtigen Preisliste, wären wir Ihnen dankbar.
We should be pleased if you would send us particulars of...	Wir wären Ihnen dankbar, wenn Sie uns Einzelheiten zu ... senden würden.
We hope to hear from you soon.	Wir hoffen, bald von Ihnen zu hören.
Offer	**Angebot**
Thank you for your enquiry.	Vielen Dank für Ihre Anfrage.

In response to your **enquiry** of...,
we enclose details of our terms of
sale and our price list.

Wir beziehen uns auf Ihre **Anfrage**
vom ... und senden Ihnen in der
Anlage Einzelheiten zu unseren
Verkaufsbedingungen sowie unsere
Preisliste.

Please find enclosed our brochure
and current price list.

Als Anlage finden Sie unsere
Broschüre und aktuelle Preisliste.

We are pleased to quote as follows:

Wir machen Ihnen folgendes
Angebot:

We thank you for your enquiry of...,
and are pleased to submit the following offer/to quote as follows:

Wir danken Ihnen für Ihre Anfrage
vom ... und erlauben uns, Ihnen folgendes Angebot zu machen:

This offer is subject to acceptance.

Dieses Angebot gilt bei Bestellung.

Order

We would like to/We are pleased to
place the following order:

Auftrag

Wir möchten gerne wie folgt bestellen:

We thank you for your offer of...,
and are pleased to place the following order:

Wir danken Ihnen für Ihr Angebot
vom ... und bestellen wie folgt:

Please enter the following order for
immediate delivery:

Hiermit machen wir folgende
Bestellung mit der Bitte um umge-
hende Lieferung:

Please send us the following items
by return.

Bitte senden Sie uns umgehend die
folgenden Posten:

Please find enclosed our order No...
for...

Anbei unsere Bestellung Nr. ...
über ...

Confirmation

We thank you for your order of...

Auftragsbestätigung

Wir danken Ihnen für Ihre Bestellung
vom ...

We are pleased to confirm the receipt of your order.

Hiermit bestätigen wir dankend den Eingang Ihrer Bestellung.

We are pleased to confirm your order.

Wir haben uns über Ihren Auftrag gefreut.

Delivery

These goods were sent on...

Lieferung

Die Waren sind am ... verschickt worden.

We are pleased to advise you that your order of... was **despatched** by rail this morning.

Wir freuen uns, Ihnen mitteilen zu können, dass die Waren laut Ihrem Auftrag vom ... heute Morgen mit dem Zug **ausgeliefert** wurden.

Non-delivery

The delivery of our order No.... is now ten days **overdue**.

Lieferverzug

Die Lieferung unserer Bestellnummer ... ist schon zehn Tage **überfällig**.

Having waited three weeks for delivery, I regret to say that your **delay in delivery** is causing us serious inconvenience.

Nachdem wir nun schon drei Wochen vergeblich auf unsere Waren gewartet haben, bringt uns Ihr **Lieferverzug** in eine schwierige Lage.

We trust you will see to the delivery as soon as possible.

Wir hoffen, dass Sie die Lieferung schnellstens auf den Weg bringen werden.

Due to a shortage of qualified labour/a strike/a fire in our factory, we shall require... to complete the order.

Wegen eines Mangels an qualifizierten Arbeitskräften/eines Streiks/eines Brandes in unserer Fabrik werden wir noch ... brauchen, um Ihren Auftrag auszuführen.

We are sorry that a slight delay will be unavoidable/inevitable.

Eine geringfügige Verzögerung ist leider unvermeidlich.

Payment

Enclosed please find invoice No...
for the goods delivered on...

The total amount **payable** is...

Zahlung

Anbei finden Sie Rechnung Nr. ...
für die am ... gelieferten Waren.

Der **zu zahlende** Gesamtbetrag
ist ...

Delays in payment

We are writing to remind you/We
regret to have to remind you that the
settlement of the above invoice
No... is already four weeks overdue.

According to our records, the above
amount of €... of/dated ... has not
yet been paid/settled.

Would you please **settle your balance,** which has been outstanding
since...

Obviously your delay in payment
must be due to an oversight.

We look forward to receiving your
remittance asap.

We shall be obliged to take legal
action if you don't attend to this
account immediately.

Mahnung

Wir möchten Sie (mit Bedauern)
daran erinnern, dass Rechnung Nr.
... bereits 4 Wochen überfällig ist.

Unseren Unterlagen zufolge, ist der
Betrag von ... € /vom ... noch nicht
beglichen.

Würden Sie bitte Ihre **Rechnung
begleichen**, die seit ... offen steht.

Wir nehmen an, dieser Zahlungsverzug beruht auf einem Versehen
Ihrerseits.

Wir freuen uns, Ihre **Überweisung**
schnellstmöglich zu erhalten.

Wir sehen uns gezwungen, rechtliche Schritte einzuleiten, wenn Sie
Ihre Rechnung nicht umgehend
begleichen.

Replies to a letter of reminder

I apologise for not clearing the balance earlier.

Antwort auf eine Mahnung

Bitte entschuldigen Sie, dass wir
unsere Rechnung nicht früher beglichen haben.

Sorry I didn't pay you earlier.

Bitte entschuldigen Sie die Verzögerung.

Please accept our apologies for the delay.

Bitte akzeptieren Sie unsere Entschuldigung.

We should like another month to settle.

Wir möchten Sie um einen Monat Aufschub bitten.

Complaints
Damaged goods

I am writing to complain about…

Beschwerden
Beschädigte Waren

Ich möchte mich über … beschweren.

We thank you for your promptness in delivering the goods. We regret, however, to have to inform you that the PCs were in a badly damaged state on arrival.

Wir danken Ihnen für Ihre prompte Lieferung, doch wir müssen Ihnen leider mitteilen, dass die PCs bei uns in einem stark beschädigten Zustand ankamen.

We assume that the damage is due to bad/wrong/inadequate packing.

Der Schaden ist anscheinend auf schlechte/falsche/ungenügende Verpackung zurückzuführen.

Please send us replacement for the damaged goods as soon as possible.

Bitte senden Sie uns so schnell wie möglich Ersatz für die beschädigten Waren.

Wrong quality

After careful examination of the goods, we found that they were faulty/did not match the samples/ were of inferior quality.

Falsche Qualität

Nach genauer Prüfung der Waren stellten wir fest, dass sie beschädigt waren/nicht den Probemustern entsprachen/von schlechter Qualität waren.

The products are not satisfactory.

Die Qualität der Produkte war nicht zufriedenstellend.

Wrong quantity
On checking the contents, we noticed a shortage/surplus of…

Falsche Menge
Nach Prüfung der Lieferung stellten wir fest, dass uns zu wenig/zu viele …. gesandt wurden.

Error in invoice
Our invoice No…. for… has been **debited** twice.

We would like a refund.

Your **statement of account**, which we received yesterday, appears to have a number of errors which refer to items we did not order.

Fehler in der Rechnung
Unsere Rechnung Nr. … wurde zweimal abgebucht.

Wir bitten um Gutschrift.

Der **Kontoauszug**, den Sie uns gestern zusandten, scheint eine Reihe von Fehlern zu enthalten, die sich auf Waren beziehen, die wir nicht bestellt haben.

Banking
Customer
We have our **business account** with…

Kindly inform us about your conditions regarding **interest rates, service charges** and **handling fees**.

As an initial deposit on our new account, we enclose a cheque for…

We enclose specimen signatures of the people authorized to sign cheques on our behalf.

As account No… is no longer needed, we would ask you to close it and to transfer the closing balance to

Bankangelegenheiten
Kunde
Wir haben unser **Geschäftskonto** bei …

Bitte teilen Sie uns Ihre Bedingungen hinsichtlich **Zinsen, Kontoführungs-** und **Bearbeitungsgebühren** mit.

Als Ersteinlage unseres neu eröffneten Kontos finden Sie anbei einen Scheck über …

Wir fügen Probeunterschriften der zur Unterzeichnung von Schecks berechtigen Personen bei.

Da Konto Nr. … nicht länger benötigt wird, bitten wir Sie um Auflösung und Transfer des

account No....

Endsaldos auf Konto Nr. ...

I would be grateful if you could arrange to **grant** me **a loan** of €... for a period of three years.

Ich wäre Ihnen dankbar, wenn Sie mir **einen Kredit** über ... € für einen Zeitraum von drei Jahren **gewähren** könnten.

You will have to pay **bank charges** if your account is overdrawn.

Sie müssen **Bankgebühren** zahlen, wenn Sie Ihr Konto überziehen.

I'm afraid we cannot extend your **overdraft**.

Leider können wir Ihren **Überziehungskredit** nicht verlängern.

Letter of application
(Applications in response to a job advertisement)

Bewerbungsschreiben
(Bewerbungen auf eine Stellenanzeige)

Dear Sir or Madam

Sehr geehrte Damen und Herren,

Dear Mr/Ms

Sehr geehrte(r) Herr .../Frau ...

I would like to apply for the post of... advertised recently in...

Ich möchte mich um die Stelle der/des ..., die ich kürzlich in ... annonciert sah, bewerben.

Please find enclosed a complete curriculum vitae and application form.

Anbei finden Sie meinen vollständigen Lebenslauf und Bewerbungsschreiben.

I would like to apply for the post of... which I saw advertised in...

Hiermit bewerbe ich mich um die Stelle einer/eines ..., die ich im ... annonciert sah.

I have seen your advertisement for... in the... and would like to apply for the post.

Ich sah Ihre Stellenanzeige in der/dem ... und möchte mich für die Stelle einer/eines ... bewerben.

(Speculative application)

(Initiativbewerbung)

I am very interested in the type of work done by your company and am

Ich interessiere mich für die Arbeit Ihres Unternehmens und suche

at present looking for a post in this particular **sector of industry**.

As you will see from my CV, I have some experience in this field, and would appreciate the opportunity of explaining how I feel I can be of use to your company.

derzeit nach einer Stelle in diesem **Industriezweig**.

Wie Sie meinem Lebenslauf entnehmen können, habe ich Erfahrung in diesem Bereich und würde mich freuen, mit Ihnen über meinen Nutzen für Ihr Unternehmen zu diskutieren.

Example endings

I look forward to hearing from you and to being granted the opportunity of an **interview**.

I trust you will consider my application favourably and grant me an interview to discuss the post in more detail.

I hope there might be an opportunity for a personal discussion.

I look forward to the opportunity of attending an interview, at which I can provide further details.

I should be pleased to attend an interview. I can be contacted on the telephone number on my CV or via my email address. I look forward to hearing from you.

Schlussformeln

Ich würde mich über die Einladung zu einem persönlichen **Vorstellungsgespräch** sehr freuen.

Ich hoffe, Sie werden mir die Gelegenheit geben, meine Fähigkeiten in einem Gespräch näher zu erläutern.

Ich würde mich über eine Einladung zu einem Gespräch freuen.

Ich würde mich freuen, wenn ich weitere Einzelheiten in einem persönlichen Gespräch mit Ihnen diskutieren könnte.

Ich würde mich über die Einladung zu einem Vorstellungsgespräch freuen. Ich kann unter der angegebenen Telefonnummer oder auch per E-Mail erreicht werden. Ich würde mich freuen, bald von Ihnen zu hören.

Invitation to attend for interview
Thank you for your recent application for the post of... We would like to invite you for an interview on Friday 26 May at 10 a.m. Will you please let me know either by phone or email whether this appointment is be convenient for you.

Termin und Einladung
Vielen Dank für Ihre Bewerbung um die Stelle einer/eines ... Wir würden Sie gerne in einem persönlichen Gespräch am Freitag, 26. Mai um 10 Uhr kennenlernen. Bitte teilen Sie mir telefonisch oder per E-Mail mit, ob Sie den Termin wahrnehmen können.

Offers of appointment
I am pleased to offer you the post of... in our... Department at a starting salary of... pounds per month. Your duties are to commence on...

Stellenangebote
Ich freue mich, Ihnen die Stelle einer/eines ... in unserer ... -abteilung anbieten zu können. Das Anfangsgehalt beträgt ... Pfund monatlich. Arbeitsbeginn ist der ...

Enclosed are two copies of the **contract of employment**.
Please sign one copy and return it to the **Personnel Department** asap.

Anbei finden Sie zwei Kopien Ihres **Arbeitsvertrages**, von denen Sie bitte eine so bald wie möglich unterschrieben an unsere **Personalabteilung** zurücksenden.

Polite refusal letters
I have read your letter and curriculum vitae with much interest but am sorry to tell you that you have not been selected for interview on this occasion.

Höfliche Absagen
Ich habe Ihre Bewerbung und Ihren Lebenslauf mit großem Interesse gelesen, doch leider muss ich Ihnen mitteilen, dass Sie nicht zu einem Auswahlgespräch eingeladen wurden.

We have had a very large number of applications and have been able to identify several candidates whose

Wir hatten eine sehr große Anzahl an Bewerbern, von denen einige für die fragliche Stelle eine geeignetere

background and experience are more closely matched to our specific requirements than your own.

Qualifikation vorweisen konnten als Sie.

Many thanks for your interest. We wish you continued professional success.

Ich danke Ihnen ganz herzlich für das Interesse an unserer Firma und wünsche Ihnen für Ihren weiteren beruflichen Weg viel Erfolg.

Refusals to cold letters

Many thanks for your recent letter and enclosed CV. Unfortunately, we do not have any suitable opportunities for you at the moment. However, we are quite impressed by your **skills** and it occurs to us that these may be of interest to one of our associated companies. I have, therefore, passed your papers on to them.

Absage bei Initiativbewerbungen

Vielen Dank für Ihre Bewerbung mit Lebenslauf. Leider haben wir jedoch keine geeigneten Stellen frei. Doch sind wir von Ihren **Fähigkeiten** so beeindruckt, dass wir Ihre Bewerbungsunterlagen an ein uns verbundenes Unternehmen weitergeleitet haben.

Letters of appreciation

I can't thank you enough for backing me/for you support.

Danksagung

Ich weiß gar nicht, wie ich Ihnen für Ihre Unterstützung danken kann.

We greatly appreciate your support during our recent crisis.

Wir sind Ihnen wirklich sehr dankbar für Ihre Unterstützung während der jüngsten Krise.

Please accept our sincere thanks for all your help and support.

Wir möchten uns ganz herzlich für all Ihre Hilfe und Unterstützung bedanken.

A big thank you to everyone involved in the marketing campaign.

Ein herzliches Dankeschön an alle, die an der Marketingkampagne beteiligt waren.

We would like to express our appreciation to the Research and Development Department.

Wir möchten unserer Dankbarkeit gegenüber der Forschungs- und Entwicklungsabteilung Ausdruck verleihen.

Thank you on behalf of the **board of directors** for all your efforts.

Wir danken Ihnen im Namen des **Vorstands** für all Ihre Bemühungen.

I am instructed by our committee to convey our sincere thanks for your assistance.

Unser Ausschuss hat mir die Aufgabe übertragen, unseren herzlichen Dank für Ihre Hilfe zu übermitteln.

Whenever there is an opportunity for us to reciprocate, please don't hesitate to let us know.

Sollten wir zu irgendeiner Zeit die Möglichkeit haben, Ihre Freundlichkeit zu erwidern, teilen Sie uns dies bitte mit.

I hope that I may soon have an opportunity to return your kindness.

Ich hoffe, dass sich bald die Gelegenheit ergibt, Ihre Freundlichkeit zu erwidern.

It was very kind of you to give me so much of your valuable time.

Es war sehr freundlich von Ihnen, mir so viel von Ihrer wertvollen Zeit zu widmen.

It was good to see you again and I want to thank you for the delightful evening I spent with you.

Ich habe mich sehr gefreut, Sie wiederzusehen, und möchte mich für den wunderschönen Abend mit Ihnen bedanken.

I wish to thank you most warmly for the hospitality extended/shown to me during my stay in London.

Ich möchte mich sehr herzlich für die mir während meines Besuches in London erwiesene Gastfreundschaft bedanken.

Congratulations
We all send you our congratulations on such an excellent result.

Glückwünsche
Wir gratulieren alle zu diesem hervorragenden Resultat.

This is to send you our warmest congratulations and best wishes on your election as vice president.	Herzlichen Glückwunsch und die besten Wünsche anlässlich Ihrer Wahl zum Vizepräsidenten.
I am writing to convey my warm congratulations on your election to the **Board**.	Ich möchte Ihnen zu Ihrer Wahl in den **Verwaltungsrat** herzlich gratulieren.
I was happy to learn that you have been appointed **Sales Manager**.	Ich habe mich gefreut, von Ihrer Ernennung zum **Verkaufsleiter** zu hören.
Heartiest congratulations on the occasion of your 65th birthday/your company's 50th anniversary.	Herzliche Glückwünsche zu Ihrem 65. Geburtstag/zum 50-jährigen Jubiläum Ihrer Firma.
With love and best wishes for your retirement.	Mit den besten Wünschen für Ihre Pensionierung.
Sam joins me in sending you our very best wishes for your future career.	Sam schließt sich meinen besten Wünschen für deine zukünftige Karriere an.
We all wish you the best of luck in your new job.	Wir alle wünschen dir viel Glück in deinem neuen Beruf.
Well done!	Gut gemacht!
Merry Christmas and a Happy New Year.	Frohe Weihnachten und ein glückliches Neues Jahr.
With season's greetings and very best wishes.	Mit den besten Wünschen für ein gesegnetes Weihnachtsfest.
All the best for the New Year!	Ein glückliches neues Jahr!
Happy New Year!	Alles Gute zum Neuen Jahr!
May I send you all our very best wishes for 2013.	Ich sende euch allen die besten Wünsche für 2013.
Happy Easter!	Frohe/Fröhliche Ostern!
Many happy returns of the day!	Herzlichen Glückwunsch zum Geburtstag!

I hope you have a lovely holiday.

Hoffentlich hast du einen schönen Urlaub.

Congratulations on your engagement/marriage.

Herzlichen Glückwunsch zur Verlobung/Hochzeit!

🔍 Final test | Abschlusstest

1. Finden Sie das richtige Wort oder die richtigen Wörter für die Leerstellen:

1. Could you please _____ on this number.

   a. reach me   **b.** speak to me   **c.** call me   **d.** contact me

2. I tried all day to_____ you, but I didn't

   _____.

   a. find... succeed   **b.** speak to... connect

   c. reach... get through   **d.** dial... find you

3. The line was always _____.

   a. out of order   **b.** engaged   **c.** not connected   **d.** unavailable

4. Hello, this is ATP Limited, _____

   a. can I be of assistance?   **b.** what can I do?

   c. what do you want?   **d.** who do you want?

5. I called previously, but I was _____.

   a. disconnecting   **b.** cut off   **c.** thrown out   **d.** cut short

6. After completing the call, I _____.

   a. cut off   **b.** cut short   **c.** hung up   **d.** left the line

7. She has been _____ the phone for hours.

   a. at   **b.** with   **c.** over   **d.** on

8. This is the number. Could you please _____ it for me.

   a. ring   **b.** dial   **c.** find   **d.** reach

2. Unterstreichen Sie den passenden Begriff!

1. How do you do? I'm very proud / relieved / pleased / honoured to meet you.

2. She has fully recovered from the operation? I must / can't / can / have to tell you how exhausted / relieved / disappointed / honoured I am.

3. Please pass on to / tell / inform / assure your father how sorry / dismayed / surprised / shocked I was to hear of his wife's death.

4. Jane's getting married? Give her my commiseration / sympathy / joy / best wishes .

5. Please tell Mr Johnson how overjoyed / pleased / surprised / encouraged I was to hear of his promotion. Oh, and give him my sympathy / fine feelings / good wishes / encouragement for the future.

6. Forgive / Listen to / Excuse / Hear me, is this seat promised / taken / used / paid for ?

7. Good morning, Polly! Could you tell Mr Smithers I shan't be in today? I'm feeling down-at-heart / down / off-putting / off colour .

8. Raise your glasses, please! I would like to say / give / propose / honour a toast to the happy couple!

9. In replying / reflection / response / answer , I have / want / desire / don't hesitate to say how happy I have been working for this company.

10. May I break out / in / down / up on this conversation? You can count in / down / on / up my support for what you are proposing.

3. Im Falle eines Todes bieten Sie den Hinterbliebenen als Beileids-bekundung „condolences" an. Welche Reaktion auf folgende Ausdrücke ist angemessen?

And the possibilities: Expressions of ...

(disappointment) (concern) (thanks) (good luck wishes)
(congratulations (2x)) (sympathy) (Good speed)

1. Announcement of an engagement or marriage

_____

2. A friend's promotion at work

_____

3. Farewell to friends embarking on a long journey

_____

4. ... and on a short journey

_____

5. A run of bad luck experienced by a friend

_____

6. Failure by a friend to honour a promise

_____

7. A road accident in which a friend is injured

_____

8. Assistance afforded by a friend

_____

4. Unterstreichen Sie die passenden Präpositionen!

1. This is supposed to be a secret, so don't let up / down / on / in to John what we have on / under / in / at mind.

2. How long can the company keep this progress on / in / up / down ? I hope we shareholders are informed on / at / in / around time if a reversal is expected.

3. You can't keep a good man in / down / up / under . Smith's talent will show at / on / in / down the end.

4. I wish I knew what this speaker is getting at / on / for / down , he seems quite on / off / at / under the mark.

5. Janet says they made that story down / up / on / off just to get at / on / over / down on us.

6. We're all feeling down / up / in / out after a very hard week at work, in fact I'm done out / in / over / under .

7. I'd like to know what they're up on / over / to / from . Can you sound them down / over / in / out for me?

8. When that department finally gets down on / over / to / from it we can count out / on / over / at some promising results.

9. You can always count in / for / with / on the company's personnel department if you're in trouble.

10. We had to bring on / up / in / down an independent company of accountants to look at / over / into / up the mysterious loss of so much money.

5. Ihre Marketing-Abteilung erhält den folgenden Brief. Wie entwerfen Sie ein Antwortschreiben?

Manchester, 28 August 2013

Dear Sirs,

We would be very grateful if you sent us all the information you have on your range of products, including a price list, delivery terms and dates, and guarantee details. Are you able to arrange with our Mr Jones a suitable time and place for a meeting to discuss the possibility of further cooperation between our two companies? We look forward to your reply.

Yours faithfully,

Thompson and Partners

_____

_____

_____

_____

_____

_____

_____

_____

6. Wird der folgende Brief dem Schreiber den gewünschten Job
bescheren, was meinen Sie? Können Sie ihn für ihn verbessern?

Dear gentlemen,

I have read with a lot of interest the announcement you positioned in the
newspaper of last week seeking an office assistant. I have much experience
of office and I sure I might be the man you require. Up to now I work as
stores manager of Hancock and Sons, just round corner from you – very
convenient! I work in stores but often in office, so I know way around. My
English not yet very good but I try to learn more. I make 300 pounds the
week. You offer me me I your man.

With many greetings,

...

_____

_____

_____

_____

_____

_____

_____

🔆 **Answers | Lösungen**

1. 1. Yours sincerely **2.** Yours faithfully **3.** With best wishes **4.** Yours sincerely **5.** Yours sincerely

2. 1. request **2.** request **3.** demand **4.** refusal

3. grateful; sent; range; products; products; developed; employ; areas; operations; scheduled; useful; arrange; reply

4. 1. banned **2.** seen **3.** several times **4.** start work **5.** stop **6.** land

5. cause; inform; defence; unaware; in question; prohibiting; assumed; used; refrain; opportunity; appeal; vicinity

6. b; c

7. has written; to complain; promised; to explain; has not turned up; tells; had suspended; looks at; says; decided to give; to call; does not do so; will strike; look

8. 1. attractive **2.** site **3.** has **4.** large **5.** recommend

9. 1. have written **2.** write **3.** will write **4.** written **5.** write **6.** wrote **7.** am writing

10. receipt; prompt; appreciate, early; assured, best; reply; grateful, sent

11. clearer; briefer/more brief, longer; more legible; more insulting; lengthier; sooner

12. BEISPIEL:
Dear Mr Green,
Thank you again for your invitation to lunch, which I originally very gratefully accepted. However, a very urgent business engagement has

since cropped up and upset my plans. I regretfully have to cancel my plan to join you for lunch. Please excuse any inconvenience this might cause. I hope I may make amends and reciprocate by inviting you to lunch at the earliest opportunity.

With best regards,

...

13. **1.** therefore **2.** Nevertheless **3.** therefore

14. An article on your company's software program, "Instantweb", which the American magazine Computer World carried, has caught our attention … This possibility particularly interested our Head Office in the United States, which has asked us to approach you with a view to obtaining the franchise for "Instantweb" in the United States.

15. **1.** but **2.** and **3.** but **4.** because **5.** but **6.** and

16. **1.** price **2.** price **3.** costs **4.** prices, costs **5.** price, costs, prices

17. **1.** consequences **2.** consequently **3.** consequent **4.** consequently

18. **1.** b **2.** c **3.** a **4.** f **5.** d **6.** e

19. **1.** f **2.** c **3.** h **4.** b **5.** e **6.** a **7.** d **8.** g

20. **1.** arrange **2.** require **3.** book

21. **1.** convenient, invite **2.** mark, inviting, reception **3.** glad, invitation **4.** kind, attend, pleased **5.** honour, company **6.** afraid, engaged

22. **1.** any **2.** any **3.** some **4.** any **5.** any **6.** some **7.** any, some **8.** Some

23. **1.** something **2.** anything **3.** something **4.** anything **5.** something **6.** anything **7.** anything

24. **1.** Before replying. **2.** after reading **3.** During, to reply **4.** after receiving **5.** While I agree **6.** after examining, meanwhile

25. **1.** effect **2.** affect **3.** effect **4.** affect **5.** effect **6.** effect

26. BEISPIEL:
Dear Sirs,

Thank you for your interest in our new product and your request for information. We are pleased to be able to send you our latest information on the product, and will be happy to answer any further enquiries you may have...

Alternativen zum zweiten Satz: We have pleasure in sending you our latest information...; We are glad to be able to send you our latest information...

27. It's; reach; left; voicemail/answerphone; mobile; call; call; get; calling

28. calling; calls; call; tell; contact; mobile; reach

29. I just called to say that I won't be at the office until later because I have a doctor's appointment, so if there are any calls for me please take messages.

30. totally happy; please; elaborate on, is not complete, when you get the chance

31. happy; care; writing; asked

32. **1.** d **2.** a **3.** b **4.** e **5.** c

33. BEISPIEL:
On Monday I was in Birmingham and called Texo, but there was no reply. I decided to call again on Tuesday afternoon. On Monday afternoon I was at Cranford Foods, where changes were made satisfactorily to

the contract. I agreed to call again on Friday. On Tuesday morning I called in at Taylor Electronics in Stratford and we arranged a meeting for Friday. I had lunch with the Stratford News Editor and described to him the new copy-editing software. He expressed interest. In the afternoon I returned to Birmingham, calling in at the telephone company en route. On Wednesday morning I had a dental appointment. In the afternoon I described the company objectives to the Birmingham Chamber of Commerce and Trade. On Thursday I drove to Stratford in order to make an early start on Friday. Early on Friday morning I called Cranford Foods and agreed to call again on Monday. The full board of Taylor Electronics turned up for the 10 a.m. meeting, indicating that prospects are good.

34. calling; had called; contacted; spoke; had... spoken; call; called; call

35. Hello; It's; am calling; call; on; Could; which; visit; visit; over the; call

36. is that; Who am I speaking; called; number; dialled; number; get/call/ reach; hang; try; get through; line/number; busy/engaged; on

37. a) over; b) off; c) by; d) on, talking

38. speak; here; wonder(ed); could; called; say; called; engaged; asked/ told; give; get/receive; will call; hang; line; speak to/talk to

39. call; mobile; busy/engaged; Could I; Could you; call; get; could you; call; Would... be

40. 1. hold 2. try 3. speak to 4. cut off 5. on 6. get off 7. on the

41. is that; calling; ask; contact; speak to; spoke; calling; asking; call; report; connected; ring; number

42. is that; am planning; put; hold/hang on; extension; put; hold/hang on; cut off; dead; by

43. 1. b 2. g 3. d 4. h 5. c 6. e 7. f 8. i 9. a

44. understand; assure; can; find; afraid; assure; give up; satisfied

45. answerphone/answering machine; satnav; dictaphone/digital recorder; laptop/notebook; mobile phone

46. 1. called 2. had called 3. would call 4. have called 5. will call
6. calls 7. call

47. Good morning; called; informed him of; decided on; very interesting; appreciate; calling; in writing; send it by fax; waiting; call

48 speak to; in; reply; out; line; hold; message; like; call back; number

49. to call/to phone/to make a call; to get through/to be put through; to hold; to hang up; to answer/to pick up

50. BEISPIEL:
The meeting discussed the Quick-Ed program, its advantages and drawbacks and reviewed complaints. Possible purchasers were listed. It was decided to assign Ken Allington, Chief Computer Analyst, to supervise the installation of a system at Metropolitan Newspapers and to familiarize staff with the system. The duration of his assignment will depend on the difficulty he has in acquainting the staff with the system. Costs and pricing will be the subject of negotiations with Metropolitan Newspapers. It was decided to meet again on Tuesday 24 August.

51. would like; doubles; occupancy; arrive; rate; reserve; have; facilities

52. hire; rate; include; inclusive; go ahead; reserve; collect; details; call; in time

53. connect; calling; leave; getting through; out of; reach; engaged/busy; line; phone; make; line; get; through/via; put me through; speaking; connected; connect; engaged/busy; hold; put me through

54. **1.** c **2.** b **3.** c **4.** b **5.** c

55. reach; out of order; say; reach; tell; postpone; getting through; on; talks; engaged; got through to; chat; on; spend; connection

56. **1.** on, off, through **2.** on, up, on **3.** up, off **4.** on, on, up, on **5.** At **6.** down

57. book; vacancy; available; reserve; reserve/book; arrive; arrive; sure; delayed; call; reserve; reserved; arrive; give; tell; reserved

58. called; asked; reserve; arriving; delayed; call; rate; served

59. **1.** persuade **2.** performed **3.** caught **4.** obtain **5.** recover from **6.** understand

60. **1.** that's enough **2.** complete **3.** complete **4.** exhausted **5.** performed **6.** covered

61. explaining; functions; install; contain; put; ranging; start; load; play; understand; straightforward

62. **1.** avoided him **2.** call me **3.** relinquished **4.** surrender **5.** quit, hinted **6.** disclose

63. **1.** patiently **2.** immediate **3.** fully **4.** promptly **5.** complete **6.** necessarily **7.** usually, prompt

64. **1.** in **2.** at, through **3.** by/in **4.** up **5.** down **6.** up **7.** into

65. **1.** break **2.** have broken **3.** break-in **4.** break up **5.** breaking down **6.** broke away **7.** broken up **8.** broken out

66. **1.** to accept **2.** of telling **3.** of reading **4.** to deliver **5.** of being

67. was born; attending; left; took; travelled; returning; enrolled; completing; joined; gained; am employed; is; am studying; include maintaining; organizing; has taken; feel

68. **1.** impressed by **2.** impressive **3.** impressively **4.** impression, on **5.** impressive **6.** impressed by **7.** to impress **8.** an impression on **9.** impressively **10.** impressed by

69. **1.** certify **2.** admit/accept **3.** confirm **4.** accepted/granted **5.** recognized

70. **1.** whom **2.** whose **3.** Who(m) **4.** who **5.** who **6.** Who(m) **7.** Whose

71. **1.** of... interest **2.** interesting **3.** interested in **4.** interest... by **5.** interesting **6.** interest **7.** interest to **8.** interested **9.** interesting **10.** interested in **11.** interest

72. **1.** I only wanted to meet her before she left. Why did she refuse?
2. They should be only too pleased they didn't take up that offer.
3. I'm only too grateful for the help you gave me.
4. It's not only the anger it causes, but also the pain.
5. We've only two miles to go before we get home.

73. **1.** mispronounce **2.** mishap **3.** misanthrope **4.** misshapen **5.** misspend **6.** miscellany **7.** misdirect

74. **1.** cooked **2.** I'm finished/defeated/I've lost **3.** exhausted/tired **4.** unacceptable/rude

75. **1.** fits and starts **2.** fit to burst **3.** fit in **4.** fit to kill **5.** fit to be tied **6.** good fit **7.** fitting **8.** fit in

76. **1.** had submitted **2.** had received **3.** knew **4.** to be **5.** had tried **6.** were/was

77. **1.** up **2.** down **3.** in **4.** on **5.** in on **6.** go

78. **1.** takes the biscuit **2.** Take note of **3.** take stock of **4.** taken heart
5. took him to task **6.** took a dim view of

79. **1.** have missed **2.** hear, have recovered **3.** have caught, boarded
4. hearing, had left (left) **5.** meet, was

80. **1.** pick on **2.** pick up **3.** pick out **4.** pick and choose **5.** picked up
(picked out) **6.** picked their way

81. Lucy: *Hello*, ARGO here. Can I *help* you?
Caller: Thatcher of North End Electronics here. I'd like to *speak* to Mr
Morgan please.
L. I'll see if he's *free*. Just *hold* a moment, please. Mr Morgan? I *have* a
Mr Thatcher of North End Electronics *on the line*. Shall I *put* him
through?
M. No, Lucy. I'm very busy at the moment. He's *calling* about sales, so
put him *through* to Steve.
L. Hello, Mr Thatcher? Mr Morgan is *busy* on another *line* at the mo-
ment. He has asked me to *put* you *through* to Mr Blackman. Sorry
to keep you *waiting*. I'll *put* you *through* right away. Oh dear! Mr
Blackman's *line* is *engaged*. Would you like to *wait*? His line should be
free very soon.
C. No. I have a *call* waiting for me on another *line*. I'll *call (call him)*
back.
M. Hello, Lucy? Is Thatcher still *on the line*? I've just remembered
something I wanted to *discuss* with him. Can you *put* him *through*?
L. No, Mr Morgan. He *rang off*. He says he'll *call back* later.
M. Lucy, this is rather important. Do you think you could *call* his number
for me?
L. Well, he said something about having a *call* on another *line*. But I'll
try to *reach* him for you.

82. **1.** must **2.** must **3.** must **4.** might **5.** must/might **6.** must

83. **1.** laid down **2.** laid up **3.** laid on the table **4.** layabout **5.** laid on

84. **1.** I didn't think the speaker was that good. His address to the forum, in fact, was *very (rather)* dull.
2. He thinks he's *very much (rather)* an expert, but he doesn't really know that much.
3. I'm *very (much)* obliged to you for your assistance, which has been *very far* beyond the bonds of friendship.

85. **1.** ever **2.** never **3.** ever **4.** never, never **5.** ever **6.** never

86. **1.** got up to **2.** comes down **3.** down at **4.** down to **5.** down on **6.** having been up against

87. **1.** made her mark **2.** markup, on the mark **3.** up to the mark **4.** on their marks **5.** marking time **6.** lost their mark

88. **1.** set up **2.** have been, haven't had **3.** has been, went **4.** had, went **5.** fell, visited **6.** has fallen, started

89. **1.** on **2.** to **3.** to **4.** for **5.** for **6.** in

Final test | Lösungen

1. **1.** c **2.** c **3.** b **4.** a **5.** b **6.** c **7.** d **8.** b

2. **1.** pleased **2.** can't, relieved **3.** tell, sorry **4.** best wishes **5.** pleased, good wishes **6.** Excuse, taken **7.** off colour **8.** propose **9.** response, want **10.** in, on

3. **1.** congratulations **2.** congratulations **3.** Encouragement **4.** good luck **5.** sympathy **6.** disappointment **7.** concern **8.** thanks

4. **1.** on, in **2.** up, in **3.** down, in **4.** at, off **5.** up, at **6.** down, in **7.** to, out **8.** to, on **9.** on **10.** in, into

5. BEISPIEL:

Dear Sirs,

Thank you for your letter of 28 July. We have pleasure in enclosing the latest complete information on our range of products, together with the additional material you requested: price list, delivery terms and dates, and guarantee details. We would be pleased to arrange a meeting with Mr Jones at his convenience to discuss the possibility of further cooperation between our two companies.

Yours faithfully,

6. BEISPIEL:

Dear Sirs,

I read with interest your insertion in last week's newspaper advertising the vacant post of office assistant, and I would be grateful if you considered my application for the job. I am currently employed by Hancock and Sons as store manager, where my employment has also given me the opportunity to acquaint myself with office routine. My salary with Hancock and Sons is 300 pounds a week. Although my English is not yet fluent, I am learning the language and hope to gain proficiency soon.

Yours faithfully,

📘 Glossar

A

account	*hier:* Kunde, auch Bericht, Rechnung, Konto
accounting	Buchhaltung
accounts	Rechnungsstelle
to acquaint oneself with sth.	sich mit etw. vertraut machen
address	Ansprache
addressee	Adressat
adequately briefed	angemessen vorbereitet/ eingewiesen
advance copy	Vorabkopie
to advertise a post	eine Stelle annoncieren
to affect	beeinflussen
agenda	Tagesordnung
all hands to the wheel	alle Mann an die Ruder
to approach a meeting	an eine Verhandlung herangehen
Asian business market	asiatischer Geschäftsmarkt
to ask to speak to sb.	mit jmd. sprechen wollen
assessment	Leistungsbericht
to assign sb. to sth.	jmd. zu etw. abstellen
at all costs	um jeden Preis
to attend a meeting	an einer Besprechung teilnehmen
attendance	Teilnahme
at your peril	auf eigene Gefahr
away	außerhalb (einer Firma etc.)

B

back in harness	wieder in der Tretmühle
to back off	zurückstellen
banking	Bankwesen
to be sb.'s cup of tea	auf einer Wellenlänge liegen; gut miteinander auskommen
to be accredited	akkreditiert sein
to be all in	völlig erledigt sein
bean-counters	Erbsenzähler (abfällig)
to become acquainted with sth.	vertraut werden mit
to be bound to be	bestimmt/sicher sein

to be dying to do sth.	„sterben" etw. zu tun (ugs.)
to be in charge (of sth.)	zuständig sein für, sich kümmern um
to be off the phone	aufgelegt haben, nicht sprechen
to be on one's way	auf dem Weg sein, wegmüssen
to be on the phone	gerade telefonieren
to be right down	gleich herunterkommen
berk	Dussel/Idiot (ugs.)
to be tied down	in etw. eingebunden sein
to be worth (one's) weight in gold	sein Gewicht in Gold wert sein
to boast	prahlen (*hier:* etw. vorweisen können)
to book	buchen
to boost sb.'s confidence	Selbstvertrauen aufbauen (umgangssprachlich)
to break a system in	ein System in Betrieb nehmen
to break down	*hier:* zerstreuen, aus der Welt schaffen
to break into the market	in den Markt vordringen
to break into the Asian market	in den asiatischen Markt eindringen
to break off	aufhören/abbrechen
bundle	Bündel/Packen
business negotiation	geschäftliche Verhandlung
(a) business-related discipline	wirtschaftliches Ausbildungsfach
by all means	aber natürlich

C

to call back	zurückrufen
to call up sth.	etw. abrufen
Can you make it?	Können Sie das einrichten? (Verabredung)
can't help	nicht umhinkommen
to catch up on letter-writing	überfällige Briefe schreiben
chief items	Hauptpunkte
to come off it	mit etw. aufhören
to come through with flying colours	mit fliegenden Fahnen durchkommen/Erfolg haben

▌ Glossar

competitive	wettbewerbsorientiert, konkurrenzfähig
to complain	sich beschweren
conference on information technology	Informationstechnologie-Konferenz
conference room	Konferenzraum
conference venue	Konferenzort
confirmation	Bestätigung
to confirm price and conditions	Preis und Lieferbedingungen bestätigen
contact	Kontakt
contribution	*hier:* (Rede-)Beitrag
to couch a complaint	eine Beschwerde formulieren
to cover (a territory)	für (ein Gebiet) zuständig sein
cross-border	Grenzüberschreitung
to cross one's fingers	Daumen drücken

D

day's proceedings	Tagesverlauf
deal	Geschäftsabschluss
to deal in American markets	auf amerikanischen Märkten verhandeln
to deal in semiconductors	mit Halbleitern handeln
to deal with sth.	etw. erledigen
degree in economics	Abschluss in Wirtschaftswissenschaft
description	Beschreibung
devoted	gewidmet
diary	Terminkalender
differences in approach	Unterschiede in der Handlungsweise/Methode
difficult market	schwieriger Markt
dire	gräßlich; *hier:* weitreichend, unangenehm
discipline	*hier:* Fachgebiet
discounted prices for larger orders	Mengenrabatt

diversification	Diversifikation/breiteres Angebot
to do business with sb.	mit jmd. Geschäfte machen
Do your stuff!	*hier:* Tun Sie, was Sie tun müssen
to draft	entwerfen
driving license	Führerschein

E

early customer	früh dran sein, ein „Überpünktlicher"
effect	Auswirkung
to elaborate points	Punkte ausarbeiten
to email sth.	etw. per E-Mail schicken
embarrassment	Peinlichkeit, Verlegenheit
to end a letter	einen Brief beenden
to enquire about	sich erkundigen nach
enquiry	Anfrage
to entail	beinhalten/nach sich ziehen
enterprise	Unternehmen
errand	Botengang
to expand one's network of contacts	das Netz von Kontakten erweitern
expenses	Kosten
expenses sheet/return	Spesenabrechnung

F

face to face	persönlich
facts and figures	Fakten und Zahlen
fairly well	ziemlich gut
to fall into (an area)	hineinfallen (im Sinne von „dazugehören")
to fare	ergehen
file (on sb.)	Akte (über jmd.)
to fill sb. in	jmd. informieren
final session	Abschlusssitzung
fine by me	gerne, ist mir recht
to fit nicely	gut passen
to follow up a lead	an einer Sache dranbleiben; eine Möglichkeit verfolgen

for all the tea in China	(Redewendung)
	etwa: Für alles Geld der Welt
forceful	*hier:* ausgeprägt (Charakter)
foreign experience	Auslandserfahrung
foreign expert	Auslandsexperte
foxed	verblüfft

G

(to be) geared up	bereit sein (etwa: seine Sieben Sachen zusammenhaben)
general impression	Gesamteindruck
generously proportioned	großzügig geschnitten
to get down to business	zum Geschäft kommen
to get down to sth. right away	sich sofort um etw. kümmern
to get hold of	erreichen
to get stuck into sth.	sich in etw. vertiefen/"hineinknien"
to get the message	die Nachricht erhalten
to get through	durchkriegen
to get to	dazukommen
to get to grips with sth.	sich mit (etw.) auseinandersetzen
Go for it!	Gehen Sie hin!/Machen Sie das!
Good for you!	Gut gemacht!
to go over	durchgehen
to go well	gut laufen
gross domestic product (GDP)	Bruttoinlandsprodukt
gross profit	Bruttogewinn

H

to hang on to	dranbleiben
to hate to lose face	es hassen, das Gesicht zu verlieren
to have a good grasp of sth.	etw. gut im Griff haben
to have a head start	einen Vorsprung haben
to have an appointment	eine Verabredung haben
to have an appointment to see sb.	einen Termin mit jdm. haben
to have bigger fish to fry	einen größeren Fisch am Haken haben (etw. Wichtigeres vorhaben)

to have in mind	vorhaben
to have sb. on the line	jmd. in der Leitung haben
head	*hier:* Vorsitzende(r)
head office	Hauptbüro
het up	aufgeregt/erhitzt
high-level delegation	hochkarätige Delegation/Abordnung
highly motivated	hoch motiviert
highly desirable	höchst attraktiv
the hot seat	im Rampenlicht
How did the conference go?	Wie ist die Konferenz gelaufen?
hype	zielgerichtete Übertreibung

I

I'm very happy to have met you!	Es war mir eine große Freude, Sie kennenzulernen!
I'm very pleased to make your acquaintance.	Sehr erfreut, Ihre Bekanntschaft zu machen.
in tray	(Post-)Eingangskorb
in a jiffy	im Handumdrehen/in Windeseile
in all seriousness	ganz im Ernst
in a state	*hier:* in einem schlechten Zustand
indisposed	unabkömmlich
to induct sb. into sth.	jdn. einführen in etw.
information desk	Informationsschalter
information pack	Infopaket
in good hands	in guten Händen
initial(ly)	anfänglich
initials	Initialen
innovative	innovativ
instructive	lehrreich
international arena	internationaler Schauplatz
international forum	internationales Forum
in the meantime	in der Zwischenzeit
in the picture	im Bild sein/Bescheid wissen
into the field	in der Praxis (hier besonders: im tatsächlichen Außendienst)

📖 Glossar

J

to join sb.	sich zu jmd. setzen

K

to keep one's appointment book clear	seinen Terminkalender freihalten
to keep sb. posted	jmd. auf dem Laufenden halten
to keep track of sth.	den Überblick behalten
knowledge	Kenntnisse

L

laid back	relaxed
to land (an order)	(einen Auftrag) an Land ziehen
to leave a message	eine Nachricht hinterlassen
to leave a number	eine Nummer hinterlassen
log	Ablaufplan
London-based company	Firma mit Sitz in London
to look at cooperation possibilities	sich nach Kooperationsmöglich- keiten umsehen
to look at the agenda	die Tagesordnung durchgehen
to look by	vorbeischauen
loudspeaker	Lautsprecher/Mithörtaste
lousy	lausig, verflixt

M

to make arrangements	Vorbereitungen treffen
to make a useful contact	einen nützlichen Kontakt knüpfen mit
Make it snappy!	Machen Sie schnell!
to make out	etw. hinstellen als, behaupten
to make up a file	einen Ordner anlegen
to manage	schaffen/in der Lage sein/ etw. in den Griff bekommen
managing editor	Herausgeber
manpower	Arbeitskraft/-kräfte; Mitarbeiter
to man sb.'s phone	jds. Telefon übernehmen
manufacturers	Hersteller

market exposure	Marktpräsenz
marketing push	Marketinginitiative
Mark my words!	Denken Sie an meine Worte!
May I introduce ...	Darf ich vorstellen ...
to meet one's match	„seinen Meister treffen"
to meet with a delegation	sich mit einer Delegation treffen
message	Nachricht
Ministry of Overseas Trade	Außenhandelsministerium
missive	Mitteilung
multinational conference	multinationale Konferenz

N

name tag	Namensschild
to narrow down	eingrenzen
new entrepreneurship	neues Unternehmertum
new technology sector	Gebiet der Neuen Technologie
non-national business acumen	nicht-nationaler Geschäftsscharfsinn

O

occurrence	Vorfall
offhand	unpersönlich
on file	in den Unterlagen
on occasion	bei Gelegenheit
on the double	in Nullkommanichts
on the spot	vor Ort
open-and-shut	klar und deutlich/eindeutig
opening vacancy	eine freie Stelle
opening of a conference	Konferenzeröffnung
to open a conference	eine Konferenz eröffnen
out tray	(Post-)Ausgangskorb
out of the blue	ohne Vorwarnung/ „aus heiterem Himmel"
overjoyed	überglücklich

P

pager/beeper	Pager/Piepser

Glossar

panic stations	Krise
to participate in a meeting	an einer Besprechung teilnehmen
payment agreement	Zahlungsbedingungen
per capita	pro Kopf
permanent location	ständiger (Wohn-)Sitz
to pick up	*hier:* aufnehmen
pocket recorder	Taschenrekorder
practical knowledge	praktische Erfahrung
to present one's business card	seine Visitenkarte überreichen
product line	Produktreihe
programme	Programm
progressive	progressiv, fortschrittlich
progress report	Erfolgsbericht
projection	Prognose
promising	vielversprechend
to punch sth. into	etw. einhacken
push	Initiative/Vorstoß (besonders im Marketing)
to put a caller through	einen Anrufer durchstellen
to put sb. in the picture	jdn. ins Bild setzen, auf den neuesten Stand bringen
to put into practice	in die Praxis umsetzen
to put sb. out of his/her misery	jmd. nicht mehr länger zappeln lassen
to put sb. through	jmd. durchstellen
to put sth. on file	etw. in die Akten eintragen

R

to raise (a point)	*hier:* etw. aufbringen (z. B. Diskussionspunkte)
to reboot	neu starten (PC)
to record	aufnehmen, aufzeichnen
to refrain from	unterlassen
to register	(sich) anmelden, registrieren
relevant papers	nötige Papiere
to reply to	beantworten

requirements	Anforderungen
retrenchment	Einschränkung/Kürzung; Kosten-reduzierung
round-up	Zusammenstellung
to run for cover	sich in Sicherheit bringen, verstecken
to run from one appointment to another	von einer Verabredung zur nächsten rasen

S

sales director	Verkaufsleiter
sales representative	Außendienstmitarbeiter
Saved by the bell!	Rettung in letzter Sekunde!
to score a hit/goal	einen Erfolg verbuchen
to scramble the brain	im Kopf herumschwirren
to seal a contract	einen Vertrag abschließen
sector	Sektor, Gebiet, Branche
to see sth. through	bei etw. dabei sein
"sell-by" date	Haltbarkeitsdatum
session	Sitzung
to settle for	sich zufriedengeben mit
shining example	leuchtendes Beispiel
to shut down	herunterfahren (PC)
to sign the book	im Buch unterschreiben
slump	*hier:* Wirtschaftskrise
to sort out	aussortieren
to sound out	aushorchen, ausfragen
speaker	Referent, Redner
to split	*hier:* teilen
(a) stack of	ein ganzer Haufen (von)
stacks	Stapel
stand-in	Vertretung
to stick to	bei etw. bleiben
stiff	steif/*hier:* rauh, umkämpft
stock	Vorrat
to streamline	rationalisieren
to strike from	ausstreichen/herausnehmen

to switch one's attention to sth.	Aufmerksamkeit verlagern
to swot	„büffeln; pauken" (ugs.)
to swot up	büffeln, sich intensiv mit etw. beschäftigen

T

tabular	tabellarisch
to tackle some letters	ein paar Briefe durchgehen
tactic	Taktik
to take a brief glance at	einen kurzen Blick werfen auf
to take a shine to sth./sb.	einen Narren gefressen haben an etw./jmd.
to take it from here	jetzt weiter vorgehen
to take off	*hier:* sich freinehmen
to take over	übernehmen
to take place	stattfinden
to take sb. off a job	jmd. von etw. abziehen
to talk through	einweisen; erklären
to tally	zusammen-, abrechnen;
telephone company	Telefongesellschaft
Tell me another!	Sie können mir viel erzählen!
to tend to	dazu tendieren/neigen
test run	Testlauf
The conference is about to start.	Die Konferenz fängt gleich an.
This is my colleague.	Dies ist mein Kollege.
time-worn	ausgedient
top sales representative	Spitzenverkäufer
to track sb. down	jmd. aufspüren
trait	Charakterzug
to type up	abtippen

U

umpteen	zig
unconditionally	bedingungslos/ohne Vorbehalte
to urge	inständig bitten, drängen
user-friendly	benutzerfreundlich

V

visitor's pass	Besucherausweis

W

to weaken	schwächen
well stocked	gut versorgt
well worded	wohlformuliert
What are you up to?	Woran arbeiten Sie gerade?/Was machen Sie gerade?
What name shall I give?	Wen darf ich melden?
to whizz about	umhersausen
to work for	arbeiten für
to work up a thirst	„sich durstig arbeiten"
worthwhile endeavours	lohnendes Bestreben/Bemühungen
to wrap things up	Sachen abwickeln
writer's cramp	Schreibkrampf

Z

zilch	Nichts (ugs.)